Detox Your Writing

There are a number of books which aim to help doctoral researchers write the PhD. This book offers something different – the scholarly detox. This is not a faddish alternative, it's not extreme. It's a moderate approach intended to gently interrupt old ways of doing things and establish new habits and orientations to writing the PhD.

The book addresses the problems that most doctoral researchers experience at some time during their candidature – being unclear about their contribution, feeling lost in the literature, feeling like an imposter, not knowing how to write with authority, wanting to edit rather than revise. Each chapter addresses a problem, suggests an alternative framing, and then offers strategies designed to address the real issue.

Detox Your Writing is intended to be a companionable workbook – something doctoral researchers can use throughout their doctorate to ask questions about taken-for-granted ways of writing and reading, and to develop new and effective approaches.

The authors' distinctive approach to doctoral writing mobilises the rich traditions of linguistic scholarship, as well as the literature on scholarly identity formation. Building on years of expertise they place their emphasis both on tools and techniques as well as the discursive practices of becoming a scholar.

The authors provide a wide repertoire of strategies that doctoral researchers can select from. The book is a toolkit but a far from a prescriptive one. It shows that there are many routes to developing a personal academic voice and identity and a well-crafted text. With points for reflection alongside examples from a broad range of disciplines, the book offers tools for thinking, writing and reading that are relevant to all stages of doctoral research.

This practical text can be used in all university doctoral training and composition and writing courses. However, it is not a dry how-to-do-it manual that ignores debates or focuses solely on the mechanical at the expense of the lived experience of doctoral research. It provides a practical, theorised, real-world guide to postgraduate writing.

Pat Thomson is Professor of Education and Director of the Centre for Advanced Studies, at The University of Nottingham, a Visiting Professor at Deakin University, the University of Iceland, and The University of the Free State, South Africa.

Barbara Kamler is Emeritus Professor at Deakin University.

Detox Your Writing

Strategies for doctoral researchers

Pat Thomson and Barbara Kamler

Routledge
Taylor & Francis Group

LONDON AND NEW YORK

First published 2016
by Routledge
2 Park Square, Milton Park, Abingdon, Oxon OX14 4RN

and by Routledge
711 Third Avenue, New York, NY 10017

Routledge is an imprint of the Taylor & Francis Group, an informa business

British Library Cataloguing in Publication Data
A catalogue record for this book is available from the British Library

Library of Congress Cataloging in Publication Data
Names: Thomson, Pat, 1948– author. | Kamler, Barbara, author.
Title: Detox your writing : strategies for doctoral researchers/authored by Pat Thomson and Barbara Kamler.
Description: 1st edition. | New York, NY : Routlege, 2016. | Includes bibliographical references.
Identifiers: LCCN 2015031879| ISBN 9780415820837 (hardback : alk. paper) | ISBN 9780415820844 (pbk. : alk. paper) | ISBN 9781315642604 (ebook)
Subjects: LCSH: Dissertations, Academic – Authorship. | Research – Methodology – Study and teaching (Graduate)
Classification: LCC LB2369 .T466 2016 | DDC 808.02–dc23
LC record available at http://lccn.loc.gov/2015031879

ISBN: 978-0-415-82083-7 (hbk)
ISBN: 978-0-415-82084-4 (pbk)
ISBN: 978-1-315-64260-4 (ebk)

Typeset in Giovanni
by Florence Production Ltd, Stoodleigh, Devon, UK

Contents

Acknowledgements and permissions

Some of this book originally appeared as posts in Pat's blog, *Patter* (patthomson. net). We have also drawn extensively on the work of other bloggers who generously share their expertise and experiences with the scholarly community – Claire Aitchison, Rebecca Coles, Adam Crymble, Sophie Coulombeau, Athene Donald, Paul Cairney, Rachael Cayley, Cally Guerin, Nick Hopwood and Ian Robson. We have used pictures that we first saw on Twitter, and we thank Simon Carter, John Goodwin, and Dave McKenna for permission to reproduce them here.

As always, our publisher, Philip Mudd, has been a source of encouragement and helpful suggestions. We always benefit from his extensive knowledge of the interactions between the academy and the publishing industry. We appreciate the ongoing support from our Routledge team and the promotion of our books at conferences around the world.

Our partners, Greg and Randy, provide continuing TLC, meals and perspective. Their tolerance of our intensive first draft writing retreats and bizarre early morning/late night international skyping habits are legend. We really couldn't have done any of this without them.

And finally, we want to thank each other. This is our third book, the fourth if you count a second edition, and it marks a 15-year collaboration. It is also our last book together and we've signed it off with very mixed feelings. Writing together has been an important part of our lives for a long time, and we'll both miss it, and each other. Love ya B. Love ya P.

1 Introduction

You have begun your doctoral studies. You're fired up about the area of study you are pursuing. You know you have to hone your research skills and you know you have to write a thesis. Exciting? Yes, but also terrifying at the same time.

Writing – this may be where the problem begins. The idea of writing. Everyone brings to the doctorate a wide array of experiences as a writer; some positive, some less so. From all your previous experience of writing essays, assignments or minor theses you have developed what we might call a disposition to writing: strategies for and habits of writing. You may have developed metaphors for how to think about working with research data or with research literatures – some productive, some not. These habits and metaphors are often developed unconsciously and you may not be aware of how they influence your actual text production. But they do.

Most doctoral researchers worry about writing. When Pat and Barbara meet with groups of doctoral or early career researchers we often ask, 'Who feels confident about writing?' No hands go up. Perhaps one. 'Who feels competent as a writer?' A few more hands. 'How many of you feel that you write adequately?' Maybe half. 'And poorly?' The other half. Despite having reached the highest level of study in the university, many doctoral researchers approach writing with some anxiety and high emotion. Can I do it? Am I up to it? How do I ever get hold of all this new stuff and make sense of it in writing? How can I write 250+ pages?

There is certainly a lot of advice about how to approach writing. Writing advice is here, there and everywhere – it's in books, on the web, in social media, at the pub. How to tell what is good and bad advice? 'Always do this. Never do that. You must, you should, what works for me is . . .' Making sense of all of the well-intentioned advice can be tricky. There are lots of urban myths out there too; the researcher who wrote for 2 hours a day and finished their thesis in record time, the researcher who never wrote anything until the last minute and passed with flying colours. Dealing with well-established textual habits, bad metaphors and writing myths can be a problem for the researcher new to doctoral writing. Clearly these need to be addressed.

What is the way forward? Our answer is the detox. The detox, as you know, is not about giving up all the things we like – but pausing to examine the over-processed, mass-produced, genetically modified things we take into our bodies and take for granted. The detox involves a period of healthy eating and drinking: crisp carrots, crunchy celery, watermelon juice. It's a time to try out some new strategies for living. Once we take a break from our usual consumption patterns, we can decide what to reintroduce and what to leave behind, what to eat sparingly and what new habits we might establish.

This book offers a scholarly detox. It is written specifically for you, the doctoral researcher and for those times when you're likely to feel out of sorts, bloated and out of shape. It asks you to stop doing things you usually do, just for a little while, and reflect. It's not that all your writing and reading is dysfunctional or incorrect. Rather, now might be a good time to take a look at the textual habits you have developed. You've probably been taught to approach reading and writing in particular ways and have developed your own coping mechanisms and your own strategies. But it's likely that none of these have been for a task as sustained, intense and demanding as the doctorate.

You might think the idea of a detox is a bit peculiar in an academic book. After all, the detox gets a lot of bad press. It's commonly associated with snake-oil salespeople peddling the latest recipe for lifelong health and happiness. And a steady diet of kale juice or spirulina wheatgrass cocktails followed by colonic irrigation can leave you feeling hungry, irritable and uncomfortable. You might even experience low energy, muscle aches, fatigue, dizziness and nausea. Feeling ravenous and deprived makes most people rebellious and resentful. It's no wonder so many people start these culinary assault courses only to stop them in very quick time. Fortunately there are many different kinds of detoxes and they don't all offer the extreme lean mean green diet.

The scholarly detox we propose is not a faddish alternative, it's not extreme. It's a moderate approach intended to gently interrupt old ways of doing things. We hope it will help you establish new habits and orientations. We intend this book to be a companionable workbook – something you can use throughout the doctorate when you feel the need to stop and examine what you're doing. We want you to ask questions about your taken-for-granted ways of writing and reading, about your disposition to writing and its effects, about the ways you structure language and the action it supports. We'll offer a range of tools to think with and practical strategies to try out. These are our detox essentials.

In Pat's blog, *Patter*, she often reflects on the critical issues and obstacles doctoral researchers face. Recently she discussed the dangers of self-diagnosing writing habits. Not a bad thing to do, as we suggest. But the risk of getting it wrong is ever present (see Commentary: Pat Thomson). The complex and sometimes terrifying aspects of academic writing are too often mistaken as individual pathology

COMMENTARY

Pat Thomson

The perils of self-diagnosis

I reckon it's very good to know about your own writing habits. It's especially good for people just starting out on an academic career. There's a bunch of pretty helpful information out there about good writing habits and writing problems enabling you to match what you see yourself doing/ not doing with helpful general writing strategies and insights. Reading about academic writing, as well as reading about the nature of the difficulties that you might be having with your writing, can lead you to some very helpful advice, new resources and productive #acwri avenues.

But observation and reading about #acwri can also make you unnecessarily anxious. And maybe you'll leap to a premature diagnosis. Stuck on writing a paper? It must be writer's block. Having difficulty sorting through the mountain of data? It must be that you're not capable. Feeling really nervous about giving that paper? Must be a crippling case of imposter syndrome. Finding yourself pausing while writing? Must have a hyperactive inner editor.

Now, I don't want to suggest that any of these things – writer's block, being incapable, imposter syndrome, hyperactive inner editors and so on – aren't real. They are, very. I don't want to suggest that these things don't debilitate and prevent some people from getting on with their PhD or with a writing project. They do. They really do. But these things aren't as widespread or as crippling as popular media headlines and online discussions might suggest.

Let's face it. Not all writing goes smoothly. Some academic writing takes a long time and is hard. But the problem might not be writer's block. It might just be that you haven't yet sorted out what you want to say. It might be that you need to talk the writing over with someone, or do some more reading, or go back to the data or the texts.

Let's be honest. Having a mountain of data is really terrifying. There is no right answer to how you analyse data, even though there are often recommended analytic procedures. It's very normal at the start of dealing with a pantechnicon of material to feel a considerable degree of trepidation. We all do. It's not unusual. It's not because you're dim-witted that it feels overwhelming.

The risk of self-diagnosis lies in the tension between knowing yourself and getting it wrong. It's clearly good to understand your own writing habits, just as it's good to watch out for changes in your body. But a rush to self-diagnose an #acwri condition isn't *always* helpful. You may well get your diagnosis wrong. You may think you have an unusual problem and feel dreadful, when in reality what's going on is a widely shared experience.

Academic writing *is* hard for most people. But, if you exercise your writing muscles, it gets easier. Words become less precious. It's not so difficult to sit down each day and write something if you just keep at it. And bad stuff doesn't have to be permanent. You can get past a crappy presentation when you acknowledge the reality that it's not always possible to be scintillating. You can get past hesitations in a meeting or saying the wrong thing when you understand that everyone messes up occasionally. You can get to love your tendency to fuss over phrases and words when it helps you to produce an elegant piece at the end of a long process of drafting and revision.

So it's always a good idea to check out what you think your writing problem is. Don't hide it away. Talk about it with other people and I'll bet you find out that the things you suspect are your problem alone are actually shared, and common. They are just part and parcel of the scholarly writing process.

We can suffer in silence, pathologise our #acwri difficulties and self-medicate, or talk with others and find out it's generally not that bad or permanent.

http://patthomson.net/2015/01/29/writing-self-diagnosis

– as a problem that needs to be cured – rather than a fact of writing life that needs strategy.

To start, we want to introduce ourselves and tell you how we think about writing and why we offer you resources and strategies, rather than techniques or skills or recipes. We make suggestions that you can take up and try out for yourself. These are not must or should prescriptions.

About us

We have to confess at the start that we know about detoxes as more than a metaphor. We have been writing together for 15 years and all our writing is punctuated by food. We come together in Australia where Barbara lives, in the UK where Pat lives, and sometimes at locations in between. Typically we work intensively on our first draft for periods of one to three weeks and the highlight of our days is food; we are consumed by where we will eat lunch and what we will buy for dinner. We started this book in Malaysia, and the Chinese noodle soups steaming with greens and mushrooms, with fancy serrated carrots at the edge of the bowl, sustained us. We are fond of food and cooking and often use it as a way of talking about writing and life in general. So it's not really surprising that we've taken a food metaphor as the idea to hold this book together.

You may think that detox as a metaphor and organisational idea is not serious enough for scholarly work, but in fact we have always enjoyed being playful about writing. We like a bit of fun and worry that a lot of the doctoral training and writing advice on offer is very, very serious. We think of writing as explorative, creative and productive.

In 2001 we gave our first conference presentation (*Talking down writing up or ten emails a day*) on the problems with the term 'writing up'. We staged a performance at a conference in Perth, Western Australia, where we stood back to back and read consecutive emails about our shared concerns. We remember struggling not to laugh at our jokes. The audience was a bit stunned, we think, at this gentle mockery of the conventional conference presentation. We argued for the central importance of writing in doctoral research. We held a strong, shared conviction that writing was too often taken for granted in academic work and treated as a transparent process that just happened.

Dear P

I hate 'writing up' because it makes the labour of writing invisible and hides the fact that it involves crafting words and ideas and identities. It implies a first draft mentality, the kind we buried years ago in debates about writing pedagogy in primary and secondary English. But it seems alive and well in university postgraduate contexts. First we think, outline, get clear and then we write. How ridiculous!

'Writing up' also obscures the fluidity of writing – how hard it is to control sometimes – and its link to inquiry itself. It's not that we do the research and then we know. It's that we know through writing and we write our way to understanding through analysis. We put words on the page, see how they look and sound, and in the process we write stuff we had no idea we were thinking before we started writing.

Dear B

I am quite sure that the 'writing up' speakers don't actually believe that they have stopped thinking after they've finished their fieldwork. And are there any people left who argue that language is a neutral transparent medium which just records something that has been 'found'? Yet both these things are implied in 'writing up' talk. We research/think/find and then we just do words about things we already know.

'Writing up' is so ubiquitous in almost any conversation about teaching postgraduates to do their own research. I want to leap up with a metaphorical mop and bucket and wash it out of our collective pedagogic mouth. Do we really want our postgrads to pick up these implied ideas as an habituated way of conceiving of research and the crafting of research texts? What would it take to write off 'writing up'? And, will talking it down suffice?

Right from the start we wanted to develop an approach to research writing that was theoretically grounded and useful. It wasn't good enough to simply argue for the importance of writing in research and writing as research. We needed to develop a way to make this idea practical, do-able, teach-able.

We are both teachers, so we knew that advice about writing – no matter how good – is not enough. There was no point telling someone what good research writing looks like if they had no idea why it's good or how they might get there. We had to combine reading, thinking and talking with actual teaching practice.

So how did we do this? We adopted a practitioner research approach. This meant that we were not only reading about writing, but also using texts produced in our own classrooms as 'data' for analysis. Early on we began to use metaphors to disrupt people's habitual ways of thinking about the writing problems they had (as in our paper on 'writing up'.) This became a trademark of our writing workshops; we ran these in many locations and cultural contexts, and with doctoral researchers across disciplines.

Our first book, the result of these workshops, was written for supervisors: *Helping doctoral students write: pedagogies for supervision* (Kamler & Thomson, 2006/2014). It is now in its second edition, and chances are, if you are reading this introduction, you may well have seen and/or used that book. Many supervisors have told us they've given it to their postgrads and we've had letters and emails from doctoral researchers who have found it useful, even though they were not our target reader.

What you may not know is that this first book had its beginnings in a liver cleansing diet. Pat's partner was on the diet and she was on it to support him. As we were writing at her house in the UK, Barbara went on it too. Daily excursions to the supermarket at lunchtime saw us ravaging the aisles for anything on the acceptable list. We could have grains, beans and brown rice, but no refined wheat, no dairy, no stimulants and no sugary anything, nothing processed, but plenty of avocados, walnuts and turmeric. High glycaemic fruit was out, as was our mutual addiction to diet cola, the Forbidden. And there were all those herbal teas filling us up – not!!

We never forget how hungry we were writing that first book together. But in the second edition, 8 years later, we were more moderate and enjoyed some of the delights of Melbourne dining out.

Our second book, *Writing for peer reviewed journals: strategies for getting published* (Thomson & Kamler, 2013) emerged from workshops we were commissioned to run because of the increasing pressure on doctoral researchers to publish. So we moved away from writing for readers like ourselves – supervisors with whom we were sharing our practice. Instead we wrote a text that could support doctoral and early career researchers to make their way into unpredictable and sometimes unfriendly territory.

For the last four years, while Barbara has been writing poetry and redesigning herself as a poet, Pat has become a blogger. In posting twice weekly about doctoral education, research policy and academic writing, she's managed to overcome our greatest worry – how to directly address the reader as YOU. We dislike the imperious, instructional tone that gets set up when we write to YOU: You must do this! You should do this or else! We know best, so listen to us! However, as in Pat's blog, here we adopt a *chatting at the bus stop* YOU. More casual, conversational. More like we sound in our actual writing workshops. So in this book, you can expect us to talk directly to YOU, the doctoral researcher. We also deliberately choose to call you, our reader, the doctoral researcher – not the doctoral student, as we want to emphasise the work (research) you are doing, rather than your unequal position (student) in the academy. And we adopt the abbreviated convention of calling you DR, the doctoral researcher now, and in future, the Doctor, with the prize title.

Over the past 10 years of writing together we've consolidated a set of principles that underpin our book. These are:

- we write pedagogically;
- we promote a conversation about good academic writing;
- we ground our work in experience and scholarship.

We write pedagogically

Pedagogy sounds grand and unapproachable. It's used differently in different places, but is often taken to mean what teachers do, that is, their methods. This is one version of pedagogy, reductive and instrumental. We understand pedagogy to mean more than teaching methods. It's about care for the learner, and it's about making learning relevant and alive. It's about the curation of experiences that lead to learning, and the animation of texts and events so that they become living practices.

This is a more European approach to pedagogy underpinned by an understanding that learning is produced by much more than snappy teaching methods. It is a more holistic approach, which involves relationships, conversations and contexts. At its heart is a 'pedagogue' who values being and becoming as much as knowing and doing. We understand this as an exercise of 'care' for persons (see Fielding & Moss, 2010; Noddings, 1986). This is why we are concerned not only with doctoral texts, the writings that are done, but also with the identity of the doctoral researcher, as we will explain in the next chapter.

Pedagogy is in the title of our first book and still informs how we approach doctoral writing. We don't simply offer maxims about what constitutes good writing. There is plenty of this normative approach about and it is important. You do need to know what the end product of academic writing looks like. But you also need to know how to get to that final product. What are the steps you might take in order to reach the desired standard?

In education, we think of these steps as scaffolding the learning. This is not the provision of a blueprint or formula, a lockstep approach. Scaffolding is a way of providing strategies that can be adapted, modified, and tailored to researchers in their particular contexts. Scaffolding is a concept that comes from a long history of educational research (Boblett, 2012; Vygotsky, 1978), but it's helpful here to picture an actual scaffold that builders use in the construction process. The scaffold helps them do things safely, step by step, without falling. When the building is finished they dismantle the scaffold and passers-by never know it was there.

The purpose of our scaffolding is to assist the DR to move from where they are now to where they need to be, without falling down a chasm or getting lost. Our scaffolding always consists of an explanation as well as some practical actions with text.

We promote a conversation about good academic writing

Let's face it. There's enough moaning and whining about how hard it is to write. It *is* difficult. But it's one thing to understand that doctoral writing isn't easy, and it's another to equate being hard with being in agony, being fearful, tortured, drowning. Common to all these metaphors is a researcher who has no control and is a passive victim. These metaphors create a bad head-space that allow you to commiserate with others, but do not support the kind of sustained effort required to get the doctorate done.

We think about writing as work. Writing work is about clarifying, capturing meaning, crafting, honing. It's hard work some of the time. But it's possible to acknowledge the difficulty of writing and still be in charge. It can be tough but manageable. However, we want more than that for you. We want you to love writing as we do. We're passionate about words. We love reading. We love writing even when we're cranking out a messy first draft. And we're committed to producing academic writing that shows we care about writing and about readers.

From both within and outside universities, academic writing is generally characterised as turgid, obscure, dense, full of hard words and empty phrases. It's said that no one reads this kind of writing and it's only done for citations. We do agree that there is a lot of academic writing that's not exactly a good read. Indeed, we've produced some of this ourselves! And we agree that this could do with changing. We return to the critique of bad academic writing in Chapter 10.

But it is possible to produce good academic writing. At the heart of every engaging and eloquent text is a scholar who sees themselves as a writer, as a craftsperson who enjoys the process and the challenges of producing elegant, comprehensible, and dare we say entertaining (or at least engaging) prose for other colleagues.

There are also well-written doctoral theses. There's a lot of mythology about theses and academic writing. It's as if a quality piece of research can only be expressed in deeply difficult prose. If it's too accessible, examiners will think it's not well theorised, not a substantial contribution. But we know that an easy read is not necessarily simple. Producing an impressive piece of work in well-crafted accessible prose is actually more difficult than writing the condensed, over-referenced and jargon-ridden text. However, it's much more enjoyable for all concerned.

Our aim is to encourage the kind of conversation that happens more often in English literature about good texts – about good academic writing not just bad academic writing. We share this ambition with other writers, such as Helen Sword (2012a), Howard Becker (1986) and Laurel Richardson (1997). We hope you like our examples and that they stimulate you to build a collection of favourite academic writings of your own.

We ground our work in experience and scholarship

There are shelves of academic books and countless blogs on academic writing. Many contain material that is helpful. We don't want to tell you not to read them. We do see ourselves as offering something else. So what do we do that is different? It's a little tricky to answer because we don't want to be in the position of critiquing the field. It always seems easier to say what we don't do than what we do. However, we have to have a go at defining our contribution because, after all, that's what DRs have to do too.

We write about writing, but not just from our experience. We offer examples but not simply because they've worked for us in workshops. The principle of reflective practice is one that we adhere to, as well as teach. It's useful to think critically about what worked for us when we wrote our own theses, what strategies we developed to supervise others, what was most effective in the workshop context. However, it's not enough. There are bodies of scholarship that can help us make sense of these experiences, that point us to important theories and to approaches that we haven't yet experienced. Writing is an established area of research – and a multidisciplinary field at that. We draw on this corpus of work.

We base our work in and on a conceptual framework, and in the systematic research that we, and others, have conducted. We see ourselves as scholars of academic writing. It is the object of our inquiry.

We therefore begin this book proper, just as you will do in your doctoral thesis and other research publications, with our theoretical toolkit. We discuss textwork/identitywork, academic writing as a conversation and academic writing as a social practice. All the strategies that we offer in the book are grounded in these Big Ideas. These are, to go back to the metaphor of the book, the detox essentials.

We never focus simply on the text without worrying about the identity of the writer. In the spirit of offering examples of good academic writing, here's Anthony Parè, a scholar of academic writing whose work we use regularly and who says this concisely:

> The text is not some sort of disembodied, independent utterance: it's an extension or expression of the writer. We are what we think, and our texts are the visible trace of our views on the world.
>
> (Anthony Parè, https://doctoralwriting.wordpress.com/2014/02/21/ supervisory-feedback-revising-the-writer-and-the-writing/).

We never just consider the text in isolation, but also in relation to its readership and field constraints. We always position the DR in conversation with the field even though they may feel very alone.

We are also concerned about the way in which thinking and writing are spoken about as if they are separate. In reality, academic writing is always thinking. We don't know what we think until we have put our ideas into language and into text. The difficulties of academic writing are therefore not simply about the technical process of writing, but are always about thinking.

The way the book is organised

We have taken the detox as a metaphor for the book, but we don't actually talk about it very much after this introduction. Instead, we begin each chapter with a common writing problem that DRs experience. We've chosen a particular set of problems – habits, dispositions, myths, emotions, metaphors – that we have seen DRs write about in blogs, that we are told about in our writing workshops, that we hear from completed DRs and that supervisors often discuss. They are not the only writing problems that DRs experience, but we think that their persistence in conversation points to the fact that they are not discussed enough.

After outlining the common problem, we then offer a Big Idea, a possible way to reframe and rename what is going on. We don't offer the Big Idea as THE way to think about a given issue, but rather as a position that you might want to adopt for a little while, to play with, to try on and try out. The Big Idea is a way to re-orient yourself to the problem, to detox previous ways of thinking and to see whether it makes a difference.

But simply thinking differently about a problem is not enough. We also offer a set of strategies that you can work with. These address the problem and provide

COMMENTARY

Richard Schechner

The boxes

Before going on, I want to point out a feature of this book. My text includes no quotations, citations or notes. Ideas are drawn from many sources, but the written voice is my own. I hope this gives the reader a smoother ride than many scholarly texts. At the same time, I want my readers to hear many voices. The voices offer alternative and supplementary opinions and interruptions. The boxes open the conversation in ways I cannot do alone. The boxes are hyper-links enacting some of the diversity of Performance Studies. I want the effect to be of a seminar with many hands or of a computer desktop with many open windows.

Schechner, 2013, p. 1

you with an expanded repertoire that you can use now and in the future. These are the research-based strategies we have found to be useful to the doctoral researchers in our writing courses and workshops.

We also offer a compendium of resources. These include writings from doctoral researchers, doctoral texts, some in draft form and some from completed theses, commentary from scholars at various career stages and research writings. These resources appear as labelled boxes in the text.

We took our inspiration for the boxes from Richard Schechner's *Performance studies* (2013), now in its third edition. This is a beautiful book. It's printed on semi-gloss paper, heavy and pleasing to the touch. It's also pleasing to the eye, with a varying arrangement of text, photographs and boxes (see Commentary: Richard Schechner). The boxes are sometimes horizontally oriented, sometimes vertical, and are of different dimensions. The basic text is presented in two columns, but the boxed materials transgress this arrangement, apparently randomly but always elegantly.

We were inspired by Schechner's book and have adopted his multiple use of boxes rather than quotations. This is not simply because we admire this layout, but because we agree with the way in which this visual arrangement embodies a philosophy about academic writing and academic books. Schechner makes a generous offer to the reader, one that we like. One of the things we want to argue for is a generosity in academic life and this way of organising a text epitomises this spirit.

We have four kinds of boxes in our book:

1   Experience boxes – these give real-life examples of the kinds of issues and problems we are discussing.

2   Writing Sample boxes – these are mainly written by DRs and ECRs, but not always. We always discuss writing samples in detail so that our reasons for including them are clear.
3   Advice boxes – these offer pithy and pointed advice to help your writing.
4   Commentary boxes – these are from a range of publications and people that we find interesting and helpful, and you may want to follow them up later.

Our book is intended to be 'teacherly'. We see Schechner's book as a teaching text. He provides a coherent narrative about performance studies, but accompanied by a set of resources about its histories, terminologies, key figures, debates and practices. This is a text with affordances – readers can take up any of the materials that they find immediately useful and they can return to them again and again to get inspiration, as well as information.

We have of course put our own spin on this approach. Our book is intended as a resource from the beginning to the end of your doctoral endeavour. The resources we offer in this book include writing strategies as well as ways to think about writing. These ideas might be grounded in creative writing or composition research, or they could be metaphors for disrupting taken-for-granted practices. We will analyse problematic and good texts in order to build up a sense of what counts as 'good' academic writing. We've also got the odd photo and narratives of academic work. We offer lists of questions and diagnostic tools that help you to revise your own writing. But these are not simply lists of things to do. Nor are they offered as a lockstep staged process. We really want you to take what we offer and make it your own. Use it on your own. Use it with groups of doctoral peers. Use it with your supervisor. Use it whenever and however makes sense to you.

Chapter 2 addresses the nature of doctoral education. Doctoral researchers often feel lost and at sea when they begin the doctorate. The expectations for thinking and writing are not the same as they were for undergraduate and taught Masters programmes. This can lead to a crisis in confidence. We argue that beginning DRs need to understand the nature of the game that they are in. We offer a conceptual reframing approach – making a modest contribution, building a scholarly identity, writing as a social and cultural practice and entering the scholarly conversation.

Chapter 3 addresses the problem of being overwhelmed by all of the reading that needs to be done to develop a research proposal and to position the research. We suggest that one way to address feeling overwhelmed is to think about doctoral research as work, writing as work, and, therefore, the need to set up good work practices. Our strategies develop new metaphors for reading, taking notes and conducting a review of literatures. We also consider workspaces and work systems.

The following chapter, Chapter 4, continues to look at literatures, and at some of the issues that can make writing about other people's words and ideas so difficult. We address the problem of the DR feeling lost in the literatures and offer the reframing idea of taking a stand. Our three strategies – diagnosing common authority problems in writing; scoping, mapping and focusing; and creating a research space – all help the DR to feel in charge of their work with the literature.

In Chapter 5 we consider the difficulties that arise for DRs when they receive confusing feedback about the inadequacies of their writing. Our reframing idea is that of the argument: to see the whole thesis as an argument. We provide three strategies to orient the DR to argument – some questions to support taking an arguer stance, using tiny texts to practise argument, and using sentence skeletons.

We then move in Chapter 6 to the imposter syndrome – the feeling of writing and talking about things you know so little about and the fear of being found out. We offer the reframing idea of performance and rehearsal to rethink being an imposter and suggest three strategies – talking to write, blogging, and the conference – as sites for performance, rehearsal and practice.

Chapter 7 addresses the conviction that writing must be right. DRs often use templates and prefabs, such as predetermined thesis structures, when they think there is one-best way to write a thesis. We counter this view with the reframing idea of form and function working together and we offer strategies that focus on moves to help the DR build structure – writing chunks, storyboarding, thesis abstracts and writing introduction and chapter abstracts.

In Chapter 8 we address the common mythology that research is always a matter for a dispassionate detached observer. Instead we offer the idea of writing with the right 'I'. We look specifically at the ways in which DRs can use their introduction and conclusion to build a credible scholarly persona.

Chapter 9 tackles one of our very favourite misconceptions – that all that is required to produce good writing is that it be carefully edited. We argue for revision, not tidying up. The strategies we propose cover the use of headings, reworking paragraphs, working with nominalisations and finding the balance of active and passive voice.

To conclude, Chapter 10 addresses the 'student' lurking within the DR. It offers the notion of styling yourself as a confident scholar. We propose four strategies which address the final stage editing of the thesis– checking your hedging, guiding the reader, quoting carefully and proofreading.

In sum

We're not going to labour the metaphor of the detox any more. We hope it's done its job in this first chapter, offering a way to think about the purpose of the book.

To sum up, our book is intended to address a number of common problems that get in the way of writing a compelling thesis. We've seen a lot of discussion about all of these problems online, and we've read quite a lot of draft theses and workshop texts that suffer from these problems.

We offer both strategies and reframing ideas for each of our identified problems because we know that it helps not simply to DO something different about an unproductive pattern of writing, but also to interrupt the usual ways in which you think about it.

We want to be reassuring. We want to assure you that you are not alone in thinking that doctoral writing can be difficult and that doing a doctorate can stretch you very thin. And, perhaps rather like the detox gurus we loathe, we want to suggest that the problems we have can actually be our friends – if we address them, see what lies at the heart of the issue, and develop ways to attend to them. A problem understood and addressed, if not ever entirely resolved, is your aim.

We don't think that the DRs who read this book will experience all of the problems we've addressed. Some of you will therefore want to find the chapter that deals with the problem confronting you right now. Others will want to read the book as a linear text, start at the beginning and move forward chapter by chapter. We hope that the book can be read in both these ways, and also be used as a source book that you can dip in and out of, casually, as a kind of companion.

2 Understanding the doctoral game

The problem: I was academically successful but now . . .

Starting the doctorate can be difficult. You are plunged suddenly into a new world where there are different sets of goals, expectations, conventions, standards and rules. You are no longer doing a course someone else has structured, no longer following someone else's body of work. Whether you are working as a graduate assistant, designing your own research proposal, or working in the field on your own project, you are now in a new game.

If you've left university and been successful in the professions or business, you're not coming back to the same place you left. Not only are you different, but what you are expected to do is too. Universities have changed. The old habits and practices that made you successful in the past won't necessarily be those that stand you in good stead now. So what has changed?

The doctorate is not the same as the other degrees you've completed. What's more, the doctorate is not the same as it once was. The doctorate was once a kind of scholarly apprenticeship. Aspiring scholars came to sit in the studies of learned professors and under their guidance produced a massive tome that sat in the bowels of the university library gathering dust. The newly doctored moved on to cloistered rooms of their own. These days DRs enter the university as a cohort, engage in numerous postgraduate classes as well as tutorials with supervisors, and write pared-down texts that are put into accessible digital repositories. Increasing numbers of Doctors find work outside higher education.

There are now many more doctoral programmes of different types and those enrolled in doctorates are a far more diverse group than ever before. Doctorates are now offered part-time, full-time, face-to-face, online, and in various mixed modes. The person enrolled in a doctorate may well be straight from their undergraduate and Masters or be a professional returning from the workplace or a retiree fulfilling a lifetime ambition.

Today, the doctorate is an important part of government policymaking, with considerations of fees, visas and reasons for study having equal billing with issues of research funding. While there is still a requirement to produce a contribution to knowledge, the emphasis on the uniqueness and singular originality of the thesis has lessened in importance. Thus, in recent times, more and more training course work has been introduced into doctorates. While this has been the norm in North America, this practice has now extended into the UK, mainland Europe, Australia and New Zealand and South Africa. This is because the PhD and the newer professional doctorates are mostly seen as general training for a career in research, either in higher education or in a public or business context. The language of 'delivery' and 'deliverables', 'outputs' and 'outcomes', 'incentivisation', 'standards', 'measurement' and 'quality' are a ubiquitous accompaniment to the contentious move away from education to 'training'.

Philosopher Peter Rickman is among many who are troubled by this shift (see Commentary: Peter Rickman).

We stand for education and see the doctorate as containing elements of training. These are mandated and there is little point suggesting to you as DRs that it is possible to get away from these requirements. But we do think that it is helpful to focus on what is possible beyond training.

We think the first action is to take stock of where you are. Understand the game and how it impacts on you. Who are you as a doctoral researcher and doctoral writer? What do examiners really expect of you? What is this high-stakes text about? What is it meant to look like? Who are you writing for? And how do you approach the vast scholarship that has preceded you?

As we suggested in the Introduction, the principle of the detox is to interrupt your patterns and habits, to reflect on common misconceptions about doctoral study, and to experiment with new ways of doing, being and understanding. So, what is it about your old thinking that might cause trouble in the new situation you are in? What does the doctorate actually ask you to do?

We offer four frameworks to aid your reflection, new tools for thinking differently about the doctoral project you have taken on. We call these reframing ideas. They are:

1   making a modest contribution
2   building a scholarly identity
3   writing as a social and cultural practice
4   entering a scholarly conversation

COMMENTARY

Peter Rickman

Education versus training

We need to consider the distinction between education and training. Broadly speaking we are familiar with the distinction. A father is supposed to have said: 'If my daughter told me she was getting sex education in school I'd be pleased. If she told me she got sex training I'd go straight to the police.' Training is about practice, about skill, about learning how to do things. Education is about fostering the mind, by encouraging it to think independently and introducing it to knowledge of the physical and cultural world. It's about theory, understanding and a sense of values. There is, of course, some overlap. Practice may require some theory and education may require some skills, such as reading and writing. To teach literature, for example, is obviously part of education as it provides insights, mental enjoyment and an appreciation of beauty; it may also improve your eloquence in selling cars but that's a fringe benefit.

It is, however, important to hold on to the different roles the two play in human life because politicians and, indeed, educators obscure the distinction and talk of education when they mean training. Of course, pleading the importance of education does not mean ignoring the pressing need for training. We can hardly do without farmers, engineers, doctors, dentists, teachers, builders and so on and each job requires skills which need to be learned. I have already mentioned that elementary education involves teaching children to read and write. Mathematics too, is at this stage not so much an intellectual exercise as the practice of dealing with money, or measuring up for the sitting room carpet. It is rightly argued that the prosperity of a country, indeed its survival and the quality of life of its citizens, depends on extensive and efficient training in a whole range of skills.

Today, few would argue against the need for training but education is, by contrast, often seen as a kind of luxury. So universities under financial pressure tend to cut theoretical subjects such as mathematics or physics, history or literature and, above all, philosophy. This, I want to argue, is a fatal mistake.

© Peter Rickman, Philosophy Now issue 47
http://philosophynow.org/issues/47/
Education_versus_Training

Reframing idea 1: making a modest 'contribution'?

You've just enrolled in the doctorate. You know one of the defining tasks of the PhD is to make an original contribution to knowledge. Something substantial. This can be a terrifying idea or possibly exhilarating. But what does it actually mean to write something new that is original? How big is a contribution? How small? Is it a cure for cancer? Something no one has ever thought of before? Or something more manageable?

One way to get some perspective on this challenge is to consider what doctoral examiners expect. Australian researchers Gerry Mullins and Margaret Kiley (2002) examined the processes that examiners go through and the judgements they make on doctoral theses. Their review of previous research suggests that examiners are not as focused on originality as DRs might think. Thesis examiners told them that their first impressions of the thesis counted – if the text was badly proofread or if the literature review was halting and limited, they were positioned to feel worried about what was to come. And examiners pointed out that there was a big difference between a 'passing' thesis and one that was 'good' or 'outstanding'. Mullins and Kiley suggest that this has implications for the ways in which DRs think about what they must achieve in their thesis (see Commentary: Gerry Mullins and Margaret Kiley).

Mullins and Kiley are not the only ones to think that the focus on original contribution can be overstated. While it might have been the test applied by learned professors sitting in their book-lined studies examining a handful of doctoral theses in a decade, the changes in the number of DRs enrolled, combined with the changed emphasis of the degree, now mean that what is generally understood as 'the contribution' has reduced.

UK Professor of Politics Paul Cairney argues that it is the view of the doctorate as training that has brought about this shift in meaning and requirements (see Commentary: Paul Cairney).

Regardless of whether we agree with the view of the doctorate as training or not, we concur with Cairney that the doctorate is not an impossible ask. It is one that is potentially within the reach of everyone enrolled. The contribution that is asked for is relatively modest, but is something where clarity of thought and rigour in process is conveyed through a well-expressed, well-organised thesis. The thesis 'text' is the evidence that the examiner uses – not to see whether the DR has found an earth-shattering idea – but to see how well they have conceptualised a problem, situated it in the relevant field and literatures, carried out their inquiry, communicated the results of their analysis – and argued for their modest and achievable contribution.

COMMENTARY

Gerry Mullins and Margaret Kiley

It's not a Nobel prize

For students, the most heartening information is that experienced examiners want them to be awarded the PhD and will go to extraordinary lengths to enable this to happen. The other information is that experienced examiners should be sought for the examination process, not avoided, because of their high degree of tolerance. These two factors arise from the examiners' experience as supervisors and their ability to judge the standard of a thesis based on a wide range of other examples. As one commented, 'As an examiner, you are not being a supervisor, but being aware of what students go through to get to that point makes one, hopefully, a wiser, less pedantic person and able to see what's being achieved. Also, you are able to see the vulnerability of the student' (SocSc/Female/7). As another said, 'I tend to be absolutely forensic when I mark a thesis and then I spend hours worrying about how harsh I've been ... have to argue myself into a sympathetic and tolerant framework. If you don't exercise tolerance it's very easy to mark a thesis' (SocSc/Male/15).

Indeed, some interviewees expressed their reluctance to send their own students' theses to examiners outside the university system because people from industry or from research institutes might not understand the limitations of the postgraduate situation. It is feared that they might examine it as if the student has had several research assistants and a large grant to set up the research—in other words 'with little understanding of the student's situation' (Sc/Female/12).

Warnings to students are also clear from the research: careful attention to detail and the avoidance of sloppiness are essential. Sloppy presentation indicates to the examiner that the research might well be sloppy. The other warning is the importance of being assiduous about actually doing what one says one is going to do, or explaining how and why changes have been made. The results of this research indicate that experienced examiners check carefully for the link between the introduction, where students outline their intentions, and the conclusions, where the intentions should have been realised.

... however, the final word of advice should go to students from one of our interviewees: 'A PhD is a stepping stone into a research career. All you need to do is to demonstrate your capacity for independent, critical thinking. That's all you need to do. A PhD is three years of solid work, not a Nobel Prize' (Maths–Eng/Female/18).

Mullins & Kiley, 2002, pp. 385–6

COMMENTARY

Paul Cairney

Being realistic about the PhD

We see the PhD (at least increasingly) as a way to demonstrate proficiency in research methods, information gathering, and presentation. So, a common answer to a problem about how you do a literature review or deal with data limitations is that you should demonstrate that you have used your training and skills to produce the right outcome. There is no right answer, but there are established ways to demonstrate that you have the skills to produce an answer. This usually starts with having a clear and realistic research question. Then, it's about showing that your engagement with the literature is geared specifically to answering that question (not a big list of points about the literature), that you have selected the most appropriate method(s), that you can write drafts and respond correctly to feedback, and that you can make oral/conference presentations and generate more feedback.

This emphasis seems preferable to, for example, trying to demonstrate some sort of awesome 'gap' in the literature or that you are challenging the conventional wisdom (imagine every PhD challenging what came before – it would be exhausting). I wouldn't rule gap-identification out completely, but I'd be careful about making exaggerated claims. Sometimes an examiner will end up thinking that the gap was there for a reason (the PhD does not demonstrate the topic's importance) or that its identification of a gap is rather artificial (which is a common ploy used by more senior academics that should really set a better example). For me, a PhD will look more convincing if you provide a quite-respectful review of the relevant literature, demonstrating how it helps guide your research (and, for example, how your case compares with cases in other fields or countries) and how your study will help improve it. This can often be about adding nuance to established findings (for example, when someone uses case studies to add depth to general assumptions about political behaviour) rather than shattering them.

The PhD will be less than perfect and that's OK. I often tell PhD students that they will be surprised about how low the bar is to successful completion – not because the bar is too low, but because it is at a realistic level, in which examiners recognise what you can do in three years when you have just begun a research career.

https://paulcairney.wordpress.com/2015/02/24/phd-chat-the-phd-as-a-record-of-research-training-not-a-perfect-achievement/

Reframing idea 2: building a scholarly identity

Through writing the thesis you are writing a new expert self, building a new researcher identity.

When you're writing the PhD you are swamped in ideas. The text is everything. How to phrase an idea, how to conceptualise in a pithy way, how to use the meta-language of your discipline, how to order ideas on the page and across chapters so they make sense. However, the framing idea we want you to consider is that you are not just writing a text. You are also writing yourself. When you are in the middle of writing page after page, it might feel like this is all there is. But in reality there is a lot more going on.

When you write the doctorate, you also produce yourself as a scholar. You are associating yourself with particular scholars and not others, you're making claims for who you are, where you stand and what you know. This is why your examiner will probably first read your introduction to find out what your question is and then read your references, to find out where you stand in the field, who you're drawing on.

Text work and identity work are inseparable (see Commentary: Barbara Kamler and Pat Thomson). Like the pink streaks in a raspberry ripple cake that cannot be prised apart from the moist yellow, the scholarly text and the scholarly identity can't be separated. Or to provide a healthier metaphor, you can't separate the ginger and mint leaves out of the watermelon juice once they have been blended.

You might not think it now, but when you look back on your completed thesis, you will see that it is not simply a big book or a collection of published articles, it embodies who you are and speaks to what you're now doing. When Helen Gunter, an education academic at the University of Manchester looked back on the thesis she wrote 10 years earlier, she saw that it was going back to a very formative time and text (Gunter, 2010) (see Experience: Helen Gunter).

Scholars are always in formation. Post-PhD you will continue to grow a scholarly self and a scholarly agenda. Other people will know you through your writing. They know who you are, what you know and what you stand for. They make decisions about you on this basis. This is why most of us feel vulnerable when we send our writing out into the world. Whether we like it or not, people equate our writing with us. These days universities have got in on this act too. They equate our writing with our quality as a scholar and this plays out in employment, promotion and quality audit regimes and success in finding and getting a job in the first place.

Pat now finds that people often come up and speak to her as if they know her well because they read her blog. In a sense this is true. The problem is that she doesn't know them. But this just goes to show there is a strong link between writing and identity – feeling that you 'know' somebody because you've read them.

COMMENTARY

Barbara Kamler and Pat Thomson

Textwork/Identitywork

The writing identity link is difficult to see. The text is tangible. The thesis or a conference paper has a materiality – of word length, margin width, page design, title. This is the text. But the process of writing that text, of drafting and crafting and struggling to find the right words has material effects. It creates the scholar who at the end of writing is different than the writer who began. Perhaps a bit more knowing and confident, perhaps still worried about having something worthy to say, perhaps a bit bolder or willing to take greater risks.

Writing a text AND writing a self at the same time is hard labour indeed. Writers often experience difficulties and textual struggles because they are negotiating text work and identity work at the same time. It is not just a matter of personal inadequacy or not being smart enough. But in university contexts such matters are rarely spoken about – because writers feel ashamed – and because there is no adequate public discourse available.

The challenge for doctoral researchers is not simply about undertaking a piece of research and producing a text. It is also about making the transition from an identity of 'student' – for those who progress from undergraduate degree to the doctorate – or 'professional' – for those who start their PhD in mid career. Both 'students' and 'professionals' need to make the transition to 'scholar', 'academic' or 'alt academic'.

Making the transition to 'scholar /academic' is about the acquisition of knowledge and competencies. It is about taking up a position of expertise and authority. The doctoral researcher often has to adopt this new expert stance before feeling ready to do so. The transition can cause anxiety. Am I going to get there? Is it ever going to happen? Am I ever not going to feel like a fraud or imposter?

Kamler & Thomson, 2014, p.16

Of course the kind of scholarly identity formed through text work is not just an individual identity. It is, as Steph Lawler, a feminist sociologist at the University of York, points out, socially framed in ways that are both enabling and limiting (Lawler, 2008) (see Commentary: Steph Lawler). You are joining an academic community, one which some critics dismiss as an 'ivory tower'. This community has expectations about your writing and theorising.

The scholarly identity that you are assuming in the thesis is highly constrained. It is shaped within particular frames and possibilities, as we discuss in the next

EXPERIENCE

Helen Gunter

My thesis, my life

In taking my bound PhD thesis from 1999 off the shelf and turning the pages I am not just removing the dust from everyday living, I am going into something that is alive and central to who I am and who others close to me are (Gunter, 1999). In looking at the blue cover, the gold lettering, the crisp white pages, the text with letters and numbers in a particular order, I can see not only an account of something that I spent five years of my life thinking and writing about, but also that there is a history here of my life.

What looks to be linear, neat and tidy, was messy, crazy and wonderfully exciting. The thesis is an archived moment that says so much more to me as I have memories about the life in which this thesis happened: I typed, I wrote with pen and paper, I talked, I thought, I cried, I drank coffee, I read, I listened, I was silent, I slept and I wept. While the pages themselves are intrinsically silent, there is a noisy biography within it and my construction of this narrative is clearly based on self-authoring in the here and now. Notably my post postgraduate experiences are an important lens through which I have emplotted this 'history-in-person' (Holland & Lave, 2001, pp. 5–6), not least how the thesis has shaped my ongoing research project.

Gunter, 2010, p. 81

section. That is, you are not simply free to choose your identity. You take action, but always within particular contexts and conventions.

Of course you are never just one 'self'. You have multiple and competing identities as student, parent, child, partner, friend, colleague, professional (Du Gay, Evans, & Redman, 2000). You are already juggling multiple 'selves' and their competing demands as you carve out time to do your doctoral coursework, read extensively, write essays, prepare your doctoral proposal defence. These multiple selves don't always sit together easily. There are lots of stories about people who not only struggle to find the time to do their doctorate, but to marry together some of their existing relationships and emerging sense of themselves (e.g. Dinkins & Sorrell, 2014; Ely, Vinz, Downing, & Anzul, 1997). *Educating Rita* is the classic example of someone who grew apart from her social milieu as she became an 'educated' person.

Supervisors acknowledge this growth. They understand that they know more than the DR at the start of the candidature. But it is the doctoral researcher who is the expert in the topic at the end. It's been a long process of growing from DR to

COMMENTARY

Steph Lawler

Identity as social

'Being made' as a person, as an identity (or, more accurately, a set of overlapping and contradictory identities), throws up troubles: It is perhaps when identity is seen to 'fail' that we see most clearly the social values that dictate how an identity ought to be. Lines are constantly drawn and redrawn between' us' and 'them', and these lines are drawn around identities such as 'they' embody all of the social disapproved forms of identity. Disapproved forms of identity vary somewhat according to the context, but their contemporary forms include inauthenticity (not being oneself), dependency and passivity (not being autonomous, not 'choosing'), unaware- ness of oneself and one's origins (not knowing 'who you are') and being part of a mob (not being an individual).

. . . although identities are seen as 'natural', and although we are enjoined to be 'true to ourselves', it is also believed that people ought in some sense to choose 'good' identities. A gap begins to open up between the concept of natural identity and the very powerful contemporary rhetoric of choice and autonomy.

The idea that we can 'be whatever we want to be' relies on an illusory eclipsing of the social world.

Lawler, 2008, p. 144.

Doctor Supervisors see the effort the DR has to make in their text to assume the required amount of authority. If the thesis reads as if it was written by a 'student' it won't be easy for the DR to get through a viva or oral defence. At the end of 3 years, the DR must act and talk like an *expert* researcher with a command of the literature, methodology, methods, results and contribution. Writing the thesis is the key site for this development.

Reframing idea 3: writing as a social and cultural practice

Another helpful approach to the thesis is to consider the ways in which the text has to work for a complex set of potential readers.

It's not just a question of you and the course and the professor or tutor, or you and the supervisor or committee. There are multiple shadowy figures who will affect how you write and what you write. Some of them are real, some imaginary, some living and some dead. Together, they constitute the social frameworks for your doctorate. Doctoral writing, in this context, is a social practice, which must meet rules, conventions, expectations of disciplines and institutions. These are determined outside of the tutorial and supervision session and precede your entry into the PhD.

The framework we've developed for understanding doctoral writing as a social practice borrows from the fields of critical discourse analysis and new literacy studies. We find Norman Fairclough's (1992) three-dimensional model of discourse useful for conceptualising the tensions and demands faced by doctoral writers and their supervisors. Fairclough uses the term discourse to refer to the way people *use* spoken and written language. Referring to language use as discourse signals that using language is social rather than individual action. Further, language as social action cannot be divorced from any other aspects of social life and social relations. It is both produced and reproduced in social contexts.

We can visualise language use in its social and cultural context as a three–part interactive structure: text, discourse practice and social practice (see Three Layer Model, Figure 2.1). This model is a powerful visual heuristic for showing that no text is ever produced in isolation from its context. It represents both the effects of broader social contexts on writing and the way writing itself is a form of social interaction, embedded in institutions and social structures.

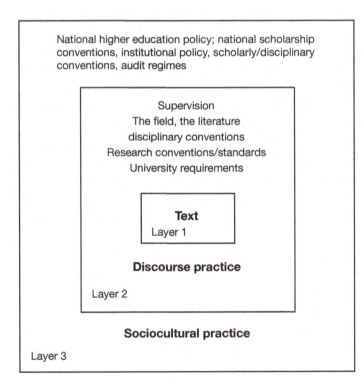

FIGURE 2.1 Three layer model of discourse

In this model the centre layer is the text, the actual spoken or written span of language that writers or speakers produce. In the outer layer is the broader cultural context, including the discipline and the university and its specific practices, histories, conventions and expectations. In the middle layer (between the text and the discipline/university) sits supervision, where supervisor or advisory committee members judge and evaluate the text as well as shape and facilitate its production.

Anthony Parè, Professor and Dean of Education at UBC, Canada, points out the important gatekeeping role supervisors play in this middle layer (Layer 2), moderating and monitoring what is acceptable to the discipline and other potential readers who are unknown to the DR (see Commentary: Anthony Parè).

COMMENTARY

Anthony Parè

Supervisory feedback and the dissertation

In a very real sense, doctoral supervisors are writing teachers. As they guide students through the dissertation process, they are introducing them to discipline-specific discourse practices. They advise on how and where certain things should be said, on what must and must not be mentioned, and on who should or should not be cited or criticized. Through feedback, questions, suggestions, and instruction, they help students locate their written contribution within the historical, intellectual, and rhetorical trends and traditions of their field. In addition, they are the arbiters of quality, and must determine if and when the student has achieved an acceptable level of specialized thought and expression. As Green (2005) notes, the doctoral supervisor 'represents, or stands in for, the Discipline itself, and also the Academy' (p. 162).

In this high-stakes, intimate tutorial – possibly the most crucial educational relationship of a student's life – new scholars are initiated into the process of making disciplinary knowledge through writing. Each discipline and subdiscipline sets its research gaze on certain phenomena, uses community-approved methods to collect relevant data, draws on different kinds of evidence, and finally crafts particular types of argument that are deployed within the discipline's set of acceptable research genres. In large part, new scholars are initiated into this process by more experienced members of the disciplinary community – by teachers, by committee members, and most particularly by doctoral supervisors.

Parè, 2011, pp. 59–60

It is not an easy thing to grasp how Layer 3 impacts on supervision when you start the PhD. Layer 3 includes influences that are not readily visible to the DR, such as university and higher education policies or global frameworks such as the Bologna Agreement and a raft of the technological, economic and cultural changes, understood as globalisation (Thomson & Walker, 2010). These seem remote from the immediate day-to-day demands of getting going. However, they are already at work, even at this early stage of candidature, shaping what you can do and say. Your topic choice, for example, and your initial proposal will be developed under the influence of Layer 3.

While you may be aware that your Supervisor and Committees shape the thesis through their comments, conversation, recommendations and track changes on your text, it is useful to understand this as doing Layer 2 work. That is, they literally embody the broader scholarly and specific disciplinary communities and their norms. You will, of course, also be supported and regulated by teachers of various graduate and postgraduate training courses, seminars and workshops.

Importantly, the examiners also sit in Layer 2 and their job is clearly regulatory. They decide if your text is acceptable – or not. They are selected because of their relative standing in the scholarly community and therefore their capacity to make decisions on its behalf. Sociologist Howard Becker, best known for his ethnographic studies of music and art, was one of the first to publish about the importance of doctoral writing within a specific discipline, in his case, Social Science (Becker, 1986). While he didn't use our three layer construct, he was clear about its importance (see Commentary: Howard Becker).

Becker clearly identifies Layer 2 considerations – the examiners who will pass judgement on the thesis. He highlights the need to consider Layer 3, how others in the community will regard the thesis in relation to their own work and to the field. Sometimes people dismiss Layer 2 as a hoop to jump through, and Layer 3 as simply a set of unnecessary and tiresome politics. While this may be partly true, it is also the case that these layers are helpful as well as obstructive, enabling as well as regulatory, and that some of these constraints are productive. As Becker notes, it is possible to shuck off these conventions and restraints – but only if one is prepared for the consequences. In the case of a doctoral thesis, this can be failure from the examiners (Layer 2) and mistrust of the scholarship and the scholar (Layer 3).

COMMENTARY

Howard Becker

Writing with Layer 3 in mind

One way to understand the problem of writing is to see it in context. We write what we write – in the case at hand, a dissertation – in the context of academic institutions. The problem's solution, in this context, requires not only putting together ideas and evidence clearly and convincingly. It also requires that we satisfy the requirements those institutions insist on for such a document.

The author, the dissertation writer, has first to satisfy the immediate readers, the people who will say yes or no, pass or don't pass, go back and do it again and we'll have another look or, for the lucky ones, 'Well done! Get it published and get on with your life and work'. People who serve as this kind of reader – for the most part reasonable, sane people – still have to consider more than the quality of the work before them. They think about the politics of their departments ('Old George will have an apoplectic fit if you attack his favorite theory') or, more commonly, of the discipline ('I agree with what you have written, but if you take that unpopular position or write in that unconventional style you will have trouble getting your work published') and as a result suggest changes in substance and style that have no reason in logic or taste, but which result purely from academic convention.

Becker(undated) www.dur.ac.uk/ writingacrossboundaries/ writingonwriting/howardsbecker/

But is this just a recipe for the status quo, for academic writing and theses never changing? Are supervisors' comments about expectations and common practices just a way to get you to conform? Some of you may well be worried about the press of convention and your desire to do something new and creative (see Experience: Anon). We share this concern. However, we know that it is possible to push the boundaries. But this requires careful strategy. Layer 3 cannot be simply ignored. It must not only be understood, but also used in order to legitimate the changes.

Change does happen. A good example can be seen in the way in which university thesis regulations are being challenged now that researchers are engaging with large amounts of digital material. As disciplines such as history, education, sociology and cultural studies have embraced the affordance of digital technologies to both analyse and represent research findings, it has become clear that thesis rules – such as those which require double-spaced texts with particular margins and fonts – are seriously out of date.

EXPERIENCE

Anon

Managing Layer 3

. . . in undertaking a PhD project not only are you honing your skills as a researcher, while discovering about the field that you are working in and what it means to be part of the academy, you are also working out who you are as a researcher, what is important to you and what your values are. These are not insignificant issues to be dealing with alongside the pressures of carrying out rigorous and original research . . . in order to work out what you the new researcher can bring to the story to be told, you must work out who you are as a researcher.

As a PhD researcher, how do you find a balance between yourself as an evolving academic who is both part of and a product of the academy, and your emerging values and beliefs as a researcher? For me, at least, there is often tension between these two forces as they pull in different ways.

By accepting my place as a PhD student I have agreed to participate in the conventions of the PhD process under the rules and regulations of the academy. But how far can PhD students go to challenge the conventions from within, whilst still adhering to the regulations that they have agreed to, in order to be 'true' to her/himself?

www.canterbury.ac.uk/education/conferences-events/constructing-narratives/docs/Graham,Matheson,Laura.pdf

Richard Andrews, Professor of English at the Institute of Education, London, is concerned that universities are not taking adequate account of the changing nature of doctoral research, in particular via serious engagement with digital materials. Together with Jude England, head of Social Science at the British Library, Andrews argues that institutional thesis regulations need to change to accommodate the pressure from disciplinary communities to inculcate new scholars into these emerging digital research practices (Andrews & England, 2012) (see Commentary: Richard Andrews and Jude England). They point out that where disciplinary communities have generated a critical mass of scholarship and advocates, they are often able to change institutional rules to accommodate new scholarly practices.

In sum, the third framing idea suggests it is a mistake to think of the thesis as the result of conversations between you and your supervisor and committee. A big mistake. They are never your only readers. They stand in for many others in guiding and framing the work that you do.

COMMENTARY

Richard Andrews and Jude England

A typology of theses

There are now a wide range of approaches to incorporating digital material into the thesis. Andrews and England suggest universities now need to consider new kinds of guidance for the examination of these kinds of dissertations. They offer two additions to the usual and conventional kind of descriptors of what counts as a thesis – those which are up to 50 per cent material other than words, and those which are up to 100 per cent artistic or technological. They suggest that dissertations can now be understood as:

1 Conventional dissertations – mostly in words and numbers, with tables and data. These are typically archived in libraries as hard copy or microfiche – the Big Book – and digital versions made available as pdfs in a thesis repository.

2 Dissertations with some typographical awareness and variation – the Big Book is designed using different forms of spacing, fonts etc. Colour may be used (this is not good for microfiche). These are typically archived in libraries as hard copy – the Big Book – and digital versions made available as pdfs in a thesis repository.

3 Illustrated dissertations – while the dissertation is still print based, there is extensive use of images produced to a high standard. A pdf is the most accurate and economical storage solution.

4 More equitable distribution of the verbal and the visual – where the visual plays an equal, or even a more substantial, part than words in the presentation of the argument. Again, pdf is the most accurate and economical storage solution.

5 Use of other modes beyond the visual and verbal – presentation includes three-dimensional and tactile and other modes of communication (such as performance) which may be presented on DVD. These can be stored as pdf – and as DVDs which have an uncertain shelf life. However the storage of three-dimensional objects on DVD reduces them to two dimensions which may affect their meaning-making capacity.

6 Fully-fledged multimodal dissertations in different media – portfolio, web-based or other kinds of non-print based installation or media presented for final examination. These are not practice-based dissertations; there is still a thesis text, but it is multimodal. The preservation of such material on cloud and other storage platforms is a complex matter, and requires ongoing attention (preservation of hyperlinks being just one of the problems that might arise).

Andrews & England, 2012, p. 9

Reframing idea 4: you are entering a scholarly conversation

The thesis can be thought of as an invitation to enter a scholarly 'conversation' (Burke, 1941). When the thesis is examined, two or three readers will engage with what you have to say at length and in depth. This is a relatively unusual occurrence in the academy. Most often scholars have to insert themselves into conversations without waiting to be asked in. The thesis is a supported way to make this first move.

The idea of entering a conversation may be new to you. In your precious undergraduate and Masters' work, you will probably have been asked to report and perhaps comment on the conversations that other scholars have had. This practice of summarising and synthesising the ideas of more learned academics got you to the doctorate. However, this is no longer adequate. You need to move away from listening in to become a more active participant. In the doctorate you are not a passive eavesdropper. You need to know and understand the conversation you're in, and also how to participate. You need to think about how to enter, what is your opening gambit and what are the most important things you want to say.

The thesis is often called a monograph, but it isn't a monologue. Far from it. At this very moment, there are lots of other people working away on topics that are not too dissimilar to your own. There are, of course, multitudes of scholars who have come before you who have something relevant to offer. There are scholarly works that you might want to answer back to, some that you want to add to, and some that you just want to forget about. This is the conversation that you are going to enter through your writing.

Thinking about the writing as a conversation is helpful because it cues you into the question of conversational etiquette. In a real-life conversation it's considered rude if you just barge into an ongoing conversation without any mind to what's been happening, fail to say hello, talk over people, take their ideas and claim them as your own, or act as if you're the only person who has anything worth saying. It's poor form as well to shuffle up to a conversation and stand there eavesdropping, waiting to be invited to speak, but without giving anything of yourself away. The first person is simply a boor, the second a bore.

The kinds of conventions that apply in real life also apply to academic conversations carried out in texts. We say more about this in the chapters to come, but for now we think it's important to stress that you need to pay attention to what else is happening in the academic conversation you want to join. As Graff and Birkenstein (2010, p.4) put it:

> To make an impact as a writer, you need to do more than make statements that are logical, well supported, and consistent. You must also find a way of

entering a conversation with others' views – with something 'they say' . . . if your own argument doesn't identify the 'they say' that you're responding to, it probably won't make sense . . . *(w)hat* you are saying may be clear to your audience, but *why* you are saying it won't be. For it is what others are saying and thinking that motivates our writing and gives it a reason for being. It follows, then. . .that your own argument – the [thesis or] "I say"moment of your text – should always be a response to the arguments of others.

The way to tell what is an appropriate contribution to a conversation is by knowing the milieu you are entering, its conventions, interests, ongoing concerns and histories. Just as you wouldn't walk into a room and simply repeat what somebody else has just said, you don't enter an academic conversation with something that is already known or something that everyone has already agreed on. You offer something more substantial. You continue the conversation either by agreeing or disagreeing with another's argument, putting a new point of view – or occasionally leading the topic elsewhere.

And this is how it is with academic conversations too. Through the thesis you establish your relationship with those already in the conversation (Clarke, 2006). To do this you must find an entry point – either 'supporting an argument, debating an argument, or announcing that an argument now needs to be made' (Belcher, 2009, p. 151). You acknowledge what has been discussed before, by referring to other people's contributions to the conversation, and you make your own position in relation to them clear. You also accept that the conversation, which was going on before you arrived, will continue after you have had your say.

ADVICE

Elizabeth Rankin

Writing into the conversation

As writers our first obligation is to think about what we are contributing to that conversation – what new information, insight, theoretical perspective, argument, application, approach, or deepened understanding we have to share with others in our field. As we write and revise it is vitally important to stay focused on that contribution and to make sure that our readers stay focused on it as well.

For our writing to be effective, there is nothing more important than this.

Rankin, 2001, p. 10

Even experienced academic writers sometimes find this hard to do. Writing group instructor Elizabeth Rankin (2001) suggests that there is one key implication of understanding academic writing as entering a conversation – you have to keep one eye on what you have to say and the other on the reader (see Advice: Elizabeth Rankin).

In sum

This chapter has focused on four interruptions to habits you may have formed in your previous university work. Even though you have been a successful student up to now, there are some habits that you may bring into the doctorate that will get in the way of success. You have been used to writing assignments, thinking of yourself as a student, and working to meet the requirements of a teacher/supervisor. These patterns are no longer sufficient. Instead we suggest that you focus on writing as an entrée into a scholarly conversation, reimagine yourself as a researcher, and locate yourself in the relevant disciplinary and institutional contexts. This textwork/identitywork is the basis of all of the scholarly writing that you will do from now on.

3 Beginning literature work

The problem: lost in the reading

Many DRs dread literature work. The more they read the more confused they get. Maybe this is your problem too.

It is likely that your supervisor has suggested a very long list of key books and papers you absolutely have to know. You do an initial search and find 2,000 plus items on your topic and nothing to help you decide which is most important. You clearly need to read now, read a lot and start making notes. You have to get on top of a whole new field.

Part of the problem is quantity. There is so much to read. There is so much written. How do you select what is relevant? Or discard what is not? Do you read everything?

However, quantity is not the only problem. DRs are not always clear about their purposes for reading. As a newcomer to the field you may have no overview of broader issues and debates to help you sift the readings. Beginners lack Layer 3 knowledge (see Chapter 2). Floundering in the dark, it is difficult to find a filter. Everything feels equally important. How do you distinguish the more pivotal readings from those that are less important, the debates and trends from the finer points of difference between scholars in your discipline?

The kinds of metaphors DRs routinely use to describe work with the literature confirm the problem. These metaphors are often about feeling out of control – floundering, drowning, being lost, sinking in quicksand. Pat and Barbara have researched and written about these metaphors (see Thomson & Kamler, 2013; Thomson podcast on *www.literaturereviewhq.com/episode-5-did-you-know-youre-a-professional-writer-expert-interview-with-pat-thomson/*). Looking for the pot of gold at the end of the rainbow is also commonly used. DRs seek magic answers – and hope to find their reward in the literature. However, the *not knowing* persists even after DRs have been reading for some time. There is no neat map to navigate the landscape. You may fear that everyone else has one, and there is something wrong with you because you don't.

The truth is there is no simple, quick recipe for getting on top of the literatures. It is a slow process of getting clear, a process characterised by uncertainty. And in order to get clear, you have to start out being uncertain. But the bad news is that you stay uncertain throughout the doctorate – even though what it is you are uncertain about changes. So there's no point fighting it, uncertainty is part of the process. It is usual. It is to be expected.

UK researchers Gordon Rugg from Keele University and Marian Petrie from Open University (Petrie & Rugg, 2011, p. 68) discuss the uncertainties that accompany different kinds of literature tasks as a set of 'stages'(see Commentary: Gordon Rugg and Marian Petrie). These are worth knowing because they help you reflect on the uncertainty that is an integral part of the research process.

COMMENTARY

Gordon Rugg and Marian Petrie

Stages of knowing and not knowing

The doctoral researcher at the beginning of their research: (1) **knows** the general area that they are interested in researching and (2) **reads** to find out what's already known about it. (3) Their **task** is to survey the field, by collecting, reading, summarising, synthesising and reporting on what's there. (4) They feel uncertain and **wonder** how they can organise these sources in a way that makes sense.

A little later in the process, the doctoral researcher: (1) **knows** what their research topic is to be. (2) They **read** to find more specific information about relevant debates, methods and blank spots. (3) Their **task** is to organise the information into categories and patterns so that they situate their topic in the field. (4) They feel uncertain and **wonder** how they can frame their topic into a question.

Further on, the doctoral researcher: (1) **knows** the research question and (2) **reads** some – the most relevant – texts more closely. (3) Their **task** is to select the groups of literatures most pertinent to the research question and to construct an argument for their research project. (4) They feel uncertain and **wonder** whether they have located all of the relevant material, as well as how their research might speak to what is already known. They can only guess at their potential contribution.

At the end of the research, the completing doctoral researcher: (1) **knows** what research is out there and (2) **reads** to clarify what is most germane to their research and what has been published since they started. But they also read for what isn't known about the topic, so that they can clarify their claims for contribution. (3) Their **task** is to construct an argument in the thesis text which establishes the antecedents for their approach, but also evaluates the field and clearly locates their contribution. (4) They feel uncertain and **wonder** how to connect what they have done with what is already known, as well as what hasn't yet been researched and all the projects that might follow on from their research.

Summary from http://patthomson.net/ 2013/07/01/working-with-literatures-you-have-to-love-the-uncertainty/

What we most like about Rugg and Petrie's heuristic is that it makes clear that there is no one moment when the doctoral – or indeed any – researcher knows everything. They/we are always in a state of both knowing and unknowing. We are always working from one position of knowing/unknowing to another. Uncertainty about something – or wondering, as Rugg and Petrie very helpfully reframe it – is the norm. It actually is the process of research. After all, if you already knew, there would be no point doing the research.

This does not mean DRs are helpless or need to feel out of control. In fact, developing good work practices is the surest way to stay buoyant in the face of uncertainty.

Reframing idea: developing good work practices

We talk a lot about working with literatures and literature work. It's the **work** word that's important here. We all know what work is – work is labour, exertion, effort. It requires diligence and focus. It means undertaking a particular task, using tools appropriate to the job. It's also often about learning what is needed in order to complete on time and produce something worthwhile at the end. Of course, work can be hard, it can be toil, drudgery and sweat, but it can equally be pleasurable, systematic and rewarding. We want you to bring these ideas about work to reading.

The work involved in reading is not about producing something already known. You are not assembling a flat-pack or following a recipe. You are doing creative and inventive work, where there is no right answer. *Your* reading will produce different understandings to another person's, even though there may be some overlap. And literature work is uncertain work, as we've said. That's the nature of it. You can't get rid of the uncertainty, that's just how it is. But there is a great deal you can do to support the process of reading and eventually produce a text that communicates the results of your reading work.

We want you to think of your reading as your professional toolkit. Work is always associated with tools, whether it is the gardener's spade and fork, the carpenter's saw and hammer, or the cook's knives. And the tools of academic work are texts. Texts in all shapes and sizes, genres and media – books, papers, websites, talks and films – these are our scholarly tools.

It's no accident that the popular stereotype of the academic office is one filled to overflowing with books. When you go into an office you are entering the academic's work environment. They have probably been amassing these books since they started doing their own doctorates, if not before. These are the books that they work with and work from over and over again. You can tell a lot about an academic from the books on their shelves: these are a statement about the scholars they stand with and the topics they stand for. Words and books are the tools of our trade.

We want you to love your tools and to take pleasure in them. Rather than seeing reading as a frightening or overwhelming task, we want you to think about it as work with tools of the scholarly trade. Your scholarly textual tools will help you to think, to make sense of your own topic and plan how to develop your own research. They are not to be feared, but to be handled with care, respect and with love.

We offer four strategies for approaching the uncertainties of literature work and for moving forward. They are:

1   understand what reading means

2   find new metaphors to guide literature work

3   create productive routines and workspaces

4   develop systems for recording your reading

Strategy 1: understand what reading means

Almost as soon as you start your PhD you'll be asked to read – and read a lot. Even if you have a clear idea of what you want to research and why, it's highly likely you'll be told to put that on hold and do some reading.

This is not a strange and unusual torture reserved only for DRs. In reality, the vast majority of research projects begin like this. Why? Are we so lacking in confidence about our own ideas and intentions that we have to see what everyone else thinks before we can begin? Or perhaps we are making sure that nobody else has done exactly what we want to do? Or is this a way of dealing with our nervousness about beginning?

There is a grain of truth in all these explanations. But there is more. When we do research we're entering a scholarly conversation (see Chapter 2). So we need to know what others have already said: the agreements and disagreements that exist; the things that are taken for granted; the things that nobody talks about; the things that everyone would love to know more about; what's considered fashionable and ahead of its time or too 'been there done that'; what terms will cause a frisson of horror and what language is preferred and perfectly acceptable. Reading allows us to understand all of these things in relation to our particular topic or interest.

But there is so much to read. So much scholarship already out there. Where to begin? Understanding the distinction between building a collective library and an inner library is a good place to begin.

You don't have to read it all

Pierre Bayard (2007), a Professor of French Literature at the University of Paris VIII, wrote a book called *How to talk about books you haven't read*. He argues that it's actually more important to understand where books fit, rather than try and read them all.

Bayard uses the term *collective library* to describe the totality of texts available on any topic. He argues that readers need to know the content of the text they are reading as well as its relationship to those that they haven't read. Let us give you an example. Suppose we ask you to think about chick lit. You might think of two of the best known examples: *Bridget Jones's diary* (Fielding, 1997) and *Sex and the city* (Bushnell, 1997). These books have in common a female protagonist who writes in the first person and has a complicated family, work and sex life. The books are a kind of second-wave feminist pilgrim's progress towards the impossible dream of marriage and children.

Now you don't need to read every piece of chick lit to know the characteristics of the genre, or to know that its lineage goes back to Jane Austen. You could probably pick up a book in a bookshop, read the blurb at the back and say 'oh that's chick lit!' So you know about the book you've picked up without having to read it. This is Bayard's point.

In the collective library there are many topics and many genres. You can understand the place of a book within the collective library by skimming the contents in order to grasp its most essential points. Bayard suggests it's important to understand the shape of the collective library as well as the relationships that elements of the whole have with each other.

So if you think of your task as establishing the collective library about your research topic, then it is clear you do not need to read everything, but rather work out the categories and genres that exist. In scholarly terms, this means understanding not only substantive common content areas, but also distinctive disciplinary and methodological traditions.

Bayard also talks about an *inner library*, a subset of the collective library. An inner library includes those books that have made a deep impression on you, as well as those that are most useful and used. These are particular books that orient your work and your contribution to the conversation. All scholars assemble their own inner library, the set of texts that help them come to grips with key ideas, debates, gaps and blind spots.

You will continue reading all the way through the doctorate, adding to your understanding of what's the collective library, while carefully selecting key texts for your inner library. It is not unreasonable for DRs to ask their supervisor or committee members to provide a few key texts that should be in their inner library. It's also a good idea to look for any work that maps the collective library. Those little 'beginner guides' and 'introductions to' guides are pretty good for giving you a quick view of the collective library. We know it's heresy, but we think one of the worst things you can do at the start of the PhD is to go to the library and do a big search that pulls up every single article and book that has been written about your topic. You need a way in and it's a long way back if you try to read everything on that enormous search document.

It's good to read surprising things outside your area

Having said that you don't have to read everything, we also want to say that it is important not to just read narrowly. Doing the PhD is a time to engage with the broader scholarship that is relevant to your area. Sometimes this means going beyond what you may conventionally understand is *relevant*. After all, becoming a DR is about becoming a well-educated person, not simply a narrow specialist. It's good to take advantage of the time you have to read some stimulating material outside your field that might, in the end, surprise you.

Lucy is a DR in politics and equity. Her story illustrates this point (see Experience: Lucy's Story).

Scholarship is highly inter-textual, that is, the texts that we write contain references to many other writings, often well beyond what is actually cited. This is writing of the kind that Bakhtin (1981) called heteroglossic. There are multiple layers of meaning in heteroglossic texts, and the more you understand the references that sit behind the actual writing surfaces, the more you get from your reading.

Here is an example. A text might contain a reference to 'surveillance'. The piece might not explore this concept in any depth, if at all, because the writer assumes that you will bring to your reading an understanding of the theory of discipline and surveillance as explicated by Foucault (1977). Even if Foucault is never mentioned, his work is there in the writing. It is hiding behind the term 'surveillance'. If you understand this reference and its hidden allusions, then you will read the piece differently than someone who doesn't have a clue that there is anything more to the term surveillance than its dictionary meaning.

EXPERIENCE

Lucy's Story

When Lucy was studying for a PhD, she joined a reading group. At the time she was enrolled at a university 500 miles away from where she lived. It was hard to travel there often or be part of the everyday research culture. So she worked largely on her own, choosing the books and articles that seemed most germane to her topic.

She was invited to join a reading group at a local university, but all of the group members were focused on youth and popular culture, while she was concerned with questions of policy and equity. There was of course some overlap between their concerns, but their primary reading list looked very different from Lucy's.

Nevertheless, she was keen to be part of a group and decided that reading 'outside' her area would not be a major distraction. And she needed the sociality of the group. Initially, Lucy was concerned that the group were reading a wide range of 'classics', many of which she'd heard of but would not otherwise have picked up, since they didn't seem to be required for her thesis. But this concern soon disappeared.

The books Lucy read with the group sparked off ideas that made her think differently about the problem she was investigating. She made friends with authors that were ultimately useful in her research, even though she hadn't imagined they would be. Indeed, they helped to provide the 'originality' of approach on which the examiners commented favourably. And some of these books and their authors have become staunch allies in the work she continues to do.

But equally important, Lucy found that, in reading these books, she gained a deeper understanding of many other books in the collective library.

The point is that reading in the social sciences and/or arts and humanities is never just a question of reading the words on the page. It is always about intertextuality and is dependent on what intellectual resources the reader can bring to the task. The more the reader understands key texts, histories of ideas, debates, traditions and trends within the discipline and field generally, the greater their appreciation and understanding of what is written.

The upshot of Lucy's early reading group experience is that she has not forgotten the importance of reading outside her field. She currently has a wide range of books on her reading pile, many of which don't seem immediately relevant to her current research, but which are providing stimulation and new resources to think with. Overall, these disparate texts are deepening her understanding of knowledge-producing traditions in related areas and creating a deeper reservoir of potential meaning-making resources.

Strategy 2: find new metaphors to guide literature work

We want to introduce you to one of our favourite strategies for taking control of literature work. This is using metaphors to frame and reframe your thinking about particular kinds of textwork/identitywork. We will be doing metaphor work throughout the book to add to your thinking resources.

We're sure you know that a metaphor is when we talk about one thing as if it is something else. Not as if it is *like* something else, but as if it *is* that something else. Metaphors get used every day. We hear regularly about pathways to success, the war on poverty, feeling under a cloud, floods of immigrants and so on. Each of these metaphors positions the speaker, and potentially the listener, in particular ways towards a material phenomenon/event/practice. None of these metaphors are neutral. All have inbuilt 'interests' and potential effects beyond speech.

Metaphors are powerful. They position us to behave in particular ways. They justify our actions and underpin them (Lakoff & Johnson, 1983). But we are not always aware of how they shape our thinking or structure our view of the world.

Metaphors have a strong effect on DRs. They work invisibly to steer thought, emotion and action. They can induce anxiety about doctoral work or alleviate it. When metaphors are made visible, however, when you bring them to light and interrogate them, you have a tool for tapping into your thoughts and feelings about research and how you might think – and act – differently.

The PhD as a journey

One of the most common metaphors that DRs use for doing the PhD is that of the journey. They start out somewhere and end up somewhere else. They feel that they have travelled a long way. It hasn't always been easy. There have been unexpected pitfalls, and surprising new places to find. The notion of the journey captures a sense of movement, personal growth and change. It can be a meaningful way of narrativising the ups and downs of the doctoral experience.

But how good a metaphor is it? Christina Hughes and Malcolm Tight (2013) suggest there are various kinds of journeys, some pleasant, some not. They argue that the most common PhD journey narrative is actually a quest, a search for a treasure, promised land and/or wisdom – the doctorate as Pilgrim's Progress, with 'staged posts of hope, loss, fear, doubt and achievement' (p. 769). Hughes and Tight argue that the Pilgrim's Progress is in some ways an apt allegory for the doctorate as it captures the loneliness, confusion, loss of voice and avoidance of temptations in the process, as well as the final arrival at the heavenly destination.

So what's the down side of the journey narrative? Hughes and Tight point out that the Pilgrim's Progress journey (the popular reading of it) is a particularly individualistic view of the PhD. It places individual motivation and spirit above all else. The pilgrim just has to believe and want hard enough to get there. What's missing from this line of thinking is anything about learning a set of new work habits – those associated with rigour, knowledge and skill acquired in social and institutional settings.

An alternative to the notion of a journey is that of 'wayfinding' – travel through a landscape that is always in motion (Ingold, 2000). It is not just the traveller who moves, but everything else around them. Wayfinding not only encapsulates the idea of movement and travel, but brings together a range of humans and non-humans in structured and serendipitous networks and power-saturated relations. It is, we think, a better metaphor for the learning undertaken during the doctorate than the journey. And of course it illustrates our point that some metaphors are more helpful than others.

So what kind of work is literature work? We offer three productive metaphors for thinking about the work of locating yourself and your research in the field – lunch with friends, making a table and the family tree.

A lunch with friends

The dinner party is a useful metaphor for rethinking the DR's relationship with the broader community of scholars she is reading and citing, and one we've talked about before (Kamler and Thomson, 2006/2014). The dinner party is a familiar domestic image. It occurs in one's own home, in the familiar territory where one belongs. The purpose of the dinner is to foster conversation with a select community of scholars. Here, however, we modify the metaphor to become a lunch with friends, because a lunch is more informal. We want you to start out being relaxed.

You will invite to the table the scholars you want to join you for a conversation over lunch. The emphasis is on the company and the conversation that happens. So the first decision is who's coming to lunch? Who do you want to invite? Whose work do you use most? Whose work is important in the field and can't be left out?

The second decision is what will you serve your guests. You don't want to offer bland, tired vegetables or deep-fried fatty stodge. Yesterday's leftovers would be unacceptable, as would rehashed and reconstituted chicken or beef. The menu needs thought, preparation and attention to presentation.

The third decision is how will you seat your guests. Who will sit with you at the head of the table? Who do you most want to engage in conversation? Whose work has most influenced yours? Who do you most want to speak back to? Who are you happy to just acknowledge and greet, but seat further away from you? Are there any guests who don't get on and should not sit next to one another?

We like this lunching metaphor because it gives the DR agency. As host to this informal lunch party, you make space for your guests to talk about their work, but *in relation* to your work. Your thesis is never disconnected from the conversation. It lies at the centre of the table – part of the offering your guests eat, chew and digest.

The lunch metaphor makes it clear that you cannot invite everyone; they will not all fit at your table. You are not just a bystander or 'reviewer' of the conversation, but the organiser. While you may not always comprehend all the nuances and complexity of the conversation, you are present. And you can reflect on these conversations later, mulling them over as you do at the end of a good day out. But having made the contact and the connection (between your work and theirs), you have a starting point for other lunches, coffees, conversations – and the option of not inviting some guests back, or including others.

The table

The table is another metaphor helpful for literature work. Howard Becker (1986) in a chapter aptly entitled 'Terrorised by the literature' uses the domestic image of the table. While this metaphor is not as sociable as a lunch, the focus is still on work and on the agency of the researcher, in this case the person making the table (see Advice: Howard Becker).

ADVICE

Howard Becker

Working with literatures

Imagine that you are . . . making a table. You have designed it and cut out some of the parts. Fortunately, you don't need to make all the parts yourself. Some are standard sizes and shapes – lengths of two by four, for instance – available at any lumber yard. Some have already been designed and made by other people – drawer pulls and turned legs. All you have to do is fit them into the places you left for them, knowing that they were available. That is the best way to use the literature. . .

You want to make an argument, instead of a table. You have created some of the argument yourself, perhaps on the basis of new data or information you have collected. But you needn't invent the whole thing. Other people have worked on your problem or problems related to it and have made some of the pieces you need. You just have to fit them in where they belong. Like the woodworker, you leave space, when you make your portion of the argument, for the other parts you know you can get. You do that, that is, *if* you know that they are there to use. And that's one good reason to know the literature: so that you will know what pieces are available and not waste time doing what has already been done.

Becker, 1986, p.142

A positive feature of Becker's table metaphor is its familiarity. We have all used tables and know what they are. The table is of a manageable size because it must fit into your room: even the grandest table can be seen in its entirety and walked around. And making a table is a crafting activity. It is pleasurable work with the hands, both mental and manual, aesthetic and utilitarian. This resonates with the notion of writing that is honed and polished through labour that is both aesthetic and functionally directed.

While the lunch party metaphor asks you to re-examine the sense of agency and authority you have as a writer, the table places your attention on the research and the conversation. It focuses attention on the re-using, crafting and the final product. And both metaphors share a sense of protracted time. A pleasurable and relaxed lunch often drifts on till it begins to get dark. Making a table takes time too – the maker often needs to leave it for periods of time while the stain dries and polish sets, for example. Both the lunch and the table can't be hurried. A hurried lunch gives the guests indigestion and truncates conversation. Rushing table-making may lead to ugly and costly mistakes and/or a wobbly construction.

The family tree

Another productive metaphor for orienting yourself to the reading is that of tracing your family tree. Most of us are familiar with the notion of genealogy – the process of researching your own background, where you come from. We have probably all sighted the television version of finding the family tree, where celebrities are helped by professional genealogists to trace their ancestors. This family tree work usually starts with parents and then grandparents. Tracking through census, births, deaths and marriage records (where these exist) often reveals surprising or sad or equally ordinary past lives which, the television programmes inevitably claim, have made the celebrities who and what they are.

Engaging with the literature can be thought of as developing your research project family tree. For instance, reading the literatures allows you trace various key influences on your work – you can map what you have inherited from your forebears. You can signal these inheritances so that readers can understand what material is yours alone and what is gleaned from what others have done. You can locate family squabbles – you can decide to ignore these, or to be part of them. You can also indicate branches of the family that have gone off on their own and have become estranged – you may or may not wish to reconnect with them. You might want to look at the ways in which broader social events connect with your individual heritage to see how your own family trajectory has been patterned and shaped.

The family you are discovering through your reading is an intellectual one. The object of all of your reading is to find out what intellectual traditions your work is based in, refers to and uses. While you are reading you are also tracing connections, lines of development and ruptures and family likenesses. You are lining up with particular vectors of thinking and of doing research.

We were inspired to think of the metaphor of the family tree when we saw a YouTube clip by Dr George Patton from Waldon University. We recommend it as further viewing if you like the metaphor of the family tree and want to pursue it further (*https://m.youtube.com/watch?v=NiDHOr3NHRA*).

You may be able to think of other metaphors for literature work that capture the sense of something that is ambitious but do-able, takes time and effort but is rewarding, and through which you learn both new skills and new 'stuff'. We encourage you to bring one of our metaphors or your own to the fore whenever you feel that the literature is going to open up and swallow you.

Strategy 3: create productive routines and workspaces

Getting control of the PhD, of course, needs more than positioning yourself as being in charge. It also means setting yourself up physically so you can enact being in control, even if you don't feel it. You need systems and processes and ways of creating a routine that work for you. So we want talk about some important activities to support your textwork/identitywork over the period of your PhD, part-time or full-time.

Organise time and space

Every productive writer has a writing routine. Most writers write in the morning, every morning. It may be before the family wakes up, or after they have gone for the day. But it is never about waiting for the right time, or the correct inspiration or the ideal conditions. Writing has to become a habit. If you don't have the writing habit before you begin the PhD, now is the time to establish one. There are a number of web-based resources that can help to do this, including www.750words.com, which asks you to sign up to write three pages a day online, gives you points and charts your progress each month. #AcWriMo (www.phd2published.com/acwri-2/acbowrimo/about/) asks people to set public targets for the month of November each year and to share successes and get support.

Mountains of interviews have been conducted with academic and fiction writers discussing their routines and habits and working environments. Many writers have regular writing targets. William Golding, Normal Mailer and Arthur Conan Doyle all claimed to write 3,000 words a day; Stephen King 2,000; Thomas Wolfe 1,800; and Jack London a mere 1,000. Anthony Trollope reportedly wrote 250 words every 15 minutes, keeping track by means of his pocket watch. And while Trollope, like many writers, started his day very early in the morning, the playwright Friedrich Schiller often wrote at night

> to ensure that no one descended on his door step while his pen flew. He'd work for hours while the stars were up and potential visitors were fast asleep. Schiller's body protested the night shift with inevitable drowsiness, but pangs of fatigue were no match for the writer. Sometimes, if he was extremely tired, more extreme action was necessary. On these occasions, Schiller would plunge his feet into a tub of cold water to avoid falling asleep at his desk.
>
> (Johnson, 2013, p.3)

Not a process we follow, nor would we recommend!

The regular writing routine also requires a particular place. Everyone now knows the story of J.K. Rowling spending the best part of the day in the coffee shop cranking out *Harry Potter* with her baby in a basket next to her. This was the writing space that she established for her work. If you haven't got a decent workspace at home or at the university, now is the time to get one. Ideally you should be able to work uninterrupted. There should be plenty of light. If you like to read and write to music, get your music organised. Invest in a decent chair and a desk at the right height, or you will end up, like too many academics, with sciatica, RSI and chronic neck/shoulder problems. And it may seem banal to say so, but it's important to get up from the computer every hour or so to walk around and give your body a break. This is part of the routine of organising time and space for writing. Some people like to buy particular kinds of stationery, notepads, notebook, pens, pencils. Pat has lots of post-its and note pads. Barbara can't write without a Uniball eye micro pen nearby to click.

It is also important to keep the desk relatively well organised and not too cluttered. The desk acts as a kind of tangible representation of how we feel about the work. You can see in the images of scholarly desks, various states of tidiness and work in progress. Don't be too judgemental about the slightly messy one – this is a writer in the very middle of a piece of work.

But, if the desk is consistently piled high with stuff, we often feel hemmed in and overwhelmed. Allow for the fact that when you are researching you will end up with piles of stuff: data, books, tables, papers, and they do get unruly. So think about where it will all go. Barbara has a spare table that she uses for stacking the piles. Pat has a big office with lots of floor space.

It's good to anticipate the sheer volume of material you are going to accumulate over the next 3–7 years and buy (second-hand) the filing cabinets, bookshelves or tables you will need now. This is your writing burrow, your den, where you will hibernate. Every morning or afternoon or evening you will crawl in and not come out until you've done a decent amount of work.

Diverse academic desks

From top: Barbara's desk; Pat's desk

Diverse academic desks

From top: @cuervoAdsi; @ sdc60

Managing email and twitter is also critical. It is easy to allow yourself to get distracted and fritter away what should be your most productive time; answering emails that can easily be left until later in the day, or getting completely engaged in social media conversations and chasing links all over the web. These are activities you only need part of your brain to do. You can do them 'after work'. Whenever you schedule your reading/writing time, make it a time to concentrate and focus, to the exclusion of other distractions.

If you work at home or at university, find ways not to be interrupted by other people. You need to place an imaginary 'do not disturb' sign on your door so people don't just barge in to tell you the trials of their day. Many universities provide full-time DRs with a place to work, but it's your task to work out how to most productively use that space. Some reading or writing may need to be done at home because a shared space is too disturbing. Some people use headphones to block out distracting noise, some prefer to work in the library where silence is policed. This may sound a bit odd, but if you work in a shared space you need to establish the rules.

Establish information systems

We've all heard the apocryphal story of people who are ready to hand in their PhDs but can't find the source of the quotation on page 98. You don't want to be this person.

If the PhD is ultimately about words and information, other people's and your own, then keeping track of these words is critical. During the PhD you will read hundreds of papers and books. You will make notebooks full of notes. You will probably write the equivalent of three or four theses in order to actually create one that can be submitted. One DR we know recently counted the words in her field notes, transcripts and analytic writing and it totalled over 250,000 words. This was before she even began writing the thesis.

Now is the time to invest in good bibliographic software. There are open access options as well as those that have student prices. We're not going to advertise any particular system, but we want to say you should have one. In fact, Pat wants to say you have rocks in your head if you don't get a good digital bibliographic system and use it from day one. The time you spend entering the details of each publication, including key words and a few key points will pay off in ways that you can't possibly imagine at the time. If you intend to continue some form of academic work, whether inside or outside higher education, the information in your bibliographic database remains your best academic writing friend.

Pat began using *Endnote* in 1997. She now has nearly 9,000 items listed. She thinks of this as a kind of adjunct brain stored on several computers and in the cloud so it never gets lost. She can retrieve her reading about a wide range of topics speedily and with very little hair-tearing and cursing. Of course, you have to be accurate in the way you enter the information, and systematic, otherwise the information retrieval capacities can't be used efficiently and the time-saving production of citations and references won't be as good as it could be. Time spent on accuracy *now* saves enormous amounts of time in the future.

There is always new software coming on the market that supports the process of brainstorming, mind mapping, data storage and analysis and writing using multiple sources of material. It's a good idea to find out who are the nerdy types in your university or online, because they will keep track of all of this software and the reviews of their effectiveness, and will always be happy to talk to you at length about a product you can try for free to make your research process more efficient. We follow Prof Andy Miah's A-Z of Social Media for Academics and subscribe to his associated mailing list (www.andymiah.net/2012/12/30/the-a-to-z-of-social-media-for-academics/), and follow @ThesisWhisperer who often reviews new software as it becomes available.

Get peer support

Isolation is killing. You need formal and informal processes to engage with peers during your PhD; people you can talk to over coffee about how things are going, people you can chat with online. As long as you don't just engage in misery stories. Be a bit wary of people who just want to have a collective moan; it is important to balance the difficulties of doctoral research with being constructive. Ideally you want to share your trials, but also have a laugh and have conversations that are affirming and intellectually lively.

There are now synchronous and asynchronous forums on twitter and Facebook where you can talk with people about academic writing or about methodology or you can find people working in exactly the same area as you. This was not possible when Pat and Barbara were DRs.

Reading and writing groups are often run by academic development staff for doctoral researchers (Aitchison & Guerin, 2014). And sometimes DRs set up their own reading and writing groups (for example, see http://patthomson.net/2015/03/19/4033/). Your institution might run 'Shut up and Write' sessions (see http://thesiswhisperer.com/shut-up-and-write/) where people come together to work companionably side by side in a coffee shop, and you can now find web-based versions of 'Shut up and Write' too. All of these forums provide a space to gather with people engaged in the same activity as you. They can provide support but also motivation, sometimes incentive and even a way of regulating your own productivity. These activities create sociable communities that feel accountable to each other for keeping going, producing text and getting through the work.

Of course, you will also be in conversation with supervisors and committee members during your PhD. But peer communities are possibly less judgemental. They are not Layer 3 spaces. Claire Aitchison discusses the strengths of the many doctoral writing groups she led at the University of Western Sydney (Aitchison, 2010) (see Experience: Claire Aitchison). She argues that talking with scholarly peers allows you to practise talking like a scholar. You can rehearse your ideas and get invaluable feedback. You can improvise answers in response to questions. It is literally a safe space, which contributes to your *being and becoming a scholar* and achieves work that does not always occur in the space of doctoral supervision.

EXPERIENCE

Claire Aitchison

Writing groups

Because our groups are multidisciplinary, participants are regularly challenged to explain what they're writing about by those from different fields. This review by other student peers from different disciplines can be just as purposefully developmental because the author has the chance to rebut, negotiate and discuss the feedback. It is common to see, through this process of questioning and being asked to explain and clarify meaning, the author return to his or her original text and rework it with a better appreciation of what the readership needs to know.

After a period of belonging to such a group, students often say they can imagine individual group members asking for clarification, critiquing and probing them for specific details: 'I knew you'd ask that!' This familiarity means that they learn to predict the questions their peers would probably raise while they are writing — and they use these internalized voices to help shape their text as they write.

By contrast, students who have had limited experience of others reading and reviewing their writing are less able to predict the kinds of queries, requirements and clarifications that unknown readers may seek. Similarly, doctoral students who show their work only to their supervisor(s) over a period of years may find that their writing can suffer from being too inward looking and decontextualized. As one student remarked: 'Many times I was surprised by the types of issues that had not previously been picked up by my colleagues or supervisor' (Survey respondent, 2007).

Aitchison, 2010, pp. 90–1

Keep track of and reflect on your progress

Writing is a good way to keep track of where you are, as well as to progress your thinking. The PhD requires sustained development of ideas and eventually an argument about the importance of your research. Right from the time you begin reading, you'll have a range of things to think about. You'll make notes in response to reading, to conversations with friends and with your supervisors/committee. You may find that writing about a series of books that you've read helps you to bring key points and themes together. Writing can also help you understand some key concepts and express them in your own words.

We are big fans of progressive abstracts, which we explain in Chapter 7, as a means of consolidating the argument about the need for your research, its location in the literature and its potential contribution. We confess a weakness for 'to do' lists and the kinds of organisational software that can now record and remind us about the things that need to get done. Lists are important not simply in relation to day-to-day activities, but also in terms of reminders about references we need to chase up, or lines of analysis we want to try. We also like the ways in which some DRs have used blogging to not only keep track of their progress and reflect on it, but also to simultaneously establish a community of DRs interested in the same areas.

All of these activities involve writing.

You may want to find a way to keep all the disparate written material together. If you are a paper and pen person, then you may need a set of folders that are organised either thematically or chronologically, with some kind of annotation so that you can find things again. You may want to keep a key journal that tracks the various other bits and pieces of text.

Keeping this material digitally is generally easier because you can search and retrieve things more effectively. These days many DRs use a wiki or blogging as the 'spine' around which they collect the various kinds of written materials they generate along the way. There are also now purpose-built writing software tools such as Scrivener which bring together all of the digital materials relevant to constructing and keeping track of a big text.

The key is to see this kind of writing as a threefold 'wayfinding' process.

1 Writing about what you are doing provides the opportunity to develop your ideas. You really don't know exactly what you think until you have to put it in words, logically and sequentially.

2 Writing about what you are doing is a way to critically interrogate ideas. As half-formed notions consolidate and appear on paper, they become available to be read and reread to see how well they stack up. Once the text

is down, you can read and re-read to check the inbuilt assumptions, blank and blind spots.

3   Writing about what you are doing is a way to evaluate your own 'learning'. It's often easy to feel that you are going round in circles in the PhD, that you haven't moved an inch since you started. Having a progressive archive of your thinking allows you to look and back and see that this is not the case.

Strategy 4: develop systems for recording your reading

When we introduced Pierre Bayard's distinction between the collective and inner library earlier in this chapter, we suggested that you don't have to read everything. You don't have to read every article in its entirety. You don't have to read every book cover to cover. Having said this, you still need a way to decide what to read and what not to read, what information you will record and what you will leave out. A systematic approach to scanning and note-taking can certainly help you address these concerns and gain control over the vast array of literatures you need to work with.

Scanning an article: don't write a word

One of the best ways to get a sense of what's out there and what might be most relevant to your study is to scan five or so articles at once. After an initial scanning, you can return to the articles that seem most pertinent and read these in more detail. To guide the process we suggest you:

- read the title of the article
- read the abstract
- read the introduction, headings, the first and last sentence of each paragraph and the conclusion
- tell a colleague DR what you think the article is about.

During this exercise the critical guideline is this: *do not highlight or write a single note.* Sit on your hands or do whatever is required to stop yourself from writing. Our aim is to interrupt your habituated practice of reading with a marker in hand, missing the forest because you are fixated on individual trees. Sometimes it's helpful to use a ruler to keep your focus on lines of text – but no pen. We think you'll be surprised by how much you know and can absorb from the article by scanning. Once you get the hang of scanning, you can build up numbers quite quickly. You can go from five to ten or so papers, and then to much larger quantities, such as fifty!

Many of us have learned that reading an article always requires underlining and noting. But we want you to try noting *after* a first reading instead. Similarly, highlighting and writing on the actual text is best left for a second detailed read, if it is required. This kind of scan-reading may show that the article belongs to the collective, rather than the inner library (Bayard, 2007).

Scanning in this way also pulls out the paper's 'skeleton' (see Chapter 5) and the argument moves. It helps you understand how academic writing works. The use of headings, topic sentences for paragraphs, titles, abstracts and conclusions are the 'red thread' that makes a piece of scholarly writing coherent.

Scanning a book: is it worth reading?

Reading a book takes far more time and commitment than a journal article. So it's important for you to decide whether a book needs to be read carefully or not. The author and the publisher leave some clues to help you decide. We suggest you:

- Read the title of the book.

  Publishers are now wary of clever book titles that make the reader guess what's inside, so they usually make the main title or its strapline quite specific.

- Read the blurb on the back.

  This has been specifically written to tell the reader about the book's purpose, something of its contents and the academic discipline to which it contributes.

- Read the titles of chapters.

  Chapter titles are not always cogently written but when they are, they give you an adequate idea of what is covered in the text.

- If the book is still of interest, then do some pre-reading.

  These days, publishers and booksellers offer sample chapters online. In a bookshop or at a publisher's stand at a conference, it is easy to scan the introduction where the writer provides a mandate for the book and outlines its chapters. Figures and tables can be checked, and if there is time, you can selectively sample the odd page here and there to get a sense of the style and tone.

This activity will help you to establish the book's disciplinary location, its intended contribution, something of its argument and a little about the way it uses evidence. It will help you form a view about whether this is a book to buy, or get from the library, or one you won't bother with now, but may come back to later.

Making notes from an article

There is only one maxim about note-taking – don't rewrite the article. It's a waste of time and it misses the point. The point is to understand what the writer is claiming and arguing. The work of note-taking is to record the most salient points so you can then categorise them, use them, build on them. It is not just to help you remember what you've read.

After reading, the DR should be able to explain succinctly to someone else what the text is about. This process of making sense and interpreting the text is important not only for immediate understanding, but for the ways it can be used to make your argument later. It is this meaning-making that is the basis of the notes, not lengthy verbatim quotes.

The first time you read the article you don't need a pen or a highlighter. You just read. Then, pick up a pen and write the argument and the claim of the paper in no more than three to four sentences. This requires disciplined thinking. It might be enough to just capture what it's about and enter it into your bibliographic software straight away.

But if the article deserves closer study, a set of questions can help. We offer seven key questions for you to consider about the article you are reading (see Table 3.1). You can bullet-point your answers in a small number of sentences or phrases. These bullets can then be entered on whatever digital referencing system you're using.

Once these questions are answered, articles can be grouped in different ways – around definitions, different aspects of the topic, methods, theoretical approaches, epistemological traditions. The doctoral researcher has created a systematic and defensible basis on which to develop their groupings and patterns.

The purpose of reading closely and note-taking is always to connect the literature to the proposed study, not simply to summarise an article or book. The synthesis must occur, but always in connection with your doctoral research.

Making notes from a book

We've just said that DRs shouldn't rewrite the article. Well, you certainly can't rewrite the book. One effective strategy is to first read the book right through, taking a minimal number of notes, perhaps using post-its.

Immediately on finishing, write a summary of the book in no more than a paragraph. This should include the purpose of the book and the problem or issue the author is addressing. It should sum up the argument and state the claim made by the author – the point you are trying to make.

TABLE 3.1 Detailed questions for note-taking

Question	The work this question is doing
1 Is the text located in the same field as yours, or another one?	The answer can help you decide the disciplinary tradition the paper is in and can help you decide whether you are drawing on other fields in order to conduct interdisciplinary research.
2 What aspect of your topic does the text address?	This helps you see that any topic is made up of multiple parts and gives you a language to differentiate what the elements are.
3 What definition is offered of the topic?	Often there are differing understandings of what appears to be the same thing. Being able to define what you take to be the meaning of the topic and why, and who else uses this definition, is important.
4 What concepts and language are used in the article that might be helpful for you?	We all build on each other's work. And if we are going to use this work, we refer to this borrowing through citations.
5 What kind of text is this? Is it theory-building? A think-piece? A meta-study or systematic review? An empirical study? How does this kind of research connect with your study?	If empirical, take note of the epistemological tradition, the methodology, the site, methods and sample, because this will allow you to discuss the kinds of empirical work already done about the topic.
	If a meta-study or review, is the conclusion helpful in creating the space for your study? Will any of the categorisations of the field be helpful either to argue for your work, or perhaps to develop your research design?
	If theory-building, what does this approach allow you to see and say? What is included and excluded? How might it be helpful to you and/or create the warrant for your study?
6 What categorisations are offered? What are the key concepts and framings used?	These may be useful in your work in building a critique in your review of literatures.
7 What connections does this text make?	The reference lists may provide links to new literature. The results may connect to what you already know/or need to know about the topic.

If the book warrants closer attention, it can be useful to write a very short outline about each move of the argument – a move may be a single chapter or more than one. This can show the way in which each chapter is related to the next and indicate any key ways in which the text is related to the DR's own study. This might include evidence used, theoretical approach, connection with other literatures. At the end, the DR will have a couple of pages of notes.

A very close read is something that is done with a relatively small number of texts – those in the inner library. You may be interested in systematically exploring the writer's language, and investigating the resources they use (citations, agreements and disagreements).

If you're looking at a writer's work rather than at a single book, you can use the note-taking process to become familiar with their overall propositions, changes in their arguments over time, and the various influences on their development and ideas.

Cornell notes

Some people swear by 'Cornell notes'. They were developed as a system for taking lecture notes but can be easily adapted for reading purposes. It can support a process of reviewing and re-reading in order to extract the most salient information from

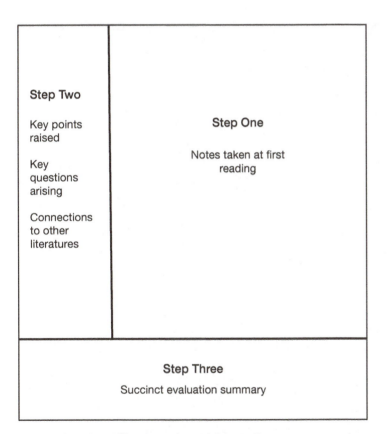

FIGURE 3.1 Cornell notes, adapted for reading

You can get free downloads of a generic Cornell notes page as a pdf from http://americandigest.org/mt-archives/004983.php

any text. We find this method of note-taking very useful for situations such as recording a conversation in a reading group or a seminar. It can be equally useful in processing what happened during a meeting with a supervisor or committee. The strategy is to divide a page into three. First you make notes about the key points. Then you extract the key points from the notes. And finally you write a summary (see Figure 3.1).

In sum

Many doctoral researchers feel lost when they begin to read. We've suggested in this chapter that the best way to deal with this feeling is to think of reading as always uncertain, and as work. It is helpful to understand what the reading is for, and to set up good systems for doing the work of reading. In the next chapter we're going to zoom in closer on the writing that happens in literature work as a result of all of this reading.

4 Finding your place

The problem: overwhelmed by the literature

You've read and read. You've taken notes on individual books and papers. But there's so much more still to read and absorb. So much interesting work that is relevant to your research. How do you make sense of it all? How do you connect it to your topic? How do you write about it?

For many DRs, writing about the literature is a formidable task. They often feel they can't manage the volume of texts and, at the same time, work out how to use these texts to locate and support their own work. They feel like eavesdroppers on conversations between expert scholars, as if the best they can do is listen carefully and regurgitate what has been said before. The result is writing that describes rather than evaluates, or writing that slavishly reports the words of others. Supervisors often write all over DR first drafts about the literature 'Put this in your own words'.

At the heart of this writing problem is the challenge of working with the words and ideas of others. Gerald Graff and Cathy Birkenstein (2010) talk about this as 'They say, I say'; a phrase that captures the tension that's inherent in the work of putting yourself and your work in relation to what other scholars have already said and published (see Commentary: Gerald Graff and Cathy Birkenstein).

You may not realise it, but when you are working with literatures and trying to figure out how to fit yourself into the conversation, your struggle always shows up on the page. You may think you can hide behind the print, or that no one will know you feel unsure, but really it's not possible. Identity struggles have a textual dimension. This is why we use the double-barrelled term textwork/identitywork. The two are intertwined and inseparable.

The identity work that goes on when DRs work with research literatures is intense. Elsewhere (Kamler & Thomson, 2006/2014) we have argued that writing literature reviews is the quintessential site of identity work, where DRs enter occupied territory – with all the danger and dread this metaphor implies – including possible ambushes, barbed wire fences and unknown academics who patrol the

COMMENTARY

Gerald Graff and Cathy Birkenstein

Working with 'they say'

For us, the underlying structure of effective academic writing – and of responsible public discourse – resides not just in stating our own ideas but in listening closely to others around us, summarizing their views in a way that they will recognize, and responding with our own ideas in kind. Broadly speaking, academic writing is argumentative writing, and we believe that to argue well you need to do more than assert your own position. You need to enter a conversation, using what others say (or might say) as a launching pad or sounding board for your own views.

Graff & Birkenstein, 2010, p. 3

COMMENTARY

Barbara Kamler and Pat Thomson

Doctoral researchers have an emergent relation to the territory (the fields which inform their research) and its occupiers (the more senior, experienced scholars of the academy). Yet they are expected to find the courage to assess the work of the occupiers – some of whom, in time, may well examine and judge their theses. The novice researcher is not only an alien in foreign fields, but is unaware of the rules of engagement, and the histories of debates, feuds, alliances and accommodations that precede her entry to the field. This is not work for the faint/feint-hearted! There are so many decisions to make. Where to start? Which fields? Which landmines to avoid? How to be 'critical', who to be critical of, and how to escape being tangled in the barbed wire? How to negotiate the complexities of power relations in a strange land? Who to include and exclude in the negotiations? Who to engage with, who to ignore and with what effects?

Kamler & Thomson, 2014, p. 31

boundaries of well-known fields (see Commentary: Barbara Kamler and Pat Thomson).

The metaphor of occupied territory is dramatic, perhaps even overstated, but it does challenge the taken-for-granted view of literature work as a relatively straightforward, if time-consuming, task. It is also a metaphor, which gets closer to the anxiety and expectation many DRs experience when 'reviewing' the literatures. Because in fact, the job of 'reviewing' is never simply about reporting and summarising what others have said. The DR must learn to use the literatures and evaluate them, in order to make a place for their own work.

But how can this be achieved? Is there a remedy for feeling lost and tentative about your place in the literature, for moving beyond the overwhelmed feeling? The first step is to learn how to take a stand, early in your writing and researching.

Reframing idea: taking a stand

Taking a stand generally means adopting a position on something – as in 'She was prepared to take a stand on the demolition of the heritage building adjacent to her office'. The term has a military history, deriving from the practice of a group of soldiers who literally dug into a piece of ground, defended it and refused to give it up. Speaking etymologically then, there's a sense of defiance and resistance in the term 'taking a stand'.

We don't want to suggest that working with literatures has anything in common with being besieged or beleaguered. It's not about defending a piece of turf to the bitter end. But we do think that the notion of staking a claim to a position, and holding it, being prepared to stand by your claim, and being able to articulate your location does have resonance with literature work. To reprise from Chapter 3, when you write about the literature you need to:

1   show you understand the history of the field and its key figures;

2   indicate which work is relevant to your proposed research;

3   establish which prior research is to be built on;

4   identify any debates that will be entered; and

5   delineate any research to be challenged.

All of this text work involves taking a stand. You must be the person who shows, indicates, establishes, identifies and delineates your work in relation to the literatures. This is a far cry from reporting or simply capturing what other scholars have done. You are not the neutral observer or the eavesdropper. You are in charge, assessing, evaluating and making sense of the scholarship that precedes you.

We like the idea of taking a stand because it is a physical metaphor that suggests strength and determination. It is as if you are saying: 'I am here. I'm a tangible presence, whether you can actually see me or not, you know I'm here. I have views that are important and that I can justify and I can convince you that these are not only sensible, but worthy of your attention. I am DR. Hear me roar. I am too big to ignore.'

The 'taking a stand' metaphor also makes tangible the identity work required to grapple with the sheer volume of texts you are reading. We don't want your writing to be flabby and insignificant, shrinking and hiding behind the many scholars you have read. We want you to tackle writing about the literatures from a confident position. If you take a stand, you have to be metaphorically and textually out there – visible and in control of the material you are writing about.

To this end, we offer you three strategies. They are:

1   Scoping, Mapping and Focusing in (ScoMaFo)
2   Creating A Research Space (CARS)
3   Diagnosing common authority problems

Strategy 1: Scoping, Mapping and Focusing in (ScoMaFo)

In Chapter 3 we suggested that it was helpful to approach your literature work with a metaphor in mind. You will of course need to operationalise your chosen metaphor. While libraries and advice, both online and in books, will offer you lots of ways to conduct a basic literature search, they often to neglect to tell you how to generate search terms in the first place. We think the approach offered by Kristin Luker in her book *Salsa dancing into the social sciences* is a helpful one, as it focuses on developing a type of Venn diagram of the relevant literatures. She calls her multi-looped diagram, in which each 'petal' represents a theme related to the research question, a 'bedraggled daisy' (Luker, 2008). 'Thesis Whisperer' offers a question-based approach to developing a search (*http://thesiswhisperer.com/2015/05/13/how-to-become-a-literature-searching-ninja/*) and we explain and illustrate a mapping strategy for literature work in an essay on working with literatures (Kamler & Thomson, 2011)(downloadable on www.academia.edu/440771/Working_with_literatures).

Here we offer a three-part strategy for attacking a relatively defined topic; this might be a specific aspect of your thesis literature work or a review you conduct for a journal article. Our strategy has the components:

Scoping: finding what's out there

Mapping: sorting and grouping into categories

Focusing in: working with a selection of texts most useful to your research topic

Scoping

One of the things that we all have to do when we start a piece of research is to find out what else has been said about our topic. What gets counted as 'literature' can be as narrow or as broad as you want, and so it's important to start by thinking about exactly *where* you are going to look, as well as for *what*. Possible sources for scoping include: peer-reviewed journal articles, books, posters, theses, print media, social media, policy documents, web resources, conference papers, letters and other kinds of archival materials.

Scoping simply means generating a rich list of these sources and doing an initial sort based on relevant criteria – chronology, discipline, methodology and/or location for example. To illustrate how this process might work, as well as the subsequent processes of mapping and focusing in, we use an extended example from Inger Mewburn and Pat's research on academic blogging (Mewburn & Thomson, 2013). Pat was responsible for the literature work and began her search with peer-reviewed journal articles (see Experience: Pat's process of scoping).

EXPERIENCE

Pat's process of scoping

To start I wanted to know just what was out there. I approached the first task of scoping with these questions: How much was written about blogging and where was it? Who was actually writing in journals about blogs and why? These questions didn't stop me noticing other things, but having them in mind meant that I wasn't going on a random scramble through articles.

I began my search by going to three major journal publishers' sites. There are many more than this, but I decided that I would use a subset first of all. My choices were Taylor and Francis, Wiley Blackwell and Sage. I did also look at Elsevier but their initial search engine wasn't as 'advanced' as the other three and wouldn't

do what I wanted, so I let it be. I went to Sage to experiment with search terms. I played with 'blog' and 'social media' and various fields, producing this result:

Sage journals 3,064 = blog in all fields, 14 in title, 28 in key words, 87 in abstract, 2,277 with social media in abstract, social media plus learning 98, social media academic = 86

In the next two journal sites I made a decision about which way to go – I searched the word BLOG in the abstract field. I reasoned that if 'the blog' was somehow central to the research then it would appear there. This is what I found:

Wiley Blackwell 193 articles with blog in abstract field

Taylor and Francis with blog in 217 abstracts

I next imported all of the 'BLOG in abstract' details from the three sites into Mendeley, the bibliographic software I was using for this co-written paper. Mendeley scooped up abstracts as well as the title, author and key words. I then read all of the abstracts and got rid of the ones where it seemed that 'blog' was not central to the research or the argument. This left me with just under 300 papers.

Now, Mendeley online has a very nice feature. You can cut and paste the list of journals in which the abstracts appear into a word document. I did that and then sorted the journals into rough disciplinary categories. As a result of this first sort, I had some idea about the disciplines where there were peer-reviewed publications about blogs. What I could write on the basis of this categorisation was something like this:

A search of three peer-reviewed commercial journal sites, using the search term 'blog' in the 'abstract' field, showed a spread of disciplinary bases for papers on blogging. The largest numbers of journals were in culture, media, education, communication, computing, health, and in associated areas like youth studies and journalism. A lesser number of journals appeared in sociology, politics and humanities. Missing from the list entirely were philosophy, archaeology, theology and most of the sciences.

But of course I knew the number of journals is not the same as the number of actual articles. This is the other nice feature of Mendeley online. When you click on a journal title, you can then see how many articles have been published in that journal. By putting this information together with the categorisation of journals into disciplinary categories I was able to write the following:

When actual articles were counted, the top three fields (bearing in mind that the classification of these journals was mine and therefore not necessarily the same as someone else's classification) the following emerged as 'top' of the leader board: cultural studies and media studies (42, with journalism an additional 16); computing /ICT (41); communication, linguistics and discourse (37); education (27); library studies and health (both on 24); business (6) and tourism (13); sociology (10); humanities (9). All others were under 5, including politics a surprising 4. However there is politics content in other disciplinary areas, particularly communication and journalism.

Mapping

Mapping is, as the name implies, a process of setting out the basic features of the research landscape. The idea is not only to identify the work that has been done but also to establish when it was done, how, and trends and connections in the substantive results. Mapping can be thought of as a kind of thematisation of ideas and/or concepts and/or arguments. Hart (2001) suggests that there are various options for mapping literatures – feature maps, tree diagrams and content maps. All of these are worth experimenting with.

We often ask DRs to think of physically mapping their reading, by constructing piles of books on the floor, and drawing lines of connection between them with string – and then to do the equivalent on chart paper, or using mind-mapping tools or post-its. A key aspect of mapping is the process of selection, not simply what goes where, and what goes with what, but what gets left out altogether. DRs often find that talking through their maps with peers can be a helpful way to make explicit why they have chosen particular kinds of groupings. Pat's explicit discussion of how she mapped the field of academic blogging illustrates what the process might look like (see Experience: Pat's process of mapping).

EXPERIENCE

Pat's process of mapping

After scoping, my next step was to do a bit more searching and downloading. I went to googlescholar and searched for the term 'blog'. There were 1,590,000 responses, far too many for me to deal with, so I decided arbitrarily to go through the first fifteen screens to see what else I might pick up that seemed relevant. I then imported these new abstracts – and in some cases papers – into my Mendeley file. This brought the total corpus of papers to 327. I then went back through this database picking out some articles that looked as if they might be relevant to my topic and downloaded these as full pdfs (also stored in Mendeley).

Now, when I say I looked for relevant papers, what exactly was I looking for? I wanted to find: (a) any blog taxonomies that people had used, or anything that might be related to the practice of developing a taxonomy or; (b) anything on academic blogging per se. I was keen to see whether there were any 'building blocks' for the paper, but I also wanted to see what kind of space there was for our contribution. What and who would we be talking to? I was also interested in (c) anything relevant to writing blogs – why people do it, any evidence about what blogs 'do' in the world and (d) anything relevant to the question of Web2 as a democratic arena or as an alternative news source.

I then reread all of the abstracts. This was my second pass through the data set.

I skimmed many abstracts and then ignored them. I made no notes as they didn't seem central to this particular project. I more thoroughly read the abstracts of those I thought were relevant, jotting down a few words about each argument. I read a relatively small number of entire papers – thirty-two only – and made more extensive notes about only a couple – including copying and pasting some potential quotations (with page numbers) into my word doc.

I then went back over my notes and sorted and categorised the papers. This time, rather than looking for disciplinary categories, I developed some THEMES. Some people might do mind mapping at this point in time in order to undertake this thematic work, but this data set was small enough for me to do it simply as bullet points in the word doc.

I finally grouped the papers under ten themes.

Because I didn't yet have all of the literatures that I needed for the review, I knew that these themes might not be the final set. I saw the mapping as having established the basic topographical features on the map, onto which other details would be introduced – that is other literatures could be added to these themes, they could be renamed, and other themes added. So I knew I would add or modify these themes, but this was at least now an ordered literatures landscape, not simply a database.

At the end of this mapping, I summarised the literatures as I knew them at that point – but only in relation to academic blogging. Writing this summary text for myself – it was not intended for final publication – was an important way of consolidating the most pertinent papers I had found.

There is a significant body of work which reports on the use of blogging for pedagogical purposes within formal learning settings – that is used in face to face or virtual classrooms (Lester & Paulus, 2011) (Manfra & Lee, 2012) (Marchi & Ciceri, 2011) (McGrail & Davis, 2011) (Miceli, Murray, & Kennedy, 2010) (Sawmiller, 2010). We are not concerned with formal learning in this paper. There appears to be relatively little written about academic blogging in peer-reviewed journals, apart from writings about their pedagogical applications.

We located one paper from an academic who blogged in the hope that the posts (about feminism) would serve as learning resources for readers who happened upon them (Sjoberg, 2012). We also found two papers about academic blogging that are highly relevant to our concerns. According to Ewins (2005), academics write blogs in order to: communicate with peers; create a single site to contain their activities; make intellectual connections across texts; make their thoughts enduring, often by referring to their own writings over time. He notes that the web offers a temporal resource which is somewhere between synchronous and drawn out as well as one which spans space/distance. He suggests that academic blogging helps to consolidate and stabilise scholarly identity through the construction of a public narrative. He notes that blogs are both representative of the scholar and a representation, and this might present a danger in job and tenure applications and promotion, as a selection committee might well know too much about the blogger.

Gregg (2005) also examined academic blogging and suggests that: 'Blogs serve as a sort of short-term ideological resolution to the contradictions of the contemporary university workplace, a safe space to share the disappointment arising from the end of guaranteed ongoing employment, the growth of casualisation and the lack of agency that persists in large organisations of the knowledge economy' (p. 471). She argues that blogs can: (a) provide support for doctoral researchers who have inadequate institutional support and supervision, (b) offer a new form of mentoring and job seeking support, and (c) provide a space distinct from the parent culture of institutions and thus provide some kind of resolution of feelings of membership of an academic community. She notes that, despite the blogger's investment in the communitarian ideals of 'the university', blogs may well also be a form of individualised self-promotion, and thus help to constitute the corporatised academic.

Focusing in

The final stage of ScoMaFo, focusing in, works with the mapping themes, potentially adding more literatures and asking additional questions related to the researcher's specific project.

Focusing in involves getting the big picture and the little picture at the same time. It's both about stepping back and moving in close. Imagine that you're in an art gallery. If you're very close up to a painting, you might be able to see brush strokes and pencil marks. But being that close means you lose the holistic appreciation of the painting. Sometimes you see things most clearly from a distance. In reality, you often have to step back to appreciate the finer details of the image in the context of the whole.

Stepping back can be conceived of as a set of three questions to gain distance on a field of scholarship.

1 What is the history of research in the field? Where has it come from and why this route?

Many DRs will work on questions that have been around for some time. Getting a handle on the way in which the field has developed helps us to think about:

- the ways in which particularities, such as time, place, and culture might have affected the development of knowledge about the topic;
- the blank spots that might have been produced through this particular knowledge-making trajectory;
- how we can avoid naïvely situating our research in a set of literatures that many in the field now see as outdated and discredited. If we want to use texts that could fall into this category, we need to do so consciously and anticipate the criticisms.

2 What are the key debates in the field?

Many fields of research have ongoing or episodic debates. Sometimes they've developed bunkered lines of inquiry and researchers find it difficult to talk to each other because they are rooted in different disciplines or different epistemological/ methodological traditions.

And some research topics do have pretty clear disciplinary strands. So, if a DR is working in a field in which different disciplinary strands exist, it is important to understand what these are, and not to bundle together disparate and conflicting texts and references. Tracing the various disciplinary trajectories can be useful work in order to position your own study.

Often, work with sharply different ontological and epistemological foundations exists in the same field. Researchers must understand the often-heated debates that these differences produce. In order to make their own contribution clear, DRs have no choice but to take a position about such sharp differences – they can't be avoided.

3 Who are the key figures in the field and why?

There are often key figures in a field – but also important minor figures – and DRs need to find out who they are. You need to acknowledge these scholars and to say where you stand in relation to their texts. Ignoring their work means you are not really located in the field at all, but off somewhere in a little world of your own, talking to yourself.

It is important to be on the lookout, as you do your scoping and mapping work, to spot recurring references and names of key figures, different kinds of disciplinary approaches, and different questions and research traditions – and of course, to consider what these might have to say to your own piece of research. (If you are interested you can see Pat's focusing-in stage on http://patthomson.net/2012/ 11/25/focusing-in-on-blogging-literatures-part-two-acwrimo-work-in-progress/)

Textualising a ScoMaFo

DRs often feel that the purpose of literature work in a thesis is to list every single thing they've read. While it is important to show you know the field and include indicative texts for the categories you've determined, you often end up leaving out a lot of 'evidence' of how much you've read. This is the rub of literature work. All the reading that you've done may not end up in the final text.

Here is our example from Pat's ScoMaFo (see Writing Sample 4.1). Having read over 300 texts for the blogging article, her end result was a much smaller number of references and citations in the finished paper. However, the final text could not have been written in the way it was, with a sense of confidence and authority about what was in the literature, without having done all this initial work.

WRITING SAMPLE 4.1

Published paper

Textualising a ScoMaFo

There is already a significant body of research which reports on the use of blogging for pedagogical purposes; this usually takes the form of case studies of face to face or virtual university classrooms. We are not concerned with that kind of formal learning in this paper. We are interested in the blogs that are 'extra-curricular', usually written by academics in addition to their main responsibilities of teaching and researching. There seems to be very little by way of research that we could draw on directly for our study. The small amount of literature that does exist however offers insights about purposes, practices and their implications.

Halavais (2006) proposes some defining characteristics of blogs: they have networked audiences with little shared interests other than that created by reading the blog, they encourage conversation and are a low-intensity academic practice which can offer thinking-in-progress. He suggests that blogging might operate as a 'third space' (Soja, 1996), or virtual university, which remains elusively outside formal institutional boundaries. Walker (2006), a veteran blogger (see also Rettburg, 2008), notes that there are different kinds of academic blogs, some of which are closer to conventional academic publishing than others. She suggests that, as a reader, her favourite blogs are those which combine research results with discussions of process and context.

One of the handful of academic blogging empirical studies by Ewins (2005) argues that academics blog in order to: communicate with peers; create a single site to contain their activities; make intellectual connections across texts; and make their thoughts enduring, often by referring to their own writings over time. He notes that the Web offers a spatial/temporal resource which is somewhere between synchronous and drawn out, as well as one which spans space/distance. He suggests that academic blogging helps to consolidate and stabilise scholarly identities through the construction of a public narrative. He notes that blogs are both representative of the scholar and a representation, and this duality might present danger in job and tenure applications and promotion (a selection committee might well know too much about the blogger for example).

Gregg (2009, p. 471) also examined academic blogging and suggests that:

Blogs serve as a sort of short-term ideological resolution to the contradictions of the contemporary university workplace, a safe space to share the disappointment arising from the end of guaranteed ongoing employment, the growth of casualization and the lack of agency that persists in large organizations of the knowledge economy. While they may not resolve these problems, bloggers voice the grievances and tensions experienced in their work lives at a time of significant structural change for the industry. Discussing these difficulties with others helps bloggers develop strategies to cope with the atomization of the workplace.

Gregg argues that blogs can: (a) provide support for doctoral researchers who have inadequate institutional support and supervision; (b) offer a new form of mentoring and job-seeking support; and (c) provide a space distinct from the parent culture of institutions and thus provide some kind of resolution of feelings of academic community membership. She notes that, nevertheless, despite the blogger's investment in the communitarian ideals of 'the university', and the conversational nature of the scholarship they promote (Gregg, 2006), blogs are also a form of individualised self-promotion. A study of PhD student blogging (Ward & West, 2008) focuses on what these written accounts might reveal about the 'hidden pedagogical processes' that underpin PhD study. While the sample size was small, this study was distinctive in that the blogs were linked in a small, private network built by one of the researchers (Ward). This allowed the participants to engage in 'painful exposure of the self'. Mewburn (2011) notes that comments on blogs can be a forum for 'troubles telling' between PhD candidates suggesting that identity work and painful self-disclosure may not need privacy to emerge. Both these papers highlight that identity work is a recurrent feature of academic blogging.

Also pertinent to our concerns are a small number of studies which show how academics can use blogs to create new research partnerships with members of the public. Shanahan's (2011) work on a new collaboration between a scientist and a farmer is a particularly convincing example.

(Mewburn & Thomson, 2013, pp. 1106–07)

The literature work in Writing Sample 4.1, taken from the finished journal article, begins with a brief assessment of the field, drawing on the scoping work. It establishes a place for this particular paper. It then draws on those papers that were most pertinent to the particular study. This literature is what we referred to in Chapter 3 as the 'inner library'. The text delineates some key points in specific texts, which, later in the paper, Inger and Pat use to show how their research results support, contradict, extend or differ from those already in the field.

Strategy 2: creating a research space (CARS)

Our second strategy, known as CARS (create a research space), is helpful as you begin to clarify exactly what your research will focus on and what it will contribute. It helps you create a warrant, or mandate as it is sometimes called, a rationale for a particular contribution to knowledge.

CARS was first developed by John Swales (1990). It's a heuristic, consisting of three sets of moves:

Move 1: establish a territory in which the work is located

Your first step is to outline how your topic sits/fits in a current policy, practice and/or scholarly debate, problem or issue. You usually do this by, first, naming the topic, and then offering some uncontentious generalisations about it. You might then make reference to the state of extant literatures, knowledge and/or policy assumptions. Sometimes DRs contrast the approach they want to take to the topic with taken-for-granted views and popular opinions.

Move 2: establish a niche for the research

Your next step is to specify what your research will do. You might make a counterclaim in relation to policy, practice or the extant literatures. You might indicate some contradictory views in policy or in practice. Or you might identify a blind spot in the literature, discussing where and how a different perspective and/or new knowledge is needed. You might offer a new theoretical take or raise questions to which there haven't been satisfactory answers. You could suggest that the research will continue a promising line of inquiry, or contribute to a particular tradition of research or writing.

Move 3: filling the niche that has been constructed

Finally, you must outline what you will do. This may be a simple outline of the research project, which gives the reader some basic information about its scope and nature. It might be a description of the theoretical approach that will be explicated. In the case of a literature-based study, it could indicate the various categories of literature that will be analysed.

To illustrate how CARS might work, we go to a short text, a thesis abstract. Writing Sample 4.2 is a psychology-based draft for a research project, which examined bullying among primary-school age girls. We look at the first three paragraphs of the abstract in which DR 4.2 accomplishes the three CARS moves.

DR 4.2 doesn't write perfectly, but she did find CARS useful in helping her structure and focus the rationale for her study. The text that you will write will sometimes be short, like this, but will also vary depending on the nature of the task.

CARS is often used to guide the writing of dissertation introductions (Paltridge & Starfield, 2007). It is also used for texts that come prior to the thesis. Most universities now have a formal process where they decide whether DRs are capable of completing a PhD hurdle to continue their candidature. It may be called a Colloquium or Confirmation or Confirmation of Status or something similar, but usually you'll be required to produce an extended document of 10,000–20,000 words. It usually occurs at the point where DRs have done a reasonably thorough job on the literature, identified their specific project, research question(s) and their research design. The text must show how the proposed study is situated, and indicate what bodies of literature the dissertation will speak with and to – in other words, the lunch with friends must be planned and the potential contribution will be specified. This is a high-stakes document. At worst, an inadequate text can result in the DR being refused permission to proceed.

Many DRs find a CARS approach very useful. It narrows their focus, allows them to make large amounts of literature comprehensible and still take a stance, make clear what they intend to research and why. However, a focus on the niche – or what is more commonly talked about as a gap in the literature – can also narrow a researcher's perspective. The gap is a gap in knowledge. So this raises the question about what new insights, perspectives and theories are going to be added by the research.

The gap is about finding new knowledge. It may not, for example, be a gap to simply study a well-researched topic in a new country or with a new group of people. If we look to DR 4.2 we can see she has established a definitional problem, a group about which not enough is known and an approach that is not often taken, namely asking the girls themselves. The gap she identifies is actually knowledge about how tweenage girls understand and experience bullying. And if we go back to Inger and Pat's article on blogging, they establish through their ScoMaFo that while there is very little on their topic, they indicate where their work fits in more generally and what few literatures they might speak to.

But minding the gap, establishing exactly what it is, is not as straightforward as it might first appear. Researchers Alvesson and Sandberg (2013) take issue with

WRITING SAMPLE 4.2

Draft thesis abstract, DR in youth studies

Abstract	*Move*

Bullying is a social phenomenon that impacts girls and boys inside and outside of school, at both primary and secondary school age. It is recognised as a social problem both by academic researchers and in the 'real world' by the media and by anti-bullying charities. Although bullying is a widely used concept, there is no universal definition.

DR 4.2 has established the territory for her research. We know that it is about bullying and is a matter of widespread concern. She has also started to establish a potential issue for her research, one of definition.

Research on bullying has been conducted over the past four decades looking at various aspects, from prevalence and severity to coping strategies and effectiveness of interventions. Studies have also considered specific types of bullying such as cyber-bullying and sex differences, for example, the view that girls find relational aggression more upsetting than boys. These studies however do not consider all the types of bullying that girls and boys use or which are most upsetting to experience. Most of the studies of girls' bullying have been conducted in secondary schools: little attention has been given to tweenage girls.

In explaining what research has already been conducted, DR 4.2 also establishes what has not yet been done. She explicitly evaluates the field, saying 'these studies do not consider . . .' this is the niche she proposes to occupy.

This research redresses this imbalance. It begins from the position that it is important for adults to listen to tweenage girls' views as they may have different understandings of bullying compared to adults and this may have policy implications. The research assumes that girls are experts on the bullying that girls their age experience in school.

Here DR 4.2 says what she is going to do. She is going to redress the imbalance and examine the experiences of tweenage girls. Furthermore, she is going to do this by listening carefully to their experiences. This is, in part, what makes her contribution 'new'.

the dominant mode of generating research questions, which they call gap-spotting. They argue that the usual process – reading the literature, finding what's been said about a particular topic and locating something that isn't done – leads to an incremental approach to research. Gap-spotting, they suggest, produces work that is predictable. It does not challenge assumptions that underlie the existing literature or produce new theories and thus continues, rather than shifts, pre-existing ways of thinking and doing research. As Alvesson and Sandberg see it, there is a kind of parasitism involved.

> Apart from directly expressing critical confrontation or proposing a new idea, much work draws upon earlier critical scrutiny and suggested revisions of theories where there may be more or fewer strongly evident elements of problematisation. A gap-spotting study can thus show its origin in the outcomes of earlier problematisation.
>
> (Alvesson & Sandberg, 2013, p. 36)

Alvesson and Sandberg argue that this kind of work applies previous theory rather than changes it. This might be work that applies a game-changing theorist (Bourdieu, Foucault and so on) to a new context, text or phenomenon. By this, they mean research that, for example, looks for the ways in which fingerprinting constitutes panoptic surveillance, or research that examines the way in which social capital helps some people get preferential treatment in university entry. These kinds of projects take the theorist as a given, they don't challenge the fundamental concepts and assumptions of the theories. This kind of research doesn't meet Alvesson and Sandberg's test of innovation and ambition. It's too predictable, too safe.

The reliable way to strengthen traditions of paradigm shifting, they propose, is to find research questions through problematisation. Problematisation is a systematic process used to challenge assumptions made within a field. It might take the form of questioning – a particular school of thought; assumptions based on a common metaphor; shared ontological/epistemological/methodological assumptions within the field; or ideological assumptions or beliefs which underpin several schools of thought. The problematising process is thus not undertaken without engagement with literatures.

Alvesson and Sandberg offer a staged strategy for problematisation – six methodological principles:

1   identify a domain of literature for assumption challenging,

2   identify and articulate the assumptions, and then

3   evaluate them. The researcher must then

4   develop an alternative,

5   consider how to present that to other researchers in the field, and also

6   carefully evaluate it.

The authors do not offer problematisation as the new one best, correct way to generate research questions. They do not argue for abandoning gap-spotting research. Rather, they propose that the wider use of a problematisation approach can strengthen fields of inquiry and generate more interesting ideas. This is as beneficial to a field as incremental research.

Writing Sample 4.3 illustrates what a problematising approach might look like, writ small.

DR 4.3 is problematising the way in which Michel Foucault theorises sexuality. She is arguing that it leaves women out. And she is proposing a way in which women's pleasure and sexuality can be theorised to produce a new erotic. This particular thesis is only available to hard copy readers in the home university library. We guess this is because DR 4.3 has provided more 'real world' examples than is possible to put in a public abstract!

It's important to say that not all theses need to take this problematising approach. It's not for everyone. And CARS used well is still a helpful strategy for

WRITING SAMPLE 4.3

Thesis abstract in women's studies

The question of pleasure is central to the later work of Michel Foucault. In setting up the question of pleasure, Foucault makes an opposition between the erotic and sexuality. This thesis is a response to that opposition. It challenges some of his philosophical assumptions about, and ethical investments in, the erotic and sexuality. Engaging with the deconstructive strategies of Jacques Derrida and Luce Irigaray it contests his conceptual oppositions and unthought gaps and examines what the costs of these are for an erotics for women. This thesis argues that there is no access to the question of pleasure other than through reason. We cannot 'know' the erotic except by resort to the discourses of sexuality. Rather than a lost paradise, prior to sexuality, the erotic is internal to and makes possible the temporal and spatial power/knowledge network that infuses sexuality. The question of pleasure includes an erotics and an ethics. While Foucault argues for a desexualisation of the erotic, sexual difference is central to a notion of pleasure that is inclusive of women. An ethics of sexual difference offers to the erotic a recognition of the other as sexually different from itself.

locating and creating the warrant for your research. But it is useful to see a variety of approaches that you can use to situate and justify your study.

Strategy 3: diagnosing common authority writing problems

It is instructive to understand what common authority-related writing problems look like. Then you can become your own textual diagnostician; identifying what you have done and considering how you might do it differently – with greater authority, and a more confident stance.

The aim of understanding common writing problems is not necessarily to avoid them in your early drafts. This may not be possible. But it is essential to be able to spot the authority problems once you have a draft. You can think of this knowledge as an essential part of your toolkit: identifying textual patterns that position the DR unintentionally as tentative, as standing outside the scholarly conversation.

We identify three common patterns: (a) he said, she said; (b) buds on the family tree; and (c) 'quotomania'. We illustrate them by looking at the texts of DRs, some early and some later in their candidature, who are working to control large bodies of literature. We are grateful for their generosity in letting us work with the specificity of their writing, as this allows other DRs to identify similar problems in their own texts and take appropriate action.

He said, she said

One of the most common patterns DRs produce when writing about literatures is what we've called 'he said, she said' (see Kamler & Thomson, 2014; Thomson & Kamler, 2013). The 'he said, she said' text is essentially a list. The DR compiles a list of ideas taken from the experts. They tell the reader what this expert has said, and what that expert has said in a cumulative fashion. They add idea after idea without making any judgement or evaluation of the work or its possible connection to their own study (see Writing Sample 4.4). Writing Sample 4.4 begins every sentence with the name of a scholar (Louise Wheelahan, Frykholm and Nitzler, Andrew Morrison) or a pronoun (she, they) to create a list of what scholars in the DR's field of Vocational Education and Training (VET) have said.

DR 4.4 presents ideas that are critical of her topic, vocational education. She has found one text that argues that VET is too narrow and another that VET just reproduces the status quo. But to introduce these two ideas she uses a 'he said, she said' format. We have put this pattern in bold.

This writing occurs early in her candidature and shows the marks of her inexperience. There is an attempt to evaluate the Fritzholm and Nitzler paper, by offering the idea that their use of Bourdieu is *useful* because it has ongoing relevance.

WRITING SAMPLE 4.4

DR early writing in Education

Louise Wheelahan (date) is highly critical of VET and **argues** that workplace learning does not give young people whole life skills. **She contends** that knowledge does not always come from practice and that learning is about putting things into practice in various situations: 'it must go beyond the work of learning for work because learning is an emergent process that engages the learner in complex relational practices that have enduring consequences that go beyond the contextual and the situational.' **Wheelahan considers** VET as giving young people access to weak forms of knowledge.

In their Swedish study, **Frykholm and Nitzler (1993) use** the educational theories of Bernstein and Bourdieu to demonstrate the reproduction of power in society under the banner of giving knowledge. **They argue** that 'vocational and career education can be regarded as part of a social and cultural reproduction'. The theory of social and cultural class reproduction comes from Pierre Bourdieu's book *Reproduction in education, society and culture* (1990, second edition) which is still influential and useful in educational research today. For example, **Andrew Morrison (2008) describes** a 'vocational habitus' which references Bourdieu's notion of habitus, arguing that gender and class are important factors in the type of vocation that young people follow.

Anyone who seriously engages with Bourdieu won't discuss the relevance of his work, but rather comment on the ways in which the authors use Bourdieu's work and to what effect. But this DR does not yet know enough about how to evaluate expert scholars.

New buds on the family tree

'He said, she said' is not the only problem DRs experience when working with other people's words. Even when DRs know they must use the literature to situate themselves and their study, there is still the problem of dealing with the sheer volume of texts with authority (see Writing Sample 4.5).

DR 4.5 tells the reader all of the things that have influenced her study. She wants to locate herself in a body of scholarly work and connect this with the knowledge derived from her personal-professional experience. There is a serious attempt to go beyond simply saying 'they said this'. The DR is trying, as we suggested in Chapter 2, to trace her intellectual family tree. However, she appears as a very tiny bud submerged under a dense arboreal canopy.

WRITING SAMPLE 4.5

DR draft colloquium text, Higher Education

Slee (2010), Barton (2000), Osler and Starkey (2005), and numerous instructive texts on research methods and processes all assert that a position is derived from a multiplicity of experiences, knowledge, policies and actions, and indeed much of my understanding of inclusion and of the pedagogic discourse that underpins it is greatly influenced by my own experience and other discourses such as social justice (Gewirtz, 2006; Fraser, 2010; Bauman, 2001; Ebert, 1991; Leonard 1997) feminism and intersectionality (Gilbert & Gubar, 2008; Valentine, 2007), race and equality, stereotyping and 'othering' (Young, 1991; Hall, 1997), gender studies (Barrow *et al.*, 2009; Woodfield & Farsides, 2006) and identity politics (Bernstein, 2005; Dworkin, 2002), all of which represents a considerable body of work within which attention has been paid to the understanding of decision and policy makers (legislators, politicians, religious leaders) and those tasked with implementing policies (educators, politicians, leaders, families, education institutions, lay workers and so on). Indeed this study is founded not only upon personal experience (heuristic perception), but is also a recognition that much of the aforementioned scholarly contributions have informed the interpretation and definition of inclusion that I offer as the foundation around which the study is to be built.

The writer begins by asserting the importance of researchers making their beliefs and position clear. Then, in an exceedingly long sentence, she lists, one after another, broad areas of research she claims to draw upon, without specifying what any of them actually mean for her work. This leaves the reader somewhat adrift. What, for example, is it about the substantial literatures on feminism and intersectionality that are most pertinent to this study? What aspects of race and equality, stereotyping and 'othering' are important to the DR and her research?

DR 4.5 has, in fact, announced her influences, but has not explained them, as a substitute for critical analysis. 'Indeed' is used twice to add emphasis and rhetorical force. But this is undercut when the DR uses the verb 'offer'. Researchers do not 'offer' their stance, they inform or tell the reader the basis on which their research has been conducted. 'Indeed' ordinarily gives the impression of an authoritative scholar, but when it is located in a laundry list of topics and citations, it fails.

Locating yourself in the research and through the writing is difficult. Sometimes DRs over-focus on themselves (see Writing Sample 4.6). This is, to strain our metaphor, an intellectual family tree where most of the branches have been cut

WRITING SAMPLE 4.6

DR thesis first draft, self study

In order for **me** to connect with the reader and to give credibility to **my** study I feel that I need to place myself in context and acknowledge that, '*I, too, lead a storied life*' (Winkler, 2003, p.399). This '*personal reality*' and '*lived experience*' is a form of, '*meditative inner work*' (Torbert, 2001, p.252) and is not offered in a self-indulgent, sentimental way (Brooker & McPherson, 1999) but as part of the process of seeking understanding through the sharing of our stories (Sparkes, 2002). By being authentic about who I am and what I bring to the research I hope to add a measure of research validity (Heen, 2005; Schein, 2001) and enable the reader to gain a sense of truthfulness and congruence with **my** intended meaning (Burgess, 2006).

off and are now dwarfed by an energetic new shoot. The reader gets a lot of me, myself and I, often with a call to the literature as a justification. We have put this pattern in bold.

DR 4.6 writes clearly. She *is* explicit about her influences, acknowledging the scholarly community to which she sees herself belonging and speaking. She wants to convince the reader that they will find her to be credible, truthful and her text congruent with these traits. But she doesn't trust her own words and uses quotations as embroidery; she expresses relatively straightforward ideas in italicised quoted phrases. These phrases appear out of context and unexplained, piled up on top of each other. We don't actually know, for example, what 'meditative work' is or how it is going to be enacted in the thesis. As a result, the reader is left in the dark.

Quotomania

A third writing issue for DRs is how to use the words of other scholars effectively. DRs often get into a bad habit of finding quotations they love and then dumping them into the text. Don't get us wrong. There's nothing wrong with a good quotation. We like them too. The problem is where and how they are used. We use the term 'quotomania' to capture two problems that occur when DRs are learning to use quotations: quotations as embroidery and quote dumping.

1 Embroidery

We saw that DR 4.6 partly got in trouble by embroidering her text with quotations. She pastes bits of italicised phrases together, in a collage-like fashion. What's the problem with embroidering? Embroidery with quotations is decorative rather than substantive. The quotations don't add meaning to what you're trying to say. They give the appearance of doing so. It's as if the writer thinks 'one of the characteristics of academic writing is that it has quotations, so I'd better put some in'. This is a common tactic used by writers who haven't yet mastered academic writing. They look at surface features of text and imitate. Instead of making a point quite simply, they embellish what is probably a straightforward comment that needs nothing more than a clear statement.

The key problem with embroidering is that each of the phrases used is decontextualised. They are lifted out of their original source and added to an entirely different piece of writing. The assumption is that they are going to fit in neatly, like a jigsaw puzzle piece. Instead they sit apart from their new text, raised out of the background by italics and by their lack of continuity in meaning. Janet Giltrow, a renowned expert on academic writing from the University of British Columbia, calls this 'copying' (Giltrow, 1997) (see Commentary: Janet Giltrow).

2 The quote dump

The quote dump – or what is sometimes also called the 'hit and run quotation' (Graff & Birkenstein, 2010, p. 44) – occurs when the DR drops a quotation into the text as if it can speak for itself. The quotation is not introduced, the writer does not say why they think it is worth quoting, or whether they agree with it, and they do not connect it with anything they are saying. The quote stands alone in the text

---

COMMENTARY

Janet Giltrow

Sometimes when you are immersed in the reasoning of another writer's argument, copying may seem a very practical solution to the problems presented by the process of putting reading to use. The original author's sentences which express the point so well are tempting: why not just repeat them?

There is a good reason for not just repeating them. They are convincing and impressive *in context*, supported, explained, modified, extended and connected by all the material that surrounds them. *Out of context* they are not nearly so powerful.

. . .

As a copier, the summarizer may still have that connected material in mind, so he (sic) may not notice the discontinuities and gaps in what he offers his reader. But, as readers, we do notice the gaps. At best, we just skim over the passage as not worth the trouble. At worst, we object to its jumps from one notion to another.

Giltrow, 1997, pp. 33–5

while the writer rushes off to something else and the reader is left to make their own reading – or more likely, left confused!!

Writing Sample 4.7 produces the classic quote dump (see Writing Sample 4.7). As in Writing Sample 4.6, the DR uses other people's words to accomplish 'I argue'. He is showing the scholars with whom he is aligned. The bad news is that he is using them to ventriloquise his own position – he allows them to speak for him. He then dumps a quotation from the key social theorist who informs his thesis, Foucault. Knowingly or unknowingly he has selected one of the most (over)used Foucauldian fragments. One might expect some discussion or explanation of how he understands this extract and what it actually means for his work.

DR 4.7 takes Foucault's point about everything being dangerous and goes on to name the implications for his work, namely that he must research with a sense of ongoing discomfort. He has tried to use the quotation as a stepping stone in his argument, but the reader falls between the cracks of the quotation and the following paragraph. Whereas Foucault talks of danger, DR 4.7 talks of discomfort. We are not clear how one leads to the other.

WRITING SAMPLE 4.7

A published PhD in sport

As Best and Kellner (1997) argue, however, such a postmodern position does not necessitate a retreat into nihilism. While we must give up the possibility of transcendental critique, we can instead seek to offer locally, socio-historically contextualised critique. Following Richardson and St Pierre (2005) I argue 'having a partial, local, historical knowledge is still knowing' (p.961). While we must give up the possibility of a future Utopia, we can strive for meaningful localised change in the contemporary moment. As Foucault (2000c) argues:

> My point is that everything is bad, but that everything is dangerous, which is not exactly the same as bad. If everything is dangerous then we always have something to do. So my position leads not to apathy but to hyper- and pessimistic activism. I think that the ethico-political choice we have to make everyday is to determine which is the main danger. (p. 256)

Whereas modernity creates a sense of assurance in the certainty offered by notions of objective knowledge and uncontested truths, I interpret post-modernity to embody a sense of discomfort which continually demands that researchers ask new questions of their selves and their research. My interest in developing a more nuanced under-standing of ethics is a response to this sense of discomfort.

The more accepted textual alternative to the quote dump is the 'quotation sandwich' (Graff & Birkenstein, 2010, p. 46). This consists of an *introduction*, the *quotation*, and then an *explanation*. The sandwich has the benefit of providing a link backward and a link forward in the new text.

The quotation sandwich can be thought of as a strategy where, first, you introduce your quotation. You might begin by saying something like 'According to Foucault . . .' You then insert the quotation, just as DR 4.7 does. However, you then need to provide an explanation by saying something like: 'In other words, Foucault argues that it is now no longer possible to take anything for granted'.

While all quotations do have to be introduced, they don't all have to be explained. Often, the move after the quotation carries the argument forward. It offers a continuation of the case being made, rather than an explanation. DR 4.7 tries to do this, but does not make a good connection between the quotation and the subsequent sentence. An alternative might be: 'Postmodernity offers a plethora of dangers that need to be assessed. Unlike modernity which created a sense of assurance in the certainty offered by . . .' and so on. Writing Sample 4.7 leaves out the follow-on step and thus lurches the reader into the body of the argument.

In sum

In this chapter we've taken a detailed look at text work and the ways in which identity work is tangled up in what and how DRs write. The problem we addressed was the difficulty of finding one's place in the literature. We offered a reframing idea of taking a stand. We then explored three strategies for getting control of the textual game: scoping, mapping and focusing in, locating your own research in the literature and diagnosing the most common authority problems when writing about the literature.

CHAPTER 5 Learning to argue

The problem: confusing feedback – your writing is too . . .

DRs are often bemused and confused by some of the feedback they get from their supervisors. They've sent off their writing and wait anxiously for it to come back. When it does, they read: 'This is too descriptive. You need to do more than tell me what happened. This is just a report of what you read – what does it mean? You need to get beyond simply summarising what people have said. So what's the point?' DRs are worried by this kind of response. They don't understand what it means. Their writing has received good responses in the past and now it seems it's just not good enough. But what are they meant to do?

The problem here is that the DR has not yet understood the kind of writing required for a successful and persuasive thesis. They are still looking in the rear-view mirror.

As we argued in Chapter 2, you cannot assume the writing strategies you've used in the past will necessarily work in the doctorate. For the most part you have been asked to write assignments and reports, and through these you have gained entry to the PhD. You will also have been expected to write essays in your doctoral coursework. However, the vast majority of doctoral writing – the proposal, conference papers, journal articles, abstracts, blogs and the thesis itself – will not be reports.

In the standard essay, set for assignments, you are often asked to:

- compare and contrast – doctoral research methods assignments typically ask you to compare qualitative and quantitative methods;
- explain a cause and effect relationship – you may be asked to address a controversy, policy or a social phenomenon and tease out how it got to be this way;

- define terminology and sift through the debates – you may be asked to address the question of epistemology and explain various views on it;

- address a contention and provide illustration – you may be asked to respond to a statement about a current trend in a field and provide information to show how it appears and/or operates.

Assignment writing requires you to do the required reading – sift and sort information, reflect critically on and integrate complex information into a coherent text (Lillis, 2001). As Anthony Parè (2010) notes, essay assignments typically need to provide: evidence that their writers understand the topic in its context; an audit trail that shows that they have read all of the relevant literatures and can use/incorporate these appropriately; a demonstration of correct referencing and in-text citations; and familiarity with the kinds of conceptual and theoretical resources typically brought to social science problems. Each of these markers of the essay garner 'points' when it is submitted for assessment purposes; lacking them may mean substantial revisions – or worse still, outright failure. At Masters level, assignments are typically assessed and graded on planning and organisation, structure, quality of writing, grounding in literature, depth of analysis and criticality.

Writers bring this repertoire of thinking, reading and writing into doctoral course work, but it doesn't always serve them well. The essay may set up a deferential attitude to prior knowledge and scholarship. The DR is tentative in making evaluative judgements and thus may well miss important debates and assume certainties where there are none (Li, 2008) (see Experience: Xiaoming Li).

Doctoral writing has a different set of expectations from everything that has gone before. You now need to show a different kind of authority and control over the vast information and scholarship you encounter. Rather than think of yourself as regurgitating material in order to show you have mastery over it, you need to be an expert and critical guide.

You are no longer just reporting and integrating, although this is important. You are also arguing. You are leading the reader through your analysis, interpretation and evaluation of other people's work in relation to your own. You are making a case for the significance of your work. This is a far cry from assignments.

Reframing idea: the whole thesis is an argument

Most DRs know that they have to argue in their thesis. After all, the word thesis means argument. But where to argue and how? Some think they have to argue for particular meanings for their data, for example. Or summarise their argument in the final chapter. However, many DRs – particularly those who get the kind of

EXPERIENCE

Xiaoming Li

Reflecting on the essay

In front of me is the Masters thesis I wrote almost two decades ago. It is a relic excavated from my last academic life. It was written, in Chinese, to meet part of the graduation requirements for the Masters degree in Modern English in the East China Normal University. Titled, 'English rhythm and sentence stress' it purports to 'understand the features of English rhythm and sentence stress, the relationships between the two, and the approaches to master them'. I selected the topic because I found most Chinese teachers of English at that time were preoccupied with the clear pronunciation of each sound, paying little attention to sentence stress and rhythm which, I believe, are just as essential to effective and intelligible spoken communication. The paper references ten publications on English phonetics, among them, Halliday's *A course in spoken English*, Daniel Jones' *An outline of English phonetics*, and Gillian Brown's *Practical phonetics and phonology*, and others, all that I could find on the university library at that time.

In the paper I borrowed extensively the terminology, theory, explanation, and even a good number of examples from those works. Over the entire 36 hand-written pages, the only part that bears my personal stamp is the final recommendation for ways to teach English rhythm and stress patterns to Chinese students. Even there, my suggestions are shielded from controversy: teach word pronunciation before teaching rhythm and sentence stress; tap the blackboard to maintain a steady rhythm as students read, etc. Although called a thesis, it actually does not have an argumentative thesis statement. I imagined myself as a conduit of knowledge, through which the wisdom of the experts was passed to the Chinese teachers. Why would a conduit argue with its sources? . . . I was not expected to argue for a particular point of view or to evaluate the sources – it would be presumptuous for me, a graduate student, to think that I had the authority or sufficient knowledge to do that. Neither did I acknowledge any diverse views or unresolved issues – it simply never occurred to me that experts would espouse different views, and thus, I did not notice any. Ironically, my inability to evaluate the sources led me to present all that I reported as universally accepted and with a tone of finality and certainty that left little room for further exploration or questioning.

Li, 2008, p. 46

mystery feedback from their supervisors that we talked about at the start of this chapter – don't understand that the *whole thesis* is an argument. It's an argument that is carefully staged, and built up step by step over a series of chapters. The whole thesis not only has to make the case that the research addresses a puzzle, niche, problem or problematisation (see Chapter 4). The thesis has to make the case that the research provides an answer and thus makes a contribution to what is already known about the particular topic.

So let's consider the question of argument. What is an argument? You may have seen the Monty Python argument sketch. A man goes into the argument clinic and purchases a one-off £5 argument. When he enters the room where his argument is located, he encounters a disagreement rather than an argument.

> Man: Is this the right room for an argument?
> Other Man: I've told you once.
> Man: No you haven't!
> Other Man: Yes I have.
> M: When?
> O: Just now.
> M: No you didn't!

Frustrated, the man says, 'Oh look, this isn't an argument!' The pattern continues with each contradicting the other. This goes on for some time until the man, exasperated, says

> M: Oh this is futile!!. . .I came here for a good argument!
> O: Ah, no you didn't, you came here for an argument!
> M: An argument isn't just contradiction.
> O: Well! It CAN be!
> M: No it can't! An argument is a connected series of statements intended to establish a proposition.
> O: No it isn't!
> M: Yes it is! It isn't just contradiction.
> O: Look, if I argue with you, I must take up a contrary position!
> M: Yes but it isn't just saying 'no it isn't'.
> O: Yes it is
> M: No it isn't! Argument is an intellectual process. Contradiction is just the automatic gainsaying of anything the other person says.
>   (Source: www.montypython.net/scripts/argument.php)

During the series of exchanges with the Arguer, the man defines his expectations of an argument as being more than simple contradiction. An argument, he says, is a connected series of statements intended to establish a position. Rather than a disagreeable exchange, it is an intellectual process. It is not emotional but rational. The sketch points to the difference between the common-sense understanding of an argument and its scholarly interpretation.

Writing a scholarly argument involves taking a position on a particular issue, event or question, and justifying that position. An argument attempts to persuade the reader to a particular point of view and to its veracity and worth. In its simplest form an argument consists of:

- a statement of position (a thesis),

- a series of points arranged in logical order, supported by evidence and examples, linked together by connections that emphasise their cumulative nature, and

- a summary in which the thesis is reaffirmed and restated. There may also be recommendations (Williams & Colomb, 2006).

While scholarly arguments generally follow this structure, they may also entertain counter points of view, in order to strengthen the case being made. They can be concise, as in the form of an abstract; in their most extended form they become a dissertation or book. Because scholarly argument does not take evidence and examples as givens, it also incorporates analysis, interpretation and evaluation. There are generally sub-arguments contained within the larger overarching case being made.

There are common problems that occur in arguments and it's as well to know what they are so that they can be avoided (see Advice: Common mistakes in argument).

In order to develop your capacity to argue, you need to imagine yourself in a new way – not merely as a reporter of work, but as an active player in the field with something important to say. This requires significant identity work. Ian Robson, an experienced early childhood researcher, explains the ongoing struggle to make an argument, and the identity work that it entails (see Experience: Ian Robson).

Argument is not easy – you have to practise. And this means stopping some habituated ways of thinking. We want you to learn to articulate what your research has to offer. We want you to make explicit the connections between your work and that of the broader community of scholars. Instead of feeling inadequate, ask yourself what is your contribution going to be? Ask yourself: Why write about this? What's the point? So what? Who cares?

The 'so what' question can be confronting because it can feel like an attack on your scholarship. But the 'so what' and 'who cares' questions are exactly what your

ADVICE

Common mistakes in argument

Arthur Asa Berger (2008) suggests that academic writers often make one or more of these mistakes in argument:

- *Adhominen argument* – attacking the person not the argument
- *Use of emotional language* to justify a position rather than evidence or reason
- *Begging the question* – assuming the answer to the question is so obvious it doesn't need to be argued
- *Overgeneralisation* – making sweeping claims that cannot be supported
- After this, therefore because of it (*Post hoc ergo propter sum*) – Just because X comes before Y doesn't mean that X causes Y
- *Appeal to false authorities* – using as evidence material from sources which do not have legitimacy in the area
- *Incorrect analogies* – a false analogy weakens not strengthens argument

- *Mispresenting the ideas of others* – cherry-picking from material and misquoting both alter the original meaning and undermine the credibility of both the original and the user
- *Pushing argument to absurd extremes* – ignoring qualifications and limitations of evidence

(Adapted from Berger, 2008, pp. 70–72)

Berger says:

When we write, we somehow become so caught up in the documents we are working on that we neglect to be careful about our logic and the argument we make. That's why taking some time away from a document we are working on is helpful; we can look at the text with a fresh mind and catch any overgeneralisations and other errors in thinking in time to correct them (p.72).

examiners and your readers will ask. What is the point of this research? How and why is it relevant? How is it significant – to whom and why? What is it offering that is new?

Another way to think about the 'so what' question is to imagine a future DR who finds your PhD in the library. In doing their literature work they write a sentence or two about your key results. What do they say and how do they describe the value of your research? Fill in the blanks: 'Your name (date) argued that . . .' When you do this exerise, you cannot avoid the challenging work of saying what you are doing and why it matters. So what . . .? So what . . .? So what . . .?

EXPERIENCE

Ian Robson

The (not so) simple act of saying something

You would think, after twenty years of speaking (latterly, writing) I would be fairly confident in putting over a point or two. Being a research student and academic sort of requires that. The honest thing is, I am struggling with it a bit at the moment, and I've caught myself saying 'I just don't think I can do it' more than once this week. It's playing on my mind.

I just had a thought: most of my drive to communicate has been to connect with people, not to put across a carefully reasoned argument. I'm happier with emotions; which is why I love mentoring people as part of professional programmes. Don't get me wrong, I've written a whole stack of essays and given a few million lectures more recently over the years but I feel the need to step up again. This time, it's about 'putting something out there', and I'm not quite prepared on some levels.

I suspect a few of us have these moments, but you see, when it's you sitting down thinking about writing an academic paper it can be paralyzing. I'm determined to get past that – I need to get that PhD – but doing that for me means I must find that confidence to speak out in an academic field populated with people who seem to speak rather authoritatively. Some of them work with me!

. . . I realise that this PhD journey is not just about accumulating knowledge, even careful critical analysis; it's also about allowing myself to say something whilst 'being myself'. Being a person who is hard on themselves, I also think I need to give myself space (physically and mentally) to start writing something, and look less at the clever stuff around me.

http://changingpractice.blogspot.com.au/2011/05/not-so-simple-act-of-saying-something.htm

We offer three strategies to help you consider and articulate the 'so what' question and stop hiding behind description:

1 Questions to guide the arguer stance
2 Learning to argue through tiny texts
3 Sentence skeletons

Strategy 1: questions to guide the arguer stance

DRs who have worked professionally between the Masters and beginning the doctorate have usually written submissions: to make a case to a superior, to make a bid for funding, to propose a change in process and organisation. They already know the importance of presenting a problem, proposing a solution and logically ordering evidence. They understand the importance of anticipating and countering contrary positions.

But because DRs often feel novice in the university context, they don't always draw on their prior knowledge to make a scholarly case. They too often feel the learner, the 'student', the beginner and resort to summarising, and describing, reporting, and telling a story instead of arguing. Clearly there is identity work involved in learning to articulate a scholarly argument. It makes you feel far more vulnerable than hiding behind description or facts. It feels risky to assert a point of view. 'Oh I can't say that. Who am I to think that? Why would anyone take notice of what I've got to say? I don't know as much as the experts. I can't.'

You may find *The craft of research* (2008) by Wayne Booth, Gregory Colomb and Joseph Williams helpful as you work at developing an arguer stance. They devote five chapters to writing arguments. They expand on the three moves of the argument we presented earlier, suggesting that an argument consists of five elements, namely:

1   A *Claim* – a statement that something is 'true'. This is sometimes called the thesis. For example:

    Claim: Some boys are leaving school at a disadvantage.

2   *Reasons* – statements that support the claim. It is helpful to think of this as the 'because statement' that follows the claim. For example:

    Claim: Some boys are leaving school at a disadvantage,

    Reason: because they have fallen behind their female peers.

3   *The Warrant* – the principle that establishes how the reason is relevant to the claim. For example:

    Claim: Some boys are leaving school at a disadvantage,

    Reason: because they have fallen behind their female peers.

    Warrant: Success at school is strongly correlated with life opportunities (work, further education).

4   *Evidence* – empirical data from your own or other studies which substantiate the reasons. In this example:

    Evidence: Exam results, post-school destinations of students sorted by class and gender

1   What is my claim?

2   What reasons support my claim?

3   What principle makes my reasons relevant to my claim?

4   What evidence supports my reasons?

5   What counterclaims might be made in response to the evidence I produce?

6   How can I refute the counterclaims?

7   How do I acknowledge and respond to alternatives/complications/objections?

FIGURE 5.1   Questions to guide the arguer stance

(adapted from Booth *et al.*, 2008, pp. 108–10)

Advice on arguments also points out the importance of anticipating and dealing with counterclaims as part of this step.

5   *Responses* – to complications/objections/alternative reasoning and/or evidence. In this example:

Responses: Dealing with the evidence of the gender-segregated labour market which reverses the pattern of school outcomes, whereby both men and boys earn more than women; some men are unemployed, but not as unemployed as women etc.

Booth, Colomb and Williams suggest that researchers ask themselves a set of questions about each of these moves as an aid to constructing their argument/ case. We have adapted their questions in Figure 5.1. These are a detox for the tentative, reluctant researcher because they force you to focus on YOU and your research.

Strategy 2: learning to argue through tiny texts

While DRs know they have to write a thesis, many tend to write around their argument. They write long slabs of text in the hope that something pithy will emerge. Our advice is: Don't do this. It is useful to write to find out what you think, but this is *only* a first step. Speedwriting, freewriting, pomodoros and writing without a parachute are strategies to get you going. At the end of a period of freewriting you will probably know what you want to say. But freewriting does not stand in for more careful elaboration of the claim and its evidence.

Writing abstracts is a useful strategy for clarifying the contribution of your research and finding a place in the scholarly conversation in your field. In a good abstract, the writer speaks with authority, not simply describing or reporting what they've done, but delineating their case and specifying their particular point of view. In other words, in writing the abstract you make yourself an active participant in the field.

We call abstracts Tiny Texts because they are relatively short in length, but high in practical yield. The intellectual and emotional labour involved in crafting a persuasive Tiny Text is invisible work, yet it has a visible impact on DRs. A good abstract asks you to write more confidently than you feel – as a scholar with something significant to say, with a perspective and a defensible base from which to speak. This may feel like a bluff. But it is the move to textualise your scholarly self with an authoritative stance, which in the end creates a more confident scholar. By doing this textwork/identitywork, you write yourself into authority.

The first time that DRs need to write an abstract is generally when they give a conference presentation. Even though conferences may have a set form for the abstract, these are formulaic and generally don't focus on argument. More often they are like a report and called a summary. Before you use the conference template, we think it is helpful to first work out what your argument is by using a Tiny Text. This work with Tiny Texts bolsters your capacity to write argument in the thesis. We offer a core strategy of four textual moves.

Four moves

We think of an abstract as having four moves. We call these Locate, Focus, Report and Argue. We show these four moves in Figure 5.2.

LOCATE: this means placing your paper in the context of the discipline community and the field in general. Larger issues and debates are named and potentially problematised. In naming the location, you are creating a warrant for your contribution and its significance, as well as informing an international community of its relevance outside of its specific place of origin.

FOCUS: this means identifying the particular questions, issues or kinds of problems that your paper will explore, examine and/or investigate.

REPORT: this means outlining the research, sample and/or method of analysis in order to assure readers that your paper is credible and trustworthy, as well as the major findings that are pertinent to the argument to be made.

ARGUE: this means opening out the specific argument through offering an analysis. This will move beyond description and may well include a theorisation in order to explain findings. It may offer speculations, but will always have a point of view and take a stance. It returns to the opening Locate in order to demonstrate the specific contribution that was promised at the outset.

FIGURE 5.2 The four moves of a Tiny Text

We now show an example of these four moves as they apply to one of our own abstracts from the *Educational Researcher* (see Writing Sample 5.1).

In the Locate we have identified an issue and suggested that it is problematic and, by inference, that we have a different view. Given this, we offer a specific Focus, which is designed to allow us to say something about the problem we have identified. In Report we detail the four findings that have resulted from our analysis. In Argue we offer a theoretical framework, and on the basis of this propose a course of action. The title clearly signals our critique in the use of the word 'failure', and our contribution in the phrase 'alternative pedagogies'.

A second example, Writing Sample 5.2, is an abstract from a paper written about academic blogging, which was published in *Studies in Higher Education* (2013). (This was the paper that we used to illustrate ScoMaFo in Chapter 4.)

The Locate in this paper is comparatively straightforward and short. It assumes that readers of the particular journal are familiar with the pressure for academics

WRITING SAMPLE 5.1

Four moves in a published paper abstract

The failure of dissertation advice books: towards alternative pedagogies for doctoral writing

LOCATE: Anxious doctoral researchers can now call on a proliferation of advice books telling them how to produce their dissertations. While these might be helpful in the short term they offer little that the doctoral researcher can use to analyse their own texts or to understand the source of their anxieties.

FOCUS: This article reveals some characteristics of the self-help genre through a textual analysis of a corpus of published books, delineating their key genre characteristics.

REPORT: Our analysis shows that the texts produce an expert-novice relationship with readers; reduce the dissertation to a series of steps; claim to reveal hidden rules; and assert a mix of certainty and fear to position readers 'correctly'.

ARGUE: We argue for a more complex view of doctoral writing as both text work-identity and as a discursive social practice. We reject transmission pedagogies that normalise the power-saturated relations of protégée/master and point to alternative pedagogical approaches that position doctoral researchers as colleagues engaged in a shared, common, unequal and changing practice.

(adapted from Kamler and Thomson, 2008)

WRITING SAMPLE 5.2

Four moves in a published paper abstract

Why do academics blog? An analysis of audiences, purposes and challenges

LOCATE: Academics are increasingly being urged to blog in order to expand their audiences, create networks and learn to write in a more reader-friendly style.

FOCUS: This paper holds this advocacy up to empirical scrutiny.

REPORT: A content analysis of 100 academic blogs suggests that academics most commonly write about academic work conditions and policy contexts, share information and provide advice; the intended audience for this work is other higher education staff.

ARGUE: We contend that academic blogging may constitute a community of practice in which a hybrid public/ private academic operates in a 'gift economy'. We note however that academic blogging is increasingly of interest to institutions and this may challenge some of the current practices we have recorded. We conclude that there is still much to learn about academic blogging practices.

(Mewburn & Thomson, 2013)

to blog. The Focus is pithy and says that the authors are going to critically examine this new phenomenon. The Report gives the results of the content analysis in a concise manner. The Argue is the most elaborated move, with three sentences. The authors contend, note and conclude, in order to make the claim that the encouragement to blog may have an array of consequences, some unintended.

We can see from these two examples that what goes into the four moves varies in length and complexity. If the research is situated in a field where there is considerable debate and the writer needs to state their position quite clearly, then the Locate, for example, will be more descriptive and sometimes more argumentative. Some arguments might lead to more than one conclusion. Some may provide a challenge to existing thinking, a new lens on the problem or a potential implication for a more general issue. These are categories of moves, not recipes for how much to say about what.

Having a clear sense of the four moves and the work they do is a useful heuristic for both constructing and analysing abstracts, written by yourself and others.

As an analytic strategy, you first divide an abstract into four moves, and see which moves are present and which are missing; which moves are developed and which are undercooked. You can ask yourself, for example: If I was to further develop the Locate, what would I need to include? How could I set the context more fully so readers will better grasp the significance of my research? Or if the abstract is too descriptive and excludes Locate and Argue, you might ask: How can I change this? How do I articulate my argument, my 'so what'?

We illustrate the power of this four-move analytic framework by applying it to a conference symposium with abstracts written by five researchers of varying experience. There is a Professor and a DR who have worked on the same research project, which is completed. There are two DRs whose research projects are half completed. There is an early career researcher who is writing from her PhD thesis.

WRITING SAMPLE 5.3

Symposium abstract

Organisational interventions with 'risky' young people: Oh to be in England?

LOCATE: The current English government can be characterised not only by its almost religious adherence to the tenets of the free market, but also by its hostility to young people. Despite espousing interest in the experiences and opinions of young people, and despite policy taking up rhetoric about equity, the prospects for many young people in the country are poor – and getting worse. The number of young people dubbed as NEET – not in education, employment or training – is the highest in Europe. The gap between the lowest and highest school achievement, strongly correlated with poverty, remains stubbornly among the widest among those participating in international testing regimes.

A range of government and third sector organisations are attempting to intervene in the production and reproduction of youthful risks and to prevent young people becoming 'collateral damage' (Bauman, 2011).

FOCUS: In this symposium we examine four of these interventions – (1) a vocational award that is alternative or complementary to more mainstream qualifications; (2) a partnership programme designed to encourage young people to participate more actively in the arts, (3) alternative education programmes offered to young people in the compulsory years of schooling, and (4) film-making projects for recreational and vocational purposes. We ask not simply what happens to young people in these programmes, but also what we can see and say about the ways in which organisations develop and challenge norms, individualise and/or collectivise risks, and do/do not steer young people towards more responsibilised self-management.

It is not uncommon for a senior academic to organise a symposium as a way of supporting and promoting the work of less experienced researchers. The Professor who organised this symposium is, or has been, the supervisor for all four co-presenters. The conference focuses on Youth Studies and has a theme of 'risk'. The conference organisers have imposed a limit of 250 words for each paper abstract and for the overall explanation of the symposium. The conference symposium itself has an abstract (see Writing Sample 5.3), which was produced by the Professor.

The symposium introduction abstract has only two moves, Locate and Focus, as its job is to introduce the subsequent papers and place them in a broader context. The Locate has to address the specific locality of the research – England, and situate it not only within Britain but also Europe more generally, as the conference is to be held in a Nordic city, and is designed to speak to European participants, practices and policies. The Focus names the four papers and pulls them together under the notion of an intervention – this provides a point of commonality between them, even though the research they report has all been developed and conducted separately. A collective purpose for the papers is also proposed, taking the focus away from young people to the organisations that cater for them. The Focus poses a problem to which the papers, read together, will provide some kind of answer. No one paper could answer the question – it is only when combined that they offer insights.

DR 5.4 has just begun her second full-time year of her PhD. She has conducted a pilot study and undertaken some document analysis. The results of this work have worried her, as she has been heavily involved in the programme she is researching (see Writing Sample 5.4).

DR 5.4 is concerned that her own experiences will colour her analysis too much and that her research may lose sight of the things she most values in the arts work with young people. These worries create a tension that shows in her writing. The Locate specifies the territory she is researching – youth, arts, vocational education. The Focus not only says what her paper will do, but also provides, for an international audience, information about the specific programme she is researching. The Report signals some hesitation to specify the results – partly because it is too early in the project to do so, but also because she may be reluctant to reveal problems with the programme e.g. putting off students, diluting content, diminishing the richness of the arts. Instead of making statements, DR 5.4 poses these concerns as a series of rhetorical questions. The end result is that questions are raised, but readers are not sure what the analysis actually produced.

The Argue is similarly ambivalent. DR 5.4 asserts what the risks in the programme might be to both young people and the arts. The possible argument – that diluted arts content runs the risk of either alienating young people or failing them – is lurking within the Report and Argue. The supervisor has been encouraging

WRITING SAMPLE 5.4

DR conference abstract

Using and abusing the arts with 'at-risk' groups

Keywords: Arts, NEET, vocational education

LOCATE: Young people at-risk of exclusion from mainstream education are often directed to alternative education programmes with a vocational content. The arts are often used as part or all of these programmes as they are seen to encompass 'softer' skills.

FOCUS: This paper surveys the policy literatures on arts programmes for 'at risk youth'. It focuses in particular on the Arts Award, a specific programme which claims to 'increase self -esteem, giving young people confidence to go on to further educational provision and improve relationships with parents and carers, by seeing their young people engaged in positive activities and celebrating achievements'. I use discourse analysis to interrogate the ways in which both the arts and young people are represented in these texts.

REPORT: The analysis raises a series of questions about the ways in which 'at risk youth' and 'arts' come together. What if some programmes, instead of benefitting young people, are simply putting the arts at-risk? When the arts content is diluted, lost amongst numeracy and literacy, behaviour management and developing 'transferable skills', the value of the arts per se is forgotten.

ARGUE: The participants risk negative experiences of instrumentalised arts programmes, which may prevent them from being life-long supporters of and/or participants in the arts. Intensive arts focused programmes could counter-productively position young people as failing to live up to programme expectations to be imaginative and creative.

this DR to be more critical of the programme, based on her results, but it is still early days in her candidature. It is difficult for her to shift from an advocacy role to a more evaluative and critical researcher stance. This will take time. Her abstract is a first step in that direction.

DR 5.5 is also in the second year of her research and is midway through an intense ethnography conducted over multiple sites (see Writing Sample 5.5).

The Focus of DR 5.5's abstract is clear. However, its relationship to the Locate is not. The Locate seems to identify some key understandings from the literature, and is trying to provide a problematisation of partnerships in general. However, there are too many complex ideas put together. As well, the problem of working

WRITING SAMPLE 5.5

DR conference abstract

Mapping risk in partnership work between visual arts organisations and youth organisations.

Key words: arts, risk, partnership, gallery, youth organisation

LOCATE: Working together across professional, disciplinary and organisational boundaries is an inherently risky process. Partnerships can develop in response to risk; they require partners to put things at risk, and they can be creatively invested in discourses of risk.

FOCUS: This paper sets out to map sites of risk in a four-year programme called (name of programme), which is led by (name of gallery) and involves galleries and museums throughout the UK, working in partnership with the youth sector to 'improve access and opportunities for harder to reach young people'.

REPORT: Like many learning initiatives in galleries, (name of programme) strives to be risk-taking in its collaborative activities. However while galleries frequently trade upon contemporary art's reputation for being daring and speculative, as institutions they typically constitute risk-averse public environments. Many youth organisations meanwhile, operate under precarious circumstances, and with young people who are regularly characterised as being vulnerable or volatile. These factors, alongside financial and bureaucratic pressures, mediate the youth sector's capacity for risk.

(Name of programme) partners put at stake resources, time, reputations and the experience of young people in order to co-construct alternative, inclusive spaces for interaction.

FOCUS: By drawing upon data generated through multi-sited ethnographic fieldwork, and employing theories of space and place, this paper describes cartographies of risk in partnership work between youth and art organisations.

The objective of this exercise is to unpick different conceptions of creative bravery, and to assess the readiness of art organisations to enable the participation of so-called 'risky' young people, while also fostering the conditions for transdisciplinary, experimental spaces of partnership.

together needs to narrow to the specific area of her research – arts organisations. A simpler way to create a problem might be to say:

'Working together across professional, disciplinary and organisational boundaries is an inherently risky process. Arts organisations are, however, increasingly asked to do just this, form new partnerships which address serious social problems.'

While the Report is ostensibly mapping the factors that mediate youth risk, the writing seems lost in detail. Each sentence shifts direction – from (name of programme) to galleries, to youth organisations, to financial and bureaucratic pressures. There are lots of ideas but they are not presented as results of her analysis. Because DR 5.5 is in her second year of candidature, it may be too early for her to be able to do so. She concludes the abstract not with Argue, but with a move back to Focus. Here there is a clearer statement of what the paper will do (describe cartographies of risk) and why. There is also a potentially interesting argument about 'creative bravery' and the readiness of arts organisations to support youth and youth organisations. But it is, as yet, unstated.

The next abstract is the only one to follow the four-move format and is written by the Professor, with DR 5.6 making suggestions for clarification. It reports on a completed research project (see Writing Sample 5.6).

Abstract 5.6 has the hallmarks of a completed research project – the results are known – and the skill of a more experienced writer. The Locate not only defines the area of Alternative Education, but offers a theoretical perspective. It has attitude, and signals a writer confident to stand by their analysis. The Focus is mercilessly brief, but unlike abstracts 5.4 and 5.5 it gives a number (17), telling the researcher this is not a piece of doctoral research but something much larger – claims are made on the basis of solid data.

The Report presents four major results. The first two tally with the disciplinary agenda set out in Locate. The third point is rarely discussed in the literatures, but the fourth point is new, thus providing the basis for argument. The Argue is still a bit tentative. This conference paper is the first outing for this argument and the writers are testing the waters. The writers *discuss* and *propose*, as often happens when researchers are presenting new material.

ECR 5. 7 completed her doctorate 7 months before writing this abstract. The abstract comes from her PhD. She has presented two methodological conference papers previously, but this is the first to draw on her results (see Writing Sample 5.7).

There is no Locate in Abstract 5.7. It begins with an extended Report of the history of an independent cinema – the site of the study. It reads like the introduction to the article rather than setting up a reason why the research was done or its significance. In the Focus, we find that the oral history interviews and archival research promises a paper that contrasts the past with the present. There is no Argue and instead a *promise to explore*. As this is the first time the ECR has written about her substantive results, and she is dealing with two separate chapters from the thesis, she is struggling with how to condense the volume of material. In this paper

WRITING SAMPLE 5.6

Professor and DR conference abstract

Hugs and behaviour points: alternative education approaches to 'risky youth'

Key words: alternative education, surveillance, therapeutic approaches, behaviourism.

LOCATE: In the UK, Alternative Education (AE) is officially defined as catering for 'risky' young people who 'do not cope' in regular schools. AE provides either reintegration into school, an alternate route to further education, training or work, or an experience complementary to schooling. This is clearly a disciplinary agenda; young people who cannot regulate themselves in 'normal' educational settings are referred to placements where different approaches are used to 'assist' them to become more adept at, and committed to, practices of self-management.

FOCUS: We conducted 17 UK case studies of AE for secondary students in the compulsory years.

REPORT: We found that this AE shared a number of common characteristics, including: (1) heightened surveillance effected through small class sizes, restrictions on movement, and continuous record-keeping, and (2) more effective regulation via the use of psychologically based techniques such as behaviour modification, behaviourism or talking therapy. However, we also saw the subordination of learning to a primary focus on managing 'behaviour problems'. Furthermore, within the full-time educational programmes on offer, Languages and Social Sciences were always the first to be abandoned to make way for vocational and recreational programmes.

ARGUE: We discuss the implications of the therapeutic and anti-social-epistemic turn in AE and the subsequent sidelining of possibilities for young people to generate broader social understandings and critique. We propose that the combined therapeutic and anti-social-epistemic turn in AE re-constitutes 'riskiness' for young people living in contexts of high unemployment and poverty, the increasing criminalization of everyday life and escalating racialised and sexualized violence.

she must do something new to fit the symposium topic and the idea of 'risky students' is mentioned at the end of the abstract, but we do not yet know why this matters.

We should point out that three of these writers (5.4, 5.5, and 5.7) did not use the four moves to write their abstracts. We have broken their texts into our moves to make visible the moves they made – which ones they included and which they

WRITING SAMPLE 5.7

ECR conference abstract

Teaching risky young people about film: art, training, recreation and politicisation

Key words: film, cinema, education, young people

REPORT: The site now occupied by (name) – (name of city) art-house cinema – has seen much of the historical development of film education: it first appeared there in the 1950s in a co-operative education centre orientated to recreation and self-betterment; the centre came to house a middle-class film society interested in enjoying meaningful film-art; and the cinema that united the two societies there in 1961 was funded by a British Film Institute attempting to nurture a critical popular culture. After (name) opened in 1990, the mixed aims of art appreciation, recreation and politicisation lived on. The cinema worked with young people in school and community settings to spread the enjoyment and knowledge of art cinema and critical, political experience. It also engaged in vocationally orientated film-making training, funded to regenerate areas of high unemployment.

FOCUS: This paper, on the basis of oral history interviews, archival research and ethnographic fieldwork, contrasts these historical modes of education with young people's contemporary experiences of film-making education.

REPORT: What they are offered today conjoins the recreational and the vocational – it is more strongly targeted at 'at risk' youth and framed as more entertaining than school and more relevant to the real world of work – but leaves aside the political. The paper explores the effects of this shift on young people's conceptions of what it means to think about and to make film.

left out. As we pointed out earlier, this is a useful strategy to analyse your own or existing abstracts written by other scholars. When we use the moves in this way, we find many abstracts do not include all of the moves we suggest.

In fact, it is the Locate and Argue that often tend to be missed out, either one or both, as is the case in these conference abstracts. This is a problem because it is these two moves that contextualise the study and allow the writer to answer the 'so what' and 'who cares' questions. Leaving them out of the abstract means that the rationale for the study, and the argument for the significance of the contribution are not clearly made in the abstract. This may well mean that readers just go past the paper because they cannot see, from the abstract, why they need to attend the conference session.

Tiny Texts are a flexible, heuristic resource. You can use them to write your own abstracts, to sort out your ideas before starting a piece of writing, or to diagnose problems in your texts. We extend our discussion of abstracts in Chapter 7 when we look at thesis abstracts.

Strategy 3: sentence skeletons

Sentence skeletons are a useful strategy for learning how to take a stand, particularly when you need to relate prior scholarship to your own. We said earlier in the chapter that your job is no longer just to report and integrate, but also to lead the reader, to be a guide, to evaluate and interpret the work of others. It is helpful to study how other more experienced scholars manage this difficult task of leading and arguing.

Your supervisor may have said to you: 'Look at what other researchers have done, try to do what they do. Use their writing as a model.' But this is often easier said than done. You are used to reading as a reader – for information, ideas, concepts. To read as a writer requires you to attend to style, syntax, approach. The sentence skeleton strategy provides one way to unpick good models of writing and see how they work. Here we draw on Swales and Feak's (1994) notion of the 'sentence skeleton'. The aim is to make explicit the linguistic patterns in any passage of writing by removing the content and identifying the skeleton of rhetorical moves.

To illustrate how it works, we've selected a passage by museum researchers Heath and von Lehn (2008) (see Writing Sample 5.8). It comes from an article where they are arguing that there is insufficient research into the ways museum visitors interact with exhibits. We show you the passage in full on the next page.

When we remove the content words we reveal the structure or skeleton of moves.

Sentence skeleton Heath and von Lehn

Despite . . . , there is surprisingly little research that examines . . . Many . . . , but in many cases these are based on . . . and provide little insight to . . . Even more wide-ranging . . . research, for example . . . , rarely addresses . . . Such research also rarely examines . . . In one sense this may not be surprising, given . . . However, with . . . , one might imagine that . . . Unfortunately this is not the case, and we still know little as to . . . , still less whether . . .

In this paper, we wish to begin to address these issues, and in particular briefly examine . . . The paper/chapter uses . . . and focuses on the ways in which . . . . In addressing . . . , we consider . . . In this way, we suggest that . . .

This skeleton makes explicit, linguistically, how the writer builds connection with the field and structures the article. In workshops we often ask DRs to insert

WRITING SAMPLE 5.8

Original text

Despite the substantial investment in 'interactive' exhibits within science centres and museums and a belief in the educational contribution of these new exhibition areas, there is surprisingly little research that examines how people use and respond to these installations. Many of the museums and science centres commission in-house evaluations and assessments, but in many cases these are based on focus groups and questionnaires and provide little insight to what actually happens at the exhibit-face. Even more wide-ranging comparative research, for example undertaken within the applied field of visitor studies, rarely addresses how people, both alone and with others, act and interact with and around these new forms of exhibit.

Such research also rarely examines the kinds of activity or interaction that arise when people confront these installations (Screven, 1986; Serrell & Raphling, 1992; Falk & Dierking, 2000; Scott, 2004). In one sense this may not be surprising, given the methodological commitments that are found within museum and visitor studies. However, with the commitment to enhancing 'interactivity' and engagement and its potential educational value, one might imagine that the action that arises at the exhibit-face might become a central empirical and analytic issue. Unfortunately this is not the case, and we still know little as to the forms of action, interaction and 'interactivity' that is occasioned by computer-based, interactive exhibits, still less whether they successfully communicate and engage people in science.

In this paper, we wish to begin to address these issues, and in particular briefly examine the forms of engagement and participation that arise within and around a small number of interactive exhibits.

The paper uses video-based field studies undertaken within a number of science centres and museums in the UK and focuses on the ways in which people use and interact with particular exhibits. In addressing 'interaction' with and around the exhibit, we consider how these 'interactive' installations delineate and constrain the engagement of visitors in ways that do not necessarily facilitate co-participation and collaboration. In this way, we suggest that the design and deployment of many computer-based exhibits in science museums and centres conflates 'interactivity' with social interaction and thereby undermines the informal educational contribution that such exhibits are thought to achieve.

(Heath and von Lehn, 2008, p. 64)

the details of their own research into skeletons like this. We see this as linguistic identity work, a way of writing yourself into an authoritative stance you may not yet be able to take in your own writing. By removing the content you are making the syntax visible.

Here is a second sentence skeleton written by Pat, which works with literatures in order to establish a 'gap' that the paper proposes to fill (see Writing Sample 5.9).

Like the first sentence skeleton, Writing Sample 5.9 is the introduction to a journal article. The introduction follows a classic CARS structure – it establishes the warrant for the research – material to be used for teaching purposes. The writer then identifies a gap in the literature it aims to fill. Pat also makes clear which tradition she is writing in – not history but cultural and literary traditions. The writer marks out their territory saying in essence: 'there's some of this and that, written from these traditions. I'm not doing that, I'm going to do this instead and here's how'. Through argument, the nature of the field is established, as well as the ways in which this particular paper differs from the work that is already published.

Sentence skeleton: Thomson

. . . scholars have suggested that . . . Drawing on scholarly traditions in . . . , these scholars have either . . . , or have . . . Some of this analysis has included . . . This work is different from that which . . . I write from . . . tradition, rather than that derived from . . .

In this paper I seek to add to . . . However, rather than . . ., I take as my object of study . . . I am particularly interested in . . .

In order to understand . . . I begin with a brief discussion of . . . I then consider . . . . I conclude with some brief comments about . . . . At the outset, I . . .

You might like to construct some of these sentence skeletons for yourself. This is not plagiarism. You are not copying content. Rather, it is a way to make explicit to yourself how experienced scholars argue and locate their work in relation to their field. It is a scaffold, a way for DRs to practise asserting and staking a claim in their field. Metaphorically, you stand in the shoes of a more experienced writer to get *inside* the patterning of language.

DRs can adapt this strategy to a wide variety of scholarly articles across disciplines to make explicit the discipline-specific conventions they need to learn.

WRITING SAMPLE 5.9

Original text

Educational administration scholars have suggested that films and television texts might be used in leadership preparation programmes as a way of promoting discussion of pressing policy and practice questions (Grant, 2002; Trier, 2002, 2007). Drawing on scholarly traditions in cultural studies and literary theory, these scholars have either examined film texts to understand the narratives that are told about education, or have deconstructed their discursive representations (Bulman, 2002, 2005; Chennault, 2006; Dalton, 1999; Ellsmore, 2005; Farber, Provenzo, & Holm, 1994; Joseph & Burnaford, 1994; Keroes, 1999). Some of this analysis has included examination of narratives and representations of educational leaders (McLay, Brown, & Ralph, 2001; Smith, 1999; Thomas, 1998). This work is different from that which examines films and novels in order to understand what they might say about the history of childhood or about schools, teachers or school principals either at particular periods of time or their change over time (e.g. Jones & Davies, 2001; McCulloch, 2009). I write from a cultural and literary tradition, rather than that derived from the discipline of History.

In this paper I seek to add to this minority educational research interest in the pedagogical use of popular texts in leadership preparation. However, rather than look at film and television programmes, I take as my object of study contemporary children's books which feature schools and headteachers. I am particularly interested in their dominant themes and how they portray leaders and the practices of leadership.

In order to understand how contemporary children's stories differ from what are often called 'traditional school stories' – and these are perhaps more familiar to those undertaking leadership programmes than contemporary stories – I begin with a brief discussion of their historical antecedents. I then consider the ways in which modern children's story headteachers are used to embody themes related to power. I conclude with some brief comments about how such texts might be used in leadership preparation. At the outset, I signpost some key theoretical assumptions and the methodological approach that underpins the discussion.

(Thomson, 2014, p. 367)

In sum

We have argued that the thesis is an argument and that DRs need to understand that the thesis presents an argument in managed stages. We have offered three different strategies – arguer questions, tiny texts and sentence skeletons – that will help you to argue well through and beyond the thesis. We are not, however, done with argument. We continue to work with the idea of argument throughout the remainder of this book.

6 Performing your research

The problem: feeling like an imposter

DRs are highly competent academics. Newcomers to the world of doctoral scholarship, perhaps, but people who have reached the highest level of study in the academy. Some have moved directly to doctoral work from Masters or Honours degrees. Others have had a break in study to pursue professional careers and/or to work in a variety of public private profit or non-profit organisations. There is, however, a core problem they share. A problem no one likes to admit. DRs often feel like imposters in a world where everyone seems to be expert. Their supervisors, their advisory committees, and their coursework professors all know more than they do.

DRs admire the scholars they read. They seek to emulate them, feel intimidated by them. Everyone seems to be more knowledgeable and intelligent. DRs often worry they will be found out and exposed. Sooner or later the inevitable will happen. At any moment, someone's going to find out they're a fraud, unable to live up to the expectations of others – and to their own.

Why is this so? Why should perfectly intelligent DRs feel tense and nervous? Endlessly doubting their capacity and skill. Painfully aware of the disjunction between how they feel and how they need to act as emerging scholars.

Certainly, there are aspects of doctoral study that contribute to feeling like an imposter. It is not simply a psychological problem of the individual DR.

1 *DRs are always surrounded by experts in their field*. DRs encounter the experts in print and in the flesh. On blogs. In academic journals and books. Whenever DRs read they are reminded of what they don't yet know. Engaging the meta-language of their discipline is challenging. The first time they say new words out loud they may feel stupid. They can't pronounce words properly because they've only ever read them. This is not cause for despair. The pressure to be expert is real for newcomers to any discipline.

2   *DRs are learning to converse in new ways.* DRs are asked by supervisors to articulate their understandings and come to terms with what they are learning – in conversation. They are engaging in new kinds of scholarly interactions. The spotlight is on their ideas and how they think, what they know and what they don't know. Learning how to talk and present oneself can feel like speaking a foreign language in a foreign land.

3   *DRs are making an ontological and identity shift.* DRS are moving from graduate student to researcher. They are engaged in new ways of thinking and being asked new kinds of questions: to think out loud and reveal their thinking. There are no ready answers available. There are no easy road maps or formulas for doing research or making a contribution to knowledge. It's a different kind of accountability and intellectual exposure. And it is challenging.

The identity shift required of the DR is articulated by Rebecca Coles, a recent PhD graduate from The University of Nottingham. Her field is anthropology and her PhD was an ethnographic study examining what counts as 'education' at an independent art house cinema. Her insightful commentary gives an insider view of what it feels like to be a new scholar and to interact with her supervisor in new ways (see Experience: Rebecca Coles).

In case you are getting depressed by all this talk of feeling tense, anxious and inexpert, you need to know you are not alone. It is not only you and your novice DR peers who suffer. Months before he died, world-shakingly brilliant Albert Einstein reportedly confided to Queen Elisabeth of Belgium that 'the exaggerated esteem in which my lifework is held makes me very ill at ease. I feel compelled to think of myself as an involuntary swindler' (Holt, 2005).

Even the most senior and experienced scholars can feel like frauds, acting and behaving in ways they don't entirely feel. This is often called the Imposter Syndrome. It's well known in academic circles – this disjunction between how academics have to act and how they actually feel. It's not fatal, it's just part and parcel of the academic game.

Professor Dame Athene Donald is a high-profile academic in the UK. She leads the prestigious Cavendish Physics Laboratory at The University of Cambridge, and Master of Churchill College. She says that Imposter Syndrome doesn't ever go away, but is a fact of life in higher education and beyond (see Commentary: Athene Donald).

We are interested in the Imposter Syndrome because it infects and inflects doctoral writing. DRs who feel their lack of expertise often display their insecurity when they engage with other people's words and ideas. We argued in Chapters 4 and 5 that when DRs work with published research and scholarly literatures they need to be evaluative. They must not simply list what other people have written

EXPERIENCE

Rebecca Coles

Before I started my PhD, I had never before been asked to sit down for an hour at a desk, facing someone I didn't know that well, and talk seriously with them. It's not that I'm not used to discussing ideas with people, but that when I do it's usually with friends and usually in small groups, in the pub or in a reading group. As an undergraduate and during my MA, I discussed more formally in group seminars. This was, in fact, central to how I learned and was the thing I most enjoyed about University. I talk a lot in group situations and often I find out what I think in the process of articulating an idea. One-to-one interactions are very different. There aren't all these ideas flying around, proposed by different people, that you follow, are inspired by, and then intervene in when you choose. You have half the responsibility to maintain a coherent flow of thought and interaction. As soon as the other person stops speaking, you have to be ready to start.

Also, I had no idea how this one-to-one interaction was supposed to go. Was it supposed to be a free flowing discussion? Or was it supposed to be more structured, more like an interview in which two people assume different roles? And if this was the case, who was supposed to be the interviewer and who was the interviewee? Who was supposed to take charge? Perhaps my slight paranoia about the situation was just a matter of personality. But whether it was me, or whether it was the way the education system had taught me to be, to begin with one-to-one supervisions made me tense and panicky.

Before I started my PhD, I had never been involved in discussing my ideas and thinking process in any kind of sustained way. In group discussions people rarely challenged me about how I knew something, in what detail I knew it, or where the thought led me. In a supervision, your ideas are under close examination, both in a good sense and a bad sense. On the one hand, you can't be flippant about an idea and declare, as you might to a friend, 'such liberal bollocks' because you have the vague idea that's the right opinion and move on. Or rather, I did, but it always met a sceptical glare. You have to justify yourself. This forced me to take myself and my ability to generate coherent analysis more seriously than I had before.

But on the other hand, the kind of thinking that supervision requires is not totally open and free. Ideas do not meet a warm reception if they are too out of step with the existent concerns of the discipline, literature or your supervisor. The point is not just to learn how to think but to learn how to produce a commodity for the academic market – a thesis, a talk, a paper, a book. Being a good academic in general, I suppose, involves negotiating between two possibly antagonistic demands – that you reflect on the reality of your thinking process, and work continually to develop it, and that your thinking process be commensurate. But the supervision process was the first time I really experienced this.

http://patthomson.net/2014/02/20/why-supervisions-can-be-hard/

COMMENTARY

Athene Donald

Getting away with it

Do you feel this phrase describes you as you go through your professional life? Do you feel as if you're a fraud and whereas everyone else knows what they are doing or deserves the position they have attained, you don't? And, on top of this, do you worry that you are about to be found out? If you answered yes to one or both these questions you are probably suffering from Impostor Syndrome. An awful lot of us do, men and women.

Although these two aspects are frequently linked in the literature, personally I don't feel that 'getting away with it' is quite the same thing as Impostor Syndrome. In part I think this is a temporal argument. Getting away with it implies you have done something with which to get away, whereas Impostor Syndrome creeps up on you beforehand, as you are about to undertake something new. So Impostor Syndrome comes first, the getting away with it bit may (or may not) be the consequence afterwards. However, the two clearly have the potential to go hand in hand.

However, most of us muddle through, just hoping that that moment of unmasking when someone says 'oh it's only you, I was expecting someone competent' never actually transpires. What matters, I suppose, is how we learn to cope with the feeling. If we don't, we may end up so paralysed with fear of the unknown and the humiliation that might conceivably come with trying and failing that we never spread our wings at all. So it is well worth recognizing the mindset as a normal state for many people, however successful they may look from the outside, not something that's unique to you indicating that you should just give up and walk away.

. . .

Let it not be thought that I have mastered Impostor Syndrome. It still rises up and bites me with monotonous regularity. If, as I believe, it is a sensation most likely to hit you the first time you do something – although it may well continue in a dull, thudding kind of way as a background to one's entire life if you're unlucky – then I still have plenty of new challenges to trip me up and to remind me that I don't know what I'm doing or why I've been asked to do it . . .

As for 'getting away with it', perhaps that too becomes less scary with time. Like a petty criminal who has got away with pilfering regularly, the next attempt will seem more matter of fact, less daunting. So if you've stood in front of 400 first year students one year and survived without more than the customary amount of critical comment about one's style of delivery/lecture notes and/or dress in the end of term questionnaires, the next year is less terrifying. If you've had to converse with a Minister of State for 20 minutes in a tense professional situation, it gives one confidence that you can hold your own in the future when confronted by politicians more generally.

So, if your knees are quaking at some new challenge, if you feel that you have achieved something by mere luck and not your innate cleverness, try to see things as others see it. I may be no academic expert on Impostor Syndrome but I do think realising that it is a common sensa-tion even amongst those – regardless of gender and way beyond academia – that you admire as confident and successful individuals may in itself be helpful. So read this and take heart.

http://occamstypewriter.org/athenedonald/2014/02/02/getting-away-with-it/

in summary form, but use it to locate and support their own project. DRs who suffer from regular bouts of Imposter Syndrome find this tricky.

Writing Sample 6.1 shows an example of a DR struggling with Imposter Syndrome as she attempts to explain her theoretical toolkit. Her research is about the disciplining of bodies through food and health regimes. While she didn't think at the start of her PhD that she would use Foucault, by the time she had generated half her data it became clear to her and her supervisor that this would be a good theoretical resource to explain what she had seen and heard in her fieldwork sites. She started reading Foucault intensively in her second year. However, in the third year, when she came to produce the first draft of the thesis, she found herself hesitating. Who was she to evaluate Foucault? How could she say in her own words things that he had said much better and that scholars who used Foucault discussed more cogently than she could hope to?

We have put in bold all the times the DR uses either the words of Foucault or of senior scholars discussing his work.

There is only one sentence, the last, where DR 6.1 presents her own interpretation in her own words. The preceding eight sentences are either all direct quotations or précis of other people's words. The DR has literally placed herself last in importance. She uses quote-dumping (see also Chapters 4 and 10) three times to avoid teasing out the concepts that are being put forward as important in her research.

This self-effacing writing occupied a full half chapter in the first draft and left the supervisor in no doubt that the DR was feeling completely overwhelmed by the task of explaining Foucault. In conversation about the problem, the DR explained that she was aware of what she was doing but didn't feel confident, competent or legitimate enough to do more than paraphrase other people's writings.

This is the writing version of Imposter Syndrome. If this is your problem, we have a real secret for you. The more you act, speak and write as if you are a scholar

WRITING SAMPLE 6.1

DR draft

An imposter discussion

In *The order of discourse*, Foucault explains how discursive rules are linked to exercises of power because, for him, 'it is in discourse that power and knowledge are joined together' (1972, p.100). 'Discursive practices are characterized by a delimitation of a field of objects, the definition of a legitimate perspective for the agent of knowledge, and the fixing of the norms for the elaboration of concepts and theories' (Foucault, 1981, p.48). Forms of discourse, he argues, are constituted by and ensure the reproduction of the social system, through forms of selection, exclusion and domination (ibid.). 'In every society, the production of discourse is at once controlled, selected, organized and redistributed' (ibid., p.52).

Foucault understands truth to be a 'system of ordered procedures for the operation, regulation, distribution, circulation and operation of statements' (Rabinow, 1984, p.74). Truth is linked to systems of power in a circular relation that produces and sustains it, and to effects of power which truth induces and which extend truth (Rabinow, 1984). This results in a 'regime of truth' which allows certain ways of being to exist (Foucault *et al.*, 1994). 'The view of the nature of power in modern societies and which Foucault develops in his genealogical studies places discourse and language at the heart of social practices and processes' (Fairclough, 1992, p.50). It is thus impossible to speak of discursive practices without also speaking of the power relations that exist around knowledge.

– regardless of how fraudulent you feel – the more you become one. This process can begin early – even before you complete your fieldwork – or start it. We think of the antidote to Imposter Syndrome as Performance.

The reframing idea: performing the scholar

The underlying issue for the academic Imposter Syndrome sufferer is that there should be congruence between their feelings and their actions. Imposters feel uncertain and act confidently. When their surface behaviour is taken as evidence that they are competent, authoritative and assured, they feel deceitful. It is as if they are deliberately pulling the wool over people's eyes – temporarily, of course, because the big fear is that other people might see through them. Or worse still, they will let the mask of expertise slip and expose the quaking incompetent behind.

The idea of performance tackles the underlying belief in congruence. If you are performing as an actor, then you generally don't expect to be the person you are portraying. You might work hard to understand the character you are meant to be – observe what people such as your character do in workplaces, communities and at home; practise the nuances of accent, posture and mannerism; construct scenarios in which they have to respond in different ways. But you know you are not actually going to *be* this character. Your aim is to present a believable and truth-like representation.

Performing opens up new possibilities for approaching the scholarly practices of speaking and writing. The DR must learn how to perform – not in a fraudulent way, but in a way that is authentic to academic scholarly practices. They must be truthful and credible in their performance. They must not be overcome by nerves, because that would spoil the performance. They must not be amateurish, because that would mean their performance had not yet reached the desired level. It does not matter if the performance is not the same as the 'self' (whatever that is). The point of the performance is to engage with the audience, not to feel authentic.

The DR's task is to learn how to perform the scholar. More expert scholars must be observed in situ so that the DR can learn the conventions and hidden rules that govern practice (see Chapter 2, on Layer 3). The trainee scholar, the DR, must also practise, rehearse, and then repeat the practice and rehearsal in order to learn how to be and do 'the scholar'. This is what we have called elsewhere 'textwork/ identitywork' – bringing into being through words and actions the embodied academic practitioner. And that practice is best accomplished through multiple avenues, through what is called an 'expansive approach' (Fuller & Unwin, 2003).

The Learning to Perform project (see Commentary: Andy Fuller and Lorna Unwin) shows some key findings from an empirical study of young musicians entering the conservatoire. Over a 3-year period, Further Education researchers Andy Fuller and Lorna Unwin investigated how musical learners developed proficiency in their chosen musical practice, but also a strong sense of identity as a musician, accompanied by a strong sense of efficacy and possibility. The most important aspect of learning was the formal provision of 'expansive approaches' – not a narrowly focused curriculum. In the case of the young musicians this meant opportunities to perform regularly in a range of musical genres and to experience the full range of musical vocations from conducting and composing to recording, staging and publicising. This expansive learning was not at the expense of deep learning within their particular pathway.

If we apply the notion of expansive learning to performing the scholar, then the ideas of practice, repetition, rehearsal, a variety of media and genre, different locations and events all have relevance. Learning to perform the DR is, as the

COMMENTARY

Andy Fuller and Lorna Unwin

The Learning to Perform project

The transition from school to conservatoire is a challenging one, forcing many students to reconsider their identity. Students entering the conservatoire frequently report feeling like a 'small fish in a big pond'. While students look forward to working with like-minded and skilful peers and teachers, they express anxiety about the high standards that such an environment will demand.

How can learning to perform be enhanced? **Through taking an expansive approach to both breadth and depth.**

The Learning to Perform findings suggest that learning outcomes, in the holistic sense in which the project conceptualises them, can be enhanced by ensuring that students engage in what other researchers have termed expansive learning (see Fuller and Unwin, 2003). Expansive learning involves participation in activities outside the immediate educational setting, and is related to extending identity – in the case of this project, allowing students to build on their concept of what it is to be a musician. Learning to Perform demonstrates that musical expertise can be developed through adopting an expansive approach to both the breadth and depth of learning.

Many music students and teachers already make use of expansive learning, both within and outside music. Learning to Perform suggests that these activities should be encouraged, and introduced flexibly into formal provision.

For learners in other disciplines, the project findings imply the need for further exploration of the role of breadth in developing expertise in any specialism.

www.tlrp.org/pub/documents/Mills%20 RB%2047%20FINAL.pdf

Learning to Perform project suggests, a matter of extending identity, and taking part in activities outside the immediate doctoral research imperatives.

We see this kind of performance work as central to writing the thesis. It achieves a great deal that is not always visible – identity work, text work. Performing will help you feel more confident in subsequent writing and presentations – even if you sometimes still feel like an imposter. This is the crux of how textwork/ identitywork operates. But you will need strategies and resources to achieve this.

We offer three performance strategies with varying degrees of riskiness and public exposure: (1) talking in order to begin the writing; (2) bridging speech and writing through blogging; (3) performing at conferences. These will allow you to build the practices of scholarly performance in ways that are not about 'faking it', but about learning how to talk and write as scholars.

Strategy 1: talking in order to begin the writing

Yes talking. Opening your mouth and speaking out loud. Talking to yourself and more importantly talking to others.

Talking is not peripheral to writing. It is the foundation. Speech came before writing. Talking before you write is critical to clarifying ideas and finding the vocabulary, terms, tone and the order in which you want to say things. The talk-think connection is at the heart of the dialogue that goes on in supervision, where the supervisor asks questions in order to get the DR to clarify and state simply what they mean. It's not about seeking a right answer, but verbal prompting to help DRs sort out what they think.

Peter Elbow, best known as an advocate of freewriting, has written about talking and writing in his book *Vernacular eloquence. What speech can bring to writing* (Elbow, 2012). Elbow doesn't argue that talking substitutes for writing – talking isn't writing. But he does suggest that there are things about talking that are helpful to writing.

Elbow points out that 'unplanned spoken language is good for pith, gists, and nutshells' (p. 90). By this he means that talking can help us to, as the common sayings suggest, 'Spit it out. Hit the nail on the head' (p. 91). Acknowledging that it's also possible to ramble around while talking, he nevertheless advocates talking as a deliberate and deliberative way of unpacking the muddle in your head – making complex ideas more accessible and separating out the detail from the major points. He calls this 'talking writing' rather than 'writing writing'.

Elbow's 'pith, gist and nutshells' talk is how we wrote this book. Our method of writing is all about the talk. We talk as much as we write. We talk a lot about the topic we are working on. We talk first of all to clarify our ideas. We often make terrible jokes, ramble around, and tell each other tangential stories about our current writing/teaching/everyday lives. But during these conversations we come up with some key ideas. We talk our way into the angle that we want to take. And by the time we have talked for an hour or so, we have worked out a metaphor or a heuristic of some kind that will help make the idea clear. This is a 'talk-as-ideas-clarification process'.

Very often, while we are engaged in one of these talk-as-ideas-clarification conversations it becomes obvious that we need to start recording. So either one or both of us will reach for a pen and paper, or one of us will sit down at the keyboard and begin to make random notes. This initial writing then becomes the basic material on which we work.

Our next stage is another kind of talk – much more focused. This is 'talking-as-writing', where we have a conversation to jointly compose the text. This is more like dictating, but it's more spontaneous, and there are often breaks in the actual talk-as-writing for more talk-as-ideas-clarification. Sometimes during this stage, we have to pause and reach for a reference book or paper to make sure that we have accurately communicated a concept or strategy.

Using both of these kinds of talk allows us to write about 4,000 words a day, sometimes less, sometimes more. The text that we produce is rough and often has to be ruthlessly pruned. It will always have gaps in it where we know we have to go back and do more thinking or researching. However, this talked text has a kind of energy that is hard to duplicate using any other method.

Elbow explains why talking helps writing (see Commentary: Peter Elbow). He discusses the richness of speaking as a resource for making meaning.

So where and how can you talk about your work?

You can begin by talking to a friend. This might sound obvious. But we have seen many DRs struggle away on a text working continually and always in silence, incommunicado from the world. This always makes us sad, because we know that some talking around the topic before and during the writing process would make the actual writing go more smoothly. The thesis is not jointly written, in the way that we write books together, but there is no reason why DRs cannot seek out opportunities for talk to facilitate and enhance their writing.

We suggest that, early on, you find a friend or two, possibly other DRs in your programme, and make a regular time to talk about your research. This is not a moan about how difficult it is to write. That can happen but it is not what we mean. We suggest talking about what you know. You can set a time, say 10 minutes each, to talk about *one* aspect of your research. It might be making sense of the literature, clarifying your research question, designing fieldwork, deciding on an analytic approach, rehearsing for a conference or presentation. After each person speaks, the others should first of all indicate a strength in what's been said and then ask questions for clarification. This discussion might take place in writing groups, more formalised structures for talking about writing; these are known to have a positive impact on the DR's textwork/identitywork (Aitchison, 2009; Wegener, Meier, & Ingerslev, 2015).

Strategy 2: bridging speech and writing through blogging

The differences between speech and writing are well documented (for example, see www.linguisticsociety.org/resource/whats-difference-between-speech-and-writing). But the reality is that talking and writing are a continuum and the binary between them is easily disrupted. Speedwriting to a timer sets out to deliberately reduce the ways in which writers stop to ponder things. It forces writers to adopt the greater spontaneity of speech. Some speaking, such as delivering a speech in Parliament or a keynote address, is written to be spoken, and can be very formal.

COMMENTARY

Peter Elbow

Speech is not the same as writing

Spoken language has more semiotic channels than writing. That is, speech contains more channels for carrying meaning, more room for the play of difference. The list of channels is impressive. For example, there is volume (loud and soft), pitch (high and low), speed (fast and slow), accent (yes and no), intensity (relaxed and tense). And note that these are not just binary items, for in each case there is a huge range of subtle *degrees* all the way between extremes. In addition, in each case there are patterned sequences: for example, tune is a pattern of pitches; rhythm is a pattern of slow and fast accent. Furthermore, there is a wide spectrum of timbres (breathy, shrill, nasal, and so forth); there are glides and jumps; there are pauses of varying lengths. Combinations of *all* of these factors make the possibilities dizzying. And *all* these factors carry meaning. Consider the example of the subtle or not so subtle pause as we are speaking, the little intensity or lengthening of a syllable – and all the other ways we complicate the messages we speak. We can't do those things in writing . . .

It's not that writing is poverty stricken as a semiotic system. But writing has to achieve its subtleties with fewer resources . . . Consider the many ways we can say the sentence, 'Listen to me' – from angry to fond – or in fact with a whole range of modes of anger. With writing, our options are comparatively small. We can underline or use all caps; we can end with a comma, a period, a question mark, and exclamation mark. We can create pauses by using the ellipsis sign. There are other textual resources of course – such as varying the spacing, sizing, or color of letters and words, playing with the shaping of letters and words, and so forth – but these are considered 'informal' and inappropriate to 'literate' writing. . . . Perhaps the main resource in writing is word choice: choose different words, put them in different orders, set a context by what comes before or afterwards to affect how readers will experience any sentence. These are the ways we convey significations in writing that we convey effortlessly in speech. In writing, we must do more with fewer channels.

Peter Elbow, pp. 3–4

www.ncte.org/library/NCTEFiles/
Resources/Books/Sample/
56347chap01.pdf

Blogging is a form of writing, but it is also speech-like. It is conversational and interactive. Bloggers, like speakers, can see how their audience react to what they are saying and they can respond, adjust. Writers, by contrast, are often solitary and have to imagine their readers. Their feedback is delayed.

Many of you may have considered the pros and cons of DRs blogging. There isn't a right or wrong answer to the question of whether you should or not. But we do want to suggest that blogging is a productive way of performing your research for a wider public. It takes you away from the isolation of your writing desk. It is not the same as the embodied speaking you might do at a conference. But it may also put you in contact with a wider public than you imagined possible. Blogging can help your more formal academic writing in the same way as talking to a friend can reduce anxiety about audience and text. Rachael Cayley teaches academic writing and speaking to graduate students at the University of Toronto. She discusses the benefits of writing on social media in her blog *Explorations of style* (see Commentary: Rachael Cayley).

COMMENTARY

Rachael Cayley

Writing for social media

At a broad level, it seems clear to me that social media is beneficial for us as writers. When we write on social media, our natural ability to express ourselves may remind us that writing per se isn't always the problem. Formal academic writing for an audience that seems both inscrutable and implacable can easily undermine our confidence. An opportunity to write more freely – with less anxiety about audience – can be a great reminder of our own writing ability. This reminder alone won't solve our *academic* writing problems, but it can help us pinpoint what they are. Similarly, blogging allows us to find smaller topics and articulate what we want to say about them in a compact format. This blog, for instance, has accumulated somewhere in the range of 100,000 words thus far; if I'd had to figure out in advance how all those words fit together, you'd never have read any of them.

. . .

As I thought over the implications of writing for social media, I came up with three ways that social media writing can inform our development as writers.

CONCISION: The first thing that will come to anyone's mind when we think of writing on social media is brevity. Trying to say something in less than 140 characters, for instance, requires that we bring a whole new level of attention to concision. Even if we don't always use those strategies in our everyday writing, we are forced to notice the potency of concision. If you regularly write extremely short sentences, you are inevitably honing your brevity skills. In doing so, you are bound to experience some of the benefits of limitation. Sometimes we will encounter the limits of limitation – i.e., the point at which something can't be any shorter – but we will also learn the value of expressing ourselves in fewer words than we thought possible.

TONE: One of the best ways to understand the role of tone in writing is by having to shift that tone. Academic prose isn't necessarily good or bad writing, but it is very particular in its tone. Social media writing, on the other hand, can give us a sense of a different style of writing and thereby help us see the distinct contours of a piece of academic writing. The benefits of this sort of relativism vis-à-vis writing seem evident to me. While people worry that the unique demands of Twitter or the text message will undermine writing ability, it seems entirely possible that the experience of writing in multiple registers will actually strengthen writing overall. Greater awareness of the conventionality of writing will increase the chance that we will be able to find ways to work productively within those conventions.

NUANCE: Short-form writing is also a great reminder of the importance of doing justice to ambiguity. For instance, I find that Twitter is great for sharing things that I like, but not so good for those things about which I have significant reservations. Without room for caveats, we are left without an easy way to disagree respectfully. Think about your average statement of scholarly reservation: 'While I found the decision to highlight X extremely helpful, I was ultimately troubled by the reliance upon traditional categories of Y'. That's 145 characters, even without actual content. So I don't share that link; Twitter becomes for me a place to talk about the things I actively like or that I like enough to forego qualification. The limits of social media writing thus confirm one of the great strengths of academic writing: the creation of a space expansive enough to contain both agreement and disagreement.

Overall, composing text for social media is instructive for our non-social media writing. By writing things that are more direct or casual or polemical, we are better able to understand how those qualities may or may not operate within our formal academic prose. And, ultimately, being able to shift registers and understand how tone, evidence, vocabulary, and syntax all affect that shift can only improve our academic writing.

http://explorationsofstyle.com/2014/04/0 2/social-media-and-writing-style/

Blogging *is* a great way to develop academic writing. All of the writing advice out there, for academic and creative writing, suggests that it's good to develop a writing habit. Write regularly, every day. Let it become as routine as cleaning your teeth. Blogging *can* be a useful part of a regular writing routine. As well, writing texts for a public can help you develop a 'voice', help you to write with some authority, and allow you to practise writing in an accessible style. Writing in public and for a public can be a key part of developing your academic identity.

Whether to blog or not depends on what you hope to achieve. Maybe you're thinking about an individual blog, something you create yourself on one of the standard platforms such as Blogger, Wordpress or Medium.

Your blog can be like a journal. You might blog about the things you are reading and thinking about. Formulating ideas into a thousand words or so and linking to relevant texts and other online resources can be helpful to your writing and thinking. It can be an archive and an aide-memoire.

However, there are potential pitfalls in using a blog as a journal. For example, when writing about fieldwork, you do need to be careful about what you say . . . 'I've just seen the most disgraceful behaviour imaginable . . . ' is not going to endear you to your research participants. You must anticipate that they might go searching for you and what you do. And why are you journalling *in public*? What do you want everyone to know, and not know? How will you feel about your first doctoral year reflections some years later – will you want your early researcher self to be obliterated from public view?

But is a personal blog what you want and/or need? The reality is that many DR blogs have quite limited readerships. Those that don't, those that are well-read and known, tend to have a focused agenda and a clear readership in mind. And even then, only some garner masses of readers. So, before you spend hours setting up your blog, it's sensible to get clear about exactly what you want to do, and why.

It's worth considering options. You could, for example, write guest posts for established blogs. You could figure out how to become a regular or semi-regular blogger for an online publication. You could form a collective with other doctoral researchers, or with others in your field, and start a newspaper-style blog.

You are always talking/writing yourself as a scholar on social media – whether it is through blogs or tweeting or LinkedIn or Facebook. There are many opportunities on social media to perform in informal text as a scholar. Twitter posts, Google hangouts, Webinars and Twitter chats, for example, offer opportunities for the DR to enter scholarly conversations in relatively low-risk ways. Because the kind of text that has to be written is more like talking, because there is often immediate feedback and engagement, and because interactions are often mediated by experienced colleagues, uncertain DRs can use these occasions to build up confidence in putting themselves forwards as knowers, rather than learners.

Performing in safer spaces, in conversations and online, may begin with the DR feeling like a fraud, but the continuous engagement and performance, makes these feelings recede.

Strategy 3: performing at conferences

Face up to the fear. A conference can act as a good dress rehearsal for more high-stakes aspects of scholarly life, such as the viva. DRs are often encouraged to present their work in conferences, and often the earlier the better. The conference paper offers an opportunity to communicate your research and it allows you to test out your arguments and get feedback. The conference also offers the quintessential opportunity to perform, behave and talk like and assume the identity of an expert scholar.

Don't think that this performance is just standing up and talking. It actually involves producing numerous written texts as well as the actual speaking on the day. You perform live and you perform in text. That is, you are doing both text work and identity work in written and spoken form.

There are many decisions to make about conference participation. First of all, you have to choose the right conference. One where there will be scholars interested in your topic and where there will be those you can learn from to enhance your research. A conference is a great place to meet your reference list in person.

To gain entry to the conference you must write an abstract (see Chapter 4). The abstract is written for referees and therefore usually addresses the conference theme, follows the conference abstract template, if there is one, and always emphasises the rigour of the approach, the significance of the results or theorisation and the potential for an interesting live performance. If the conference abstract could speak it would say 'include me!'

The abstract you submit may not be the same as the text for the conference programme. You may be asked to write a short summary of the paper for that publication. If you have to do this, then that summary is saying to the reader 'pick me, I'm interesting and worth you investing your time'. You may also have to write these kinds of summaries in future for websites or bid applications. They are generally written from a more catchy, promotional stance.

Then you have to write the conference paper itself. The conference paper is always the best text you can produce at the time, written as well as you can. The conference paper may be submitted for peer review or it might be the first draft of a potential journal article or chapter (see Thomson & Kamler, 2013) or it may be a place to test out ideas (see Chapter 5). You might choose to lodge the paper in an online conference repository or to put it up on a site such as academia.edu or researchgate. Whatever end you have in mind, the paper says 'take me seriously, talk with me . . . ' and maybe even 'cite me'.

The paper presentation

Of course, you will need to decide whether you want to visually display your research, using one of the standard platforms, for example PowerPoint or Presi. The display is a very different kind of text from the paper and may not follow the same order as the conference abstract. Displays usually begin with a full title slide, then provide information about the Locate, Focus, Report and Argue of the work. A visual display is intended to provide information complementary to what you say during your live presentation. For this reason presenters often choose to show some of their data and its analysis in visual presentations, graphically saying to the audience 'trust me and my research'.

Most conferences also ask presenters to prepare a handout. Sometimes this is a full paper, but very often it is an extended abstract. The Locate, Focus, Report and Argue framework is a useful way to structure the handout. The handout is something that people can take away with them and refer to later. It is basically an invitation that says 'follow my research further'.

Then there is the actual presentation – the live performance you make at the conference. This is usually *not* a reading of the paper. If any of the paper is read it will have been highly edited so that only the most pithy points are offered. Remember, this is not a teaching performance. You're not lecturing people, you're sharing. People often present with their paper in hand, so they can consult it if they go blank. Generally the presentation is more colloquial than the paper because it's spoken. The presentation is intended to say 'listen to me, engage with me'.

The pitfalls in conference presentations are numerous. People reading their paper and not looking at the audience. People with too much information packed on slides that the audience has to try to read while listening at the same time. People reading their slides verbatim, adding nothing to them. People with too many slides. People who assume that everyone in the audience is able to follow a really complex argument without any guidance. People who assume the audience is as familiar with the extant literatures and/or a specialised vocabulary as they are. People who go way over time and make it hard for every other presenter in the session, and eat up the time for questions (see Advice: Anthony Weston). The critical advice for any performance is this: be well prepared.

But you may choose to present something other than a paper.

The conference poster and roundtable

You may opt to present a research poster instead of a written paper. A research poster requires a different kind of performance mindset because the poster must grab people's attention, as well as be informative. It's important to understand something about visual presentation when preparing the poster – all the relevant information

ADVICE

Anthony Weston

Rules for conferences

In his book *A rulebook for arguments* (2001) Anthony Weston offers six rules that people who talk at conferences should adhere to.

Rule One: Reach out to your audience

Weston suggests that you have to show some enthusiasm for the topic, be respectful of the audience, be patient with them, never talk down to them. After all, he says, you are asking for a hearing, and the audience doesn't have to give that to you. You have to do what's required in order to get and keep their attention.

We think this means that you need to talk enthusiastically and knowledgably.

Rule Two: Be fully present

Being there means not reading something that people can read for themselves, but engaging with the audience. This is achieved by making eye contact, speaking with expression and energy – walking around even. Even if you do read, you can still do these things. Weston reminds us that oral presentations are a face-to-face experience and that people will be dissatisfied if that's not what they get.

We think this means that you need to talk with people not at them.

Rule Three: Signpost your argument

When people read, they can go back over the bits they don't understand, or choose to skip over things that are difficult. Weston argues that an audience can't do this and so they need more signposting than in a written paper – the speaker stating what the argument to come is going to be, repeating the various steps of the argument, summarising what's just been said. He also points to the importance of the speaker making sure that they allow the audience time to follow what's being said, to make notes if that's what they want to do, and to make the transition from one point in the argument to another. Weston suggests that speakers need to start by saying something like – my basic argument is – and conclude with something like – I've argued that . . .

We think this means you do have to talk more formally than if you are explaining your research to a friend.

Rule Four: Offer something positive

Weston proposes that just presenting an audience with critique leaves them feeling depressed and that the speaker needs to moderate the negativity and offer some direction forward. He doesn't mean 'spin' by this. We think in academic presentations this rule means making sure that the implications of the argument – the 'so what' and 'now what' of the presentation – are made clear at the end. There shouldn't be the slightest opportunity for the audience to be left wondering why they needed to know what it is you have said.

We think this means you need to think beforehand about the order of things you say, and the take-home message.

Rule Five: Use visual aids sparingly

We'd probably say sensibly and sensitively here rather than sparingly. But Weston has clearly suffered from conference PowerPoint overdose and he argues that if it is used it needs to be engaging. He argues for variety in presentations rather than reliance on one medium; using a range of techniques such as inserting a short reading from a text, a bit of audience participation, the use of handouts. Above all, he says, don't let the slide-show substitute for you.

We think that talking at conferences needs to be thought of as a multimedia presentation – there is you, your visuals and the talk. You have to think about how these work together.

Rule Six: End in style

Weston says this means keeping to time and not petering out. Having a snappy ending that reinforces the major point you are making is the way to go. Talking at a conference is a performance, so it's important to pay as much attention to the ending as to the start!

must go in, but in a way that is easy to read. Posters lend themselves to the visual display of data. You can take advantage of this feature and not jam up the available space with text.

It is customary for conferences to offer specific poster sessions where presenters stand by their posters at the allotted time to talk about the work. They often have handouts to distribute at this time too. This kind of performance is informal and while there might be a short presentation, most often presenters chat to poster readers and answer any questions. A poster session can be more interactive than a paper presentation and presenters need to respond to a range of queries and comments. If you have a poster presentation you must really know your stuff, and be prepared for in-depth probing as well as the occasional and possibly unwanted gratuitous supervision session!

The roundtable is the other common conference format. Roundtables, as the name implies, occur when the presenter talks to people who come to sit at their table. Unlike a conference session when there are multiple presentations, you are *it* at the roundtable. You can assume that everyone at the table is there because they are interested in your topic. A roundtable performance usually consists of a short input from the presenter – minus visual display but often with a handout – followed by a conversation, which may have some questions and answers. As with the conference poster, the roundtable is more informal and this is both a good and bad thing – you can be more relaxed and at ease with people and there can be a real conversation rather than a ritualised question and answer format. However, there is unlikely to be a chairperson and so you do have to engage with whoever turns up and whatever they want to say. This is not a lunch with friends.

The conference performance builds identity. Continuous conference practice places the body and speech of the DR in the spotlight. A key aspect of this performing is that the DR gets direct feedback. This helps the feeling of being an imposter recede. An audience takes your work seriously. What you say matters enough for them to bother to respond. Adam Crymble works in the field of Digital History at the University of Hertfordshire (see Experience: Adam Crymble). He describes the benefits of conference feedback, and he also makes a connection between blogging and conferencing – since both performances produce external confirmation of the DR as a scholar worthy of interaction.

EXPERIENCE

Adam Crymble

Comparing different kinds of presentations

Last year I delivered a couple of research papers on the history of crime. The first was in October at the Institute of Historical Research or the IHR as it's known, here in London. The second was in January, on a beach in Belize.

Now before you start looking for tropical conferences on 18th century crime, I should qualify that the first paper was delivered to a room full of people. The second was posted on my blog while I was on vacation – and yes, sadly, I DID write about 18th century crime while gazing out over the Caribbean Sea. For some people, speaking to a room and blogging are probably significantly different activities. But for me they aren't all that dissimilar. Let me explain why by talking about what I got out of both experiences as well as what went into them.

At the IHR, I presented an hour-long paper based on three chapters from my PhD thesis. It was about two years' worth of work that I had condensed down and tried to make engaging for a room full of people. For about two months before I gave the talk I didn't do much other than scramble to get the research done, create the graphs, build the powerpoint presentation, and craft the 8,000 words that I was to deliver. It was an incredible amount of work. I wore a jacket and tie, and I think I might have even gotten a haircut. Good thing because some of the most eminent crime historians in the world happened to be in town and decided to come to my talk. In all, I think there were about 50 historians in the room, most of whom knew far more about crime and the eighteenth century than I do.

The talk was followed by a really engaging discussion – at least from my perspective. I had a number of people offer suggestions for improving my argument, or on sources and archives

I should visit. A couple of scholars who also write on similar topics challenged my findings – though were collegial and offered their own suggestions. Afterwards we continued on to the pub and to dinner as a group and over the course of the evening I must have heard ideas, criticisms, and praise from about 25 individuals on what I was doing.

The beach was a very different experience. The paper itself was just shy of 3,000 words, so somewhere in the 20–25 minute range if I had delivered it orally. This time my paper was based on some quick research I'd done just before Christmas. In total I'd invested a little more than a week analyzing the use of language in the Old Bailey Proceedings over a two hundred year period. It was really nothing more than an idea I'd wanted to test out, based on a conversation I'd had at the pub concerning the size of the lexicon over time.

The results I came up with were what you might call half-baked. Not that I'd been lazy, or that I didn't know what I was talking about, or that the results were wrong. Just that I hadn't spent weeks or months revising my methodology and my prose as I had at the IHR. Nor did I do an in depth literature review. Instead it was more an activity in play. I had some sources, I had an idea, I tried it out, I wrote it up – with a reasonable amount of care – and I posted it to the world, curious to see what it thought. When I posted my paper on the blog, there was no beer and pizza afterwards – though I did have a nice swim. And in the end I got one comment on the post from Ben Schmidt at Harvard who offered a suggestion for improving the methodology and the results.

On the surface it looks like the blog post was significantly less successful, since the number of comments I got were 25 at the physical presentation, and only one on the blog. But I don't think that's quite fair, for a couple of reasons.

Firstly, the talk at the IHR was a formal affair presenting years of research, with a moderator that gazes around the room encouraging more questions from the audience. The blog post was a way to test an idea, which is shouted into the great wilderness. That level of anonymity readers of blogs enjoy means there isn't the same pressure to respond. But just because they don't respond doesn't mean they didn't engage with the content. It's difficult to know how many people engage with content on the Internet. I know 50 people were in the room for my seminar paper at the IHR, and I didn't notice anyone sleeping, but even then I can't be sure who disappeared into the recesses of their mind as I talked away.

My blog however offers statistics, and though I know not everyone who visits a blog post reads it, I do know about 600 people came to take a look. That's about 12 times more than showed up to hear my seminar, and because a blog post is printed on the Internet rather than delivered orally, vanishing on the wind as it's spoken, my blog readers could be anywhere in the world, and could even have been sleeping when I delivered it . . .

I think the blog and twitter provide diversity for me. In my case, my blog attracts a lot of digital humanists, but blogs aren't just a way to get feedback from digital humanists. I posted another blog post a few weeks later on the same research material, this time focused on using criminal records to measure immigration. I again got one comment, but this time it was from Tim Hitchcock, a historian of 18th century Britain, who offered a historical interpretation that might explain what I had found. Tim's expertise with the provenance of the records meant he knew things about the sources I didn't.

I posted a third blog post again on a slightly different topic, and received different types of comments again from linguists, computer scientists, and Sharon Howard, the project manager from the Old Bailey Online project. With three blog posts and roughly the same number of words as my seminar paper, I'd engaged a number of different types of people from all over the world with very different sets of expertise, and different types of feedback than I could ever expect to get from a room full of crime historians.

Which experience was more valuable? The seminar or the blog posts? For me, I don't think there's much that can compare with a room full of world experts devoting their combined experience to listening and critiquing years of your hard work. I also don't think you can beat the type of connections that can only be made in a face-to-face meeting at the pub, or over pizza with people who share your interests. But I also don't think we should sniff at a model that allowed me to test 3 ideas in an informal setting, get a broad range of feedback from interdisciplinary experts all over the world, and all without costing anyone a penny.

I've taken on board all of the feedback I've received from these two papers. My PhD thesis is stronger for having delivered the seminar paper, and I've decided to pursue the ideas expressed in my blog more formally as a future research project. So these papers were both valuable in their own right, and I think I'm a better historian for having delivered them.

http://adamcrymble.blogspot.co.uk/2013 _05_01_archive.html

Conference presentations, be they papers, roundtables or posters, can all have a transformative effect. At the start, you may well feel the terrors of imposter-hood. However, at the end, it is highly likely that you will feel better about yourself and your work. And the more performing you do, the more likely it is that you will take your growing scholarly identity into other forms of doctoral text work.

In sum

When DRs write they often feel as if they don't have the authority to write. They compose tentative sentences, hide behind other people's words, feel dreadful when they are asked to speak about their work.

It may seem paradoxical to say that the way to beat Imposter Syndrome is to perform. However we suggest that thinking like a performer, an actor, is helpful. An actor doesn't have to *be* the person they are representing, they just have to be believable. Finding some less risky places to perform as a scholar is helpful. We suggested three strategies – talking to friends, using blogging as a place to write about your work in a more informal way, and presenting at conferences. Even though the DR might feel nervous trying these strategies out, the pay-off is likely to be immediate feedback, enhanced networking. The feeling of playing at someone you're not retreats into the background more and more often.

7 Structuring the thesis

The problem: get a template, get control

DRs are often encouraged to use a structured template to frame their writing. They are nervous about how to capture and make sense of all the data they are generating, or how to reduce the mountains of material they are reading. How can they pull it all together in a coherent way? How can they write about their research so it makes sense to an external reader – to an examiner? This is a real anxiety. And anxious DRs seek solutions. This is only natural. But the premature use of templates or formulae to make sense of your research can create as many problems as it solves.

If you start with a structure before you know what you have to say, you shut down meaning. If you start with the premature creation of chapters before you complete your analysis, you pay less attention to content than form. It's like squeezing what you have to say into a brace that squashes you, rather than opening out the argument of your thesis.

We can illustrate the problem by looking at conventional wisdom about structuring a thesis. The traditional format is often described as IMRAD (Swales, 1990) – Introduction, Methods, Report and Discuss. You may wonder where the Literature Review and Conclusion have gone. The answer is they haven't gone anywhere, but it's probably just too awkward to say/write ILMRADC.

IMRAD can be useful because it focuses attention on: Why this research (Introduction), How will it be done (Methods), What was the result (Results) and How does this make sense in relation to the literatures in the field(s) (Discussion). DRs do need to provide a justification for the study, locate it within a field of literature and possible policy and/or practice. They do have to say how the research was designed and conducted and they need to report the results. In the discussion and conclusion, DRs not only need to say what the thesis was about and did, but also argue this as a contribution to knowledge and maybe policy and/or practice.

IMRAD captures much of this work. It is, however, only one way to accomplish the necessary work of arguing the contribution. There are variations on IMRAD

(Paltridge & Starfield, 2007). There's a topic-based thesis, which is more typical of arts and humanities, where there is a general introduction, followed by a series of topic-based chapters, ending with a conclusion. And in the social sciences, the results can be organised in different ways too. Often there are two or three thematic chapters, but there might also be three case studies or three accounts of the phenomenon being studied or three stages of a project.

But the IMRAD structure is not straightforward. For example, a thesis may not need a literatures chapter per se. Work with literatures may be better divided up and spread around the text. A recent thesis we've read provided a policy context, a history of the field of research and a history of practice, all of which used literatures extensively and made up the first three chapters. The DR could not have made her argument if she'd crushed all of the literature into one ritual offering.

Sometimes, even when IMRAD appears to work, it can result in a text that is tedious to read and seems disjointed. But perhaps the greatest worry is that it doesn't foreground argument. IMRAD fosters description. We argued in Chapter 4 that the whole thesis is an argument and needs to be structured as a carefully staged set of moves that make your case. IMRAD encourages the writer to present pieces of argument in isolated pieces rather than develop an extended and overarching argument to follow. This means the reader must piece together the bits and pieces of argument along the way to make their own coherence. This is a lot to ask of any reader. However, if that reader is also an examiner, they may become impatient with the expectation that it is their job to do the hard work of tying sections of the dissertation together.

The IMRAD default structure can be rather like a package holiday. A package holiday gets you away, often to an interesting location. However, all of your days are organised, as are most of your meals. While you make some decisions about whether to laze by the pool or go on an unescorted tour of the local batik factory, these decisions occur within a predetermined framework. Of course, sometimes the package holiday is just the thing. At other times, you may find yourself yearning for escape from the group and the relentless activity plan. You think longingly about the time when you planned your own adventure and chose exactly what you wanted to do – when and where and how.

So is there a thesis equivalent to the self-planned holiday? Perhaps. But that's not what we want to suggest here. Rather than offer you an alternative structure, we propose a different idea – that you attend to your content before finally deciding on the form in which it should be organised and presented. Work out what you want to say in conjunction with thinking about the structure.

The reframing idea: form with function

The notion of form with function is generally attributed to the field of architecture. Rather than design a building from an existing blueprint, or design a structure in order to display particular built forms, architects were urged, by the likes of Frank Lloyd Wright, to understand the uses to which a building was to be put, and then design accordingly. Wright argued that 'form and function are one' and this can be seen in his design for the Guggenheim museum in New York. As the Guggenheim website explains, the principle of form and function being one

> is thoroughly visible in the plan for the Guggenheim Museum. According to Wright's design, visitors would enter the building, take an elevator to the top and enjoy a continuous art-viewing experience while descending along the spiral ramp.
>
> www.guggenheim.org/new-york/education/school-educator-
> programs/teacher-resources/arts-curriculum-
> online?view=item&catid=730&id=120

We believe that the unity of form and function is a maxim that also applies to the thesis. We want you to attend to content before finalising form. To focus on what you have to say first of all. You have to understand the substantive argument you will make before you consolidate the structure through which it will be written. This means you begin with writing, not with templates. And in this attention to content, writing is your biggest research friend. Writing provides the opportunity to be innovative and insightful – to explore meanings and possibilities, rather than close them off prematurely. It's your companion in generating data, in making sense of it and presenting the case for why it matters.

We are arguing that writing is research. This is not simply our idea, but one shared by researchers (e.g. Lee, 1998; Richardson, 1997) who argue that putting our ideas into language, the primary way we make meaning in academic research, happens through talking – and writing. Laurel Richardson, Professor Emeritus at Ohio State University, has argued this cogently (see Commentary: Laurel Richardson box).

Writing occurs at every stage of the research process, but this is often not recognised in formal research methods texts and courses. And DRs often find there is just so much going on that writing takes second place in their minds until it comes to writing the actual thesis text. As Aitchison and Lee (2006, p. 268) have it, DRs

> are often concerned simultaneously with the major questions of thinking, learning, knowing, engaging, positioning, becoming and writing that constitute

---

COMMENTARY

Laurel Richardson

Research is writing

I write because I want to find something out. I write in order to learn something that I didn't know before I wrote it. I was taught, however, . . . not to write until I knew what I wanted to say, until my points were organised and outlined. No surprise, this static writing model coheres with mechanistic scientism and quantitative research. But, I will argue, the model is itself a sociohistoric invention that reifies the static social world imagined by our nineteenth century foreparents. The model has serious problems: It ignores the role of writing as a dynamic, creative process; it undermines the confidence of beginning qualitative researchers because their experience of research is inconsistent with the writing model; and it contributes to the flotilla of qualitative writing that is simply not interesting to read because adherence to the model requires writers to silence their own voices and to view themselves as contaminants.

Richardson, 1994, p. 517

---

their extended experience of research degree candidature and their transaction with the thesis text. For students, the problems of knowledge production, text production and self-formation are complexly intertwined at the point of articulation. Data analysis, principles of selection and focus, the structuring of the text, the performance and defense of an argument – are all questions of writing.

When we research we write. Our thinking proceeds in, through and with our writing even though we don't always recognise its importance. Elizabeth St Pierre provides an example of how writing was integral to her research. She examined the lives of thirty-six older white southern women in a small rural town and relied on writing as both data collection and as analysis (see Experience: Elizabeth St Pierre).

Now we aren't suggesting that you have to use your dreams as data, as St Pierre does. We do, however, agree strongly with her that the writing we do about our data *is* integral to the thinking and meaning-making that we do.

Together with researchers such as Richardson and St Pierre, we are standing against a view of research which is about collecting data as if it's just out there ready to be picked up, like a bunch of wildflowers – against a view of analysis as simply a process of picking things out and coding them through predetermined programmes or statistical procedures that seem straightforward. Against a view that

EXPERIENCE

Elizabeth St Pierre

Writing as data collection and analysis

In my study, I used writing as a method of data collection by gathering together, by collecting – *in the writing* – all sorts of data I had never read about in interpretive qualitative text books, some of which I have called *dream data*, *sensual data*, *emotional data*, *response data* (St Pierre, 1997b), and *memory data* (St Pierre, 1995). Such data might include, for example, a pesky dream about an unsatisfying interview, the sharp angle of the southern sun to which my body happily turned, my sorrow when I read the slender obituary of one of my participants, my mother's disturbing comment that I'd gotten something wrong, and very real 'memories of the future' (Deleuze, 1986/1988, p.10), a mournful time bereft of these women and others of their generation. These data were neither in my interview transcripts nor in my fieldnotes where data are supposed to be, for how can one textualise everything one thinks and senses in the course of a study? But they were always already in my mind and body, and they cropped up unexpectedly and fittingly in my writing – fugitive, fleeting data that were excessive and out of category. My point here is that these data might have escaped entirely if I had not *written*: they were collected only *in the writing*.

I used writing as a method of data analysis by using writing to think: that is, I wrote my way into particular spaces I could not have occupied by sorting data with a computer program or by analytic induction. This was rhizomatic work (Deleuze & Guattari, 1980/1987) in which I made accidental and fortuitous connections I could not foresee or control. The point here is that I did not limit data analysis to conventional practices of coding data and then sorting it into categories that I then grouped into themes that became section headings in an outline that organised and governed my writing in advance of writing. *Thought happened in the writing.* As I wrote, I watched word after word appear on the computer screen – ideas, theories, I had not thought before I wrote them. Sometimes I wrote something so marvellous it startled me. *I doubt I could have thought such a thought by thinking alone.*

Richardson & St Pierre, 2005, p. 970 (italics in original) this activity yields findings as if these are somehow self-evident and all you have to do is present them. We do not believe you 'write them up' as if the meaning is already crystal clear. And IMRAD is strongly connected to this instrumental approach to research.

We stand with a group of scholars who believe the researcher is entirely implicated in all stages of the research. Nothing is a research project until we create one. We generate the data, not collect it. We sort and devise interpretations, categories and definitions that allow us to analyse data, using writing at every stage. And we interpret the data. We continue to work on what it might mean through writing all the way through the research and the production of the thesis text.

We've been critical of IMRAD because it is formulaic, closes down meaning when used too early and detours you away from developing your argument. We offer four strategies to help you find a more organic way to structure your thesis. These are:

1   writing chunks instead of chapters,

2   storyboarding to create the moves,

3   writing thesis abstracts,

4   writing the introduction and chapter abstracts.

Strategy 1: writing chunks instead of chapters

DRs often refer to the writing they do throughout their candidature as chapters: 'I'm doing the literature review chapter or the methodology chapter now.' Obviously there is some satisfaction and even a sense of relief in thinking you can write chapters and complete pieces of the dissertation early. It seems to automatically reduce the labour so that the thesis seems more manageable.

Premature elaboration of chapters often coincides with the IMRAD approach. The difficulty is that there is no context into which the chapters fit. No overarching story. No continuous and sustained argument. The most likely result is that these early chapters will either sit awkwardly in the overall text, or they will require extensive rewriting in order to produce 'flow' later on.

We suggest instead that you produce *chunks* of writing, not chapters. Chunks are more *provisional* groupings around key ideas, data, methodologies. These chunks may or may not end up being incorporated into the thesis, but they provide the groundwork for eventual chapters. Chunks may be written and rewritten. You can write about the problem you are researching, about the field of knowledge production, about the methodology – often several times. These chunks are important for sorting out ideas and developing the 'readerly' stance (Barthes, 1975) you will take in your final text.

Chunks have substance. They are not just a few pages in length. They are substantive pieces of text that probe, test out, argue and interpret specific aspects of the research. We have written chunks in order to construct some of the chapters in this book. We find that getting out the ideas, so that we know what we have to say, is a helpful precursor to putting those ideas into sequence and framing them through a key idea.

When DRs finally come to the end of their fieldwork, and begin to worry about how to construct the actual dissertation text, their supervisor may well ask them to write some chunks about their data, to develop their analysis and theoretical ideas.

Once you have chunks of writing and various bits of data analysis, these have to be put together. The next step is storyboarding.

Strategy 2: storyboarding to create the moves

Traditionally, storyboarding is a process used in film-making. Each camera shot is plotted using a single frame and these are organised sequentially to show the way the story unfolds. Directors may very well film individual shots out of sequence, but they can be reassembled using the storyboard. Cutaway close ups, for example, are generally shot separately from wide angle takes of the same event. So storyboards not only allow you to organise a sequence of events – what follows what – but also allow you to produce chunks in a random order and sequence them later.

Storyboarding is also used by novelists, particularly those who write detective fiction, where they need to create a complex plot, manage multiple characters, red herrings and false trails. In the days before computers, this novelistic plotting was often accomplished via library index cards. Vladimir Nabakov was a great fan of the index card method. He apparently wrote all of his novels on index cards, not on paper (see Experience: Vladimir Nabakov).

However, you are not writing a whodunnit or any other kind of narrative. You are constructing an argument. The argument is the major organiser of your thesis text. Argument provides the opportunity for you to make your mark, to state your case, stake a claim.

A joint study by Vernon Trafford and Shosh Leshem in the UK, South Africa and Israel, which examined the conclusions of 100 PhD theses, found that 46 per cent made no claims to have contributed to knowledge (www.timeshigher education.co.uk/news/half-of-theses-fail-to-show-how-they-advance-to-knowledge/2003278.article). The researchers concluded that candidates assumed their readers would recognise the merit of their thesis. They are adamant that this is unacceptable. We agree. However, we think the problem is not simply understanding that a thesis needs to make a contribution to knowledge. The problem is that DRs do not understand how to argue their contribution from start to finish.

EXPERIENCE

Vladimir Nabokov

The Russian born novelist's writing habits were famously peculiar. Beginning in 1950, he composed first drafts in pencil on ruled index cards, which he stored in long file boxes. Since, Nabakov claimed, he pictured an entire novel in complete form before he began writing it, this method allowed him to compose passages out of sequence, in whatever order he pleased: by shuffling the cards around, he could quickly rearrange paragraphs, chapters, and whole swaths of the book. (His file box also served as a portable desk; he started the first draft of Lolita on a road trip across America, working nights in the back seat of his parked car, the only place in the country, he said, with no noise and no drafts). Only after months of this labour did he finally relinquish the cards to his wife Vera, for a typed draft, which would then undergo several more rounds of revisions.

Vladimir Nabokov, in Currey, 2013, p. 180

The storyboard can help construct the moves of your extended argument. As with your thesis, the storyboard will present a problem, justify the importance of attending to that problem, and persuade a reader that the evidence you have accumulated sheds new light on the problem.

It is easy to get bogged down in detail because you have been completely immersed in the data you are analysing. You need distance in order to find pattern, order and stance. Storyboarding helps you to do this.

In storyboarding, your aim is to make explicit and sensible how your argument is staged *across* chapters. It offers a technique for finding larger groupings in the data than you may have found to date. You look for flow and for the logic of the moves and find an angle on the substantive work that you've done. You capture the big idea and break that into two or three bits that will become the results chapters or topic chapters.

We suggest you begin your storyboard in the middle, with your results, and then work out to the beginning and ending moves. If you've done this 'middle work', you know what the argument is that runs through the entire text.

Storyboarding can be done in any number of ways. There are digital mind-mapping tools, Scrivener's corkboard, and MAC has a program called storyboard. Here we suggest a way of doing storyboarding with paper and post-its (see Advice: Storyboarding the results).

ADVICE

Storyboarding the results

Top-down

You have the big idea that will hold the thesis together. You came to this idea by writing chunks and you know the two or three or four big meta-categories, resulting from your analysis. These are now chapters. Make a page for each one. Lay them out on the floor or on a big table or pin them on the wall with a label. What sequence should they be in? Put them in order and number them. Now get a pack of post-its. Convert the smaller bits of data analysis and chunks into no more than two or three sentences per post-it. These smaller pieces might be, for example, themes in qualitative analysis or clusters of survey results. Put the post-its together on the relevant chapter pages. Then arrange them in order on the page to make the chapter argument. This is a way to consider the internal set of moves. You may find that you have to move post-its from page to page in order to get the best sequence. Finally, name each page by trying to capture the Big Move.

Bottom-up

Pull all the bits of stuff that you have onto post-its – two or three sentences only for a theme or cluster of analysis. Now start to make patterns from the post-its. Which ones clump together logically? Try to work up to two, three or four sets of post-its. Transfer these to a page and think of it as a chapter. What is the overall meta-category? What is its name? Pin the pages on a wall, or put them on the floor or table. Now arrange the post-its in logical order as in the top-down process, moving them around to see if they work better elsewhere.

As you are sorting through the order of post-its for each chapter, it can help to talk through what an abstract of the chapter might be. Talk this out loud, not in your head. Yes, aloud.

The next step is to write a long abstract for each of the pages. You can, of course, simply use the pages and post-its as the outline to guide your writing, but a further iteration of the internal chapter argument via an abstract provides a good road map for the larger task.

An alternative approach to storyboarding, developed by Patrick Dunleavy, can be found on: https://medium.com/advice-and-help-in-authoring-a-phd-or-non-fiction/story-boarding-research-b430cebd5ccd

There are other tools that you can use to do the storyboarding process. You may want to use PowerPoint to make a series of slides about the various chunks that stage your argument. Just like post-its, these can be shuffled around until you get the sequence you want. You can use blank postcards, or buy ready-made blanks such as ©Artefact Cards (see http://markcarrigan.net/2015/02/16/how-to-use-artefact_cards-for-academic-writing/). Or you might put the entire map of your research onto a single diagram. This is what Dave McKenna, a DR researching policy-making practices, did (see Writing Sample: Dave McKenna).

But before you launch into the whole text, it is helpful to write an abstract for the dissertation to make sure that your argument hangs together and flows.

WRITING SAMPLE

Dave McKenna

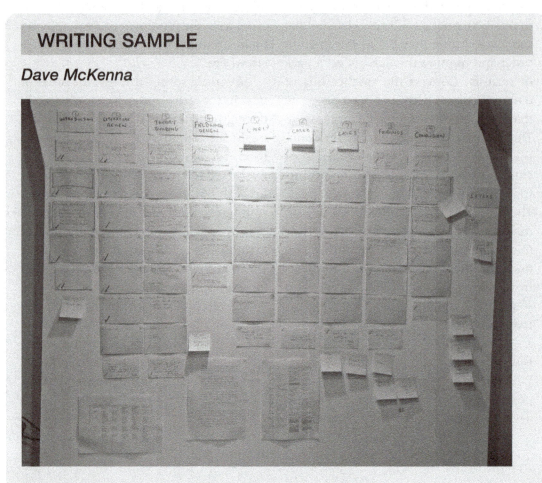

http://patthomson.net/2015/11/09/buffering-your-thesis

Strategy 3: writing thesis abstracts

We argued earlier in this chapter that there are pitfalls in using IMRAD. So too are there misconceptions about the thesis abstract.

Cooley and Lewkowicz (2003, p. 112) give this advice on the thesis abstract:

> [The Abstract] is written after the research has been completed and the writer knows exactly what is contained in the body of the text. It is a summary of the text and it informs readers of what can be found in the dissertation and in what order, functioning as an overall signpost for the reader. Although it is the last part of a dissertation to be written, it is generally one of the first a reader will look at. Indeed, if the Abstract is not well written, it may be the only part of the dissertation a reader will look at!

We disagree with this advice. The abstract is not a summary, it is an argument, writ small. And it is not best left until the bitter end. We see thesis abstracts as an iterative process: begun early and revised/revisited until the end.

We trawled many writing advice sites to examine the advice DRs are offered about how to write abstracts. We don't want to name and shame anyone here, but we saw too many dubious handy hints. A lot of advice does suggest that the abstract is a summary. We also saw a lot of technical advice – such as assigning one sentence to capture each chapter in a cumulative fashion, cutting and pasting sentences from key passages of the thesis to get a first draft. This confuses the road map for the thesis with the abstract.

It is more useful to think of the thesis abstract as a mini-statement of the thesis. It presents *all* of the moves that are in the larger text. The thesis abstract is not a trailer. It's not an advertisement for what is to come. It's not a foreword, preamble or introduction. It's not the blurb on the back of the book or a sales pitch per se. It's also not the same as the research proposal: it's not about what you're going to do, but what you've done, how, in what way, what this means and how it constitutes a contribution to knowledge. The thesis abstract is a tiny version of the bigger whole.

And it is a very important little text. It is the first thing your examiner reads. It must be written with authority. It sets the tone for what is to come. On the basis of the abstract alone, before they start the text proper, the examiner will form expectations about what is to follow – how well the thesis is likely to be written, whether it is going to be well argued and evidenced, whether it is going to be lively or dull.

Thesis abstracts are also important for readers beyond the examiners. They might be reprinted in indexes such as ERIC or PsycInfo. People doing literature searches generally read an abstract in a digital thesis collection before deciding whether the whole thing is worth reading. So the thesis abstract quite often stands in for the entire thesis. It's actually a high-stakes bit of writing.

It's a mistake to dash off the abstract at the last minute before handing in the thesis. No matter how desperate you are to be rid of it, no matter how sick and tired you are of it, you need to spend time fine-tuning this tiny bit of prose. We say fine-tune, because we see the thesis abstract as a text you write and rewrite continuously.

Our approach is to treat the abstract as an extended argument. It must therefore state the problem, establish its importance, show what you've actually done, and make the case that this is a sound piece of research which adds to knowledge. We use the four moves we introduced in Chapter 5 to achieve this work: Locate, Focus, Report, Argue. We specify these moves for the thesis abstract in Figure 7.1.

We now look at three published thesis abstracts from three different universities in Australia. We've used the four moves as an analytic tool to show what their authors, now graduated DRs, have included and omitted. They didn't use the four moves when they were writing, and we don't know what framework they were required to use. We found these abstracts by searching digital theses online. We use them not to suggest that they are 'bad abstracts', but rather to illustrate which are more informative, why and how. We want you to assess the benefits of using the four moves for yourself.

The first abstract is for research in the interdisciplinary field of 'development studies' (see Writing Sample 7.1).

This abstract has a very extended Locate. It explains the relevant maritime boundaries and establishes that there is more at stake than simply establishing them. They need to be maintained administratively. A warrant for the research is thus created but it is more like a CARS structure than a Locate. The Focus however is

LOCATE – Place the thesis within the discipline and the field. Relate the topic to relevant issues, debates, practice problems or social trends and from a critical perspective. Create an explicit warrant for the research, its significance and the contribution.

FOCUS – Identify the particular questions, issues or kinds of problems or problematisations that you will investigate.

REPORT – Provide a short economical statement of the research design – e.g. the nature of the research, participants and/or the corpus of data, how these were chosen, the method of analysis – to show the thesis is credible and trustworthy. Outline the major findings that form the basis of the argument to come.

ARGUE – Explain the results and their significance. Connect to the current state of knowledge, show what the research has added. This may go beyond analysis to some form of new conceptual or theoretical framing. You must answer the 'so what', and the 'now what' questions.

FIGURE 7.1 Moves in a thesis abstract

WRITING SAMPLE 7.1

Completed doctoral thesis abstract

Challenges and opportunities in the delimitation of Indonesia's maritime boundaries: a legal and technical approach

LOCATE: Indonesia officially recognises ten neighbours with which maritime boundaries are required. The ten neighbours are, clockwise from the northwest, India, Thailand, Malaysia, Singapore, Vietnam, Philippines, Palau, Papua New Guinea, Australia and Timor-Leste (East Timor). At the time of writing, Indonesia has, either fully or partially, signed 17 maritime boundary agreements with seven neighbours and no maritime boundaries with Philippines, Palau and Timor-Leste. There are more than 20 segments of maritime boundaries to be delimited in the future.

It is evident that pending maritime boundaries between Indonesia and its neighbours have repeatedly caused issues and tensions in international relations between Indonesia and its neighbours. Incidents around maritime boundary areas have taken place from time to time and remind us that settled maritime boundaries are required. Interestingly, such incidents take place not only in areas where maritime boundaries are missing but also in areas where maritime boundaries have apparently, formally at least, been settled. This indicates that settling maritime boundaries is not the end of the story. Administration and management are essential for good ocean governance in the future for Indonesia.

The delimitation of Indonesia's maritime boundaries with its neighbours in accordance with the international law of the sea is required. FOCUS: This thesis provides options of maritime boundary between Indonesia and its neighbours by REPORT: critically analysing three relevant case studies which are located in the Sulawesi Sea, Singapore Strait and Malacca Strait. The most recent trends in delimitation methods, particularly the three-stage approach, were used in analysing options of delimitation. The approach consists of three steps, which is the construction of a provisional line based on equidistance, followed by adjusting the provisional line by considering relevant circumstances and lastly by conducting a disproportionality test to ensure that the delimitation does not cause inequality to parties in question. This thesis does not come up only with options of maritime boundary delimitation between Indonesia and its neighbours, but also critical evaluation of the three-stage approach which may be considered as one of the novel contributions of the research.

I Made Andi Arsana, December 2013, University of Wollongong

not as clear as it might be in linking back to the problem established in the Locate. The Report is both extensive and truncated. We are told that the case study is used to examine how the ongoing boundary work is conducted in three sites using a three-step approach. We don't know why this approach has been chosen, nor do we know the results. We don't know if this is a new approach devised by the researcher, or where it has been used previously if it isn't new. We do know that some kind of evaluation of this three-stage approach has been undertaken, but we are not told the results.

To understand the significance of the study and its 'so what', the reader needs to know exactly what the new understandings are about maritime boundaries and their maintenance. We expect to read something about the way in which this research might be applied to resolve the problems identified at the outset of the abstract.

Thesis abstract 7.2 is from urban planning, again in a 'development' context (see Writing Sample 7.2).

Abstract 7.2 is considerably longer than 7.1 – 505 words compared to 256. While we are not fans of putting the Focus first, it is a very common strategy and it does have the virtue of telling the reader right at the outset what the thesis does. The Focus in this abstract is clearly stated. The Locate however is presented in two places and interrupted by some of the Report. This makes the reader work to make sense of the situation and the problem that the thesis addresses. The second Locate causes the confusion. When we came across it we did not know at first whether it was a report of results or something else. Eventually we worked out that it was a statement of the key policy imperatives that the thesis investigates in two Lombok districts. The remainder of the abstract, the second Report and Argue are informative, easy to read and compelling. The Argue offers a clear and strong statement of the DR's stance, and also proposes a way forward. We have a clear sense of the contribution that this study makes to the implementation of development policy in this context.

The final thesis abstract, 7.3, comes from traffic studies (see Writing Sample 7.3).

The Locate in Abstract 7.3 is very clearly stated. The reader understands the problem, and the fact that several people have tried to resolve it without success. The Focus is crystal clear and makes an effective link back to the problem. It also makes a bold claim – *a new approach*. The contribution is thus established early on and can now be elaborated and evidenced through the Report. We are told that this is a case study, and the steps that were taken. We are also succinctly informed of the results. Even though this abstract is shorter than the first we examined, it actually does more work. The reader is better informed about the study because the first three moves have been accomplished so well. The Argue is under-developed somewhat truncated. We are told the relevance of the results and how they might be used, but no larger point is made about the utility of decision trees more broadly, nor the importance of a focus on decision making per se in sites with similar problems. And is there any big city that doesn't have a traffic problem, we ask?

WRITING SAMPLE 7.2

Completed doctoral thesis abstract

Decentralization and development planning in Indonesia: a case study of two districts in Lombok

FOCUS: This thesis is a critical analysis of the contemporary development planning system in Indonesia, institutionalized in parallel with democratization and decentralization policies. It examines to what extent local development planning exhibits practices of good governance, through its features of transparency, responsiveness, accountability and inclusive-participative procedures. The central research question is to what extent does decentralization promote good governance in development planning?

LOCATE: Scholars have investigated decentralization outcomes in Indonesia from various angles, portraying both scepticism and optimism. This study contributes to understanding about how local government in Indonesia uses its new powers within a broader context of democratization, in an area which has received less attention, i.e. development planning. This includes understanding about how participative, pro-poor and gender-sensitive policies, the contemporary vocabulary of Indonesian politics, are put into practice in instituting development planning, in particular for the education sector.

REPORT: In this thesis the practices of development planning are investigated in two districts in Nusa Tenggara Barat (NTB) province, i.e. Central and West Lombok. The research involved a critical review of development planning policies, interviews with government officials at the national, provincial and district levels, project/donor funding agency staff, and members of local NGOs, and observations of Musrenbang, the multi-stakeholder forum for development planning at the village and supra-village levels.

LOCATE: The contemporary regulations for development planning build a foundation for more transparent and responsive practices, and require governments to be accountable to their local constituents. Public engagement is a core value, obligating governments to consult the public through all phases in designing development plans.

REPORT: In general the research findings demonstrate complex relations between democratic political institutions, devolved power and the realities of political practice. Planning procedures in the two districts showed unprecedented transparency, as required by regulations: program planning along with the budget was exposed to the public, through local media and during the sessions of Musrenbang. Another obvious sign of progress is the involvement of the public, which contrasts with the previous practice which was restricted to the elites. Women's involvement was also more obvious than before, although this was not the case for the poor. Participants played active roles in Musrenbang, asking questions, demanding modifications or posing criticism, although this varied across areas.

However, the participative process was characterized by less than satisfactory practical and strategic preconditions, which compromised the quality of the process. The development planning process cannot be dissociated from the dynamics of local politics, which in Lombok have politicized government institutions and had unexpected implications for how decisions on development programs were made.

ARGUE: Overall, this study concludes that there has not been much progress towards good governance in development planning in the two districts observed. Judging from this example, decentralization is important but insufficient in establishing good local governance for development planning. Political will from local bodies is essential, and it was lacking in these two districts of Lombok. Although so far it is under-utilised, an invited space like Musrenbang can be an important entry point for both the officials and the public to engage in critical collaboration in development planning.

Rasita Purba, April 2013, Monash University

We'd hazard a guess that there are potentially much broader implications of this study than the author is prepared to claim.

These three thesis abstracts appear to be written within the confines of the word limits set by their institutions, but are of very different lengths. However, even the two that are of a similar length achieve very different ends for the reader. Abstract 7.3 makes the contribution abundantly evident, even if it could go further. Abstract 7.1 leaves the reader in some doubt about what's new and why. Abstract 7.2 is almost twice as long, but for the most part the additional words have allowed the author to provide useful detail which enhances the argument for the contribution.

Some people opt for a one-page thesis abstract, as is the case with 7.1 and 7.3, so that the examiner or thesis browser can get it all at once. It is a visual representation of the coherent whole. Other people opt for more words to elaborate their argument, as does 7.2. But it is important not to go on too long, because it suggests to the examiner that the rest of the thesis may well not be as concise as it should.

Armed with their storyboard and thesis abstract, DRs might also like to experiment with a strategy offered by Umberto Eco.

Strategy 4: writing the introduction and chapter abstracts

In addition to being a highly successful novelist and academic, Umberto Eco wrote a book about writing a thesis (Eco, 1977/2015). Recently translated into English,

WRITING SAMPLE 7.3

Completed doctoral thesis abstract

Modelling traffic accidents using duration analysis techniques: a case study of Abu Dhabi

LOCATE: One of the main aims of Traffic Incident Management (TIM) is to reduce the duration of the disruption to traffic caused by an accident. Several approaches have been applied in the past in order to analyse and predict this. Incident duration can be broken down into four time intervals: reporting, response, clearance and recovery. Accurate models of each interval allow traffic controllers to deploy resources efficiently, thereby minimising an accident's effect on traffic flow and congestion. This may, in turn, lead to a reduction in other adverse impacts of traffic accidents such as air pollution, fuel consumption and secondary crashes. **FOCUS**: A new approach to this problem, based on the accidents' characteristics, was developed using a fully parametric hazard based modelling technique to predict accident durations. **REPORT**: The road network around Abu Dhabi, capital of the UAE, was used as a case study. Data was obtained from the UAE Federal Traffic Statistics System (FTSS) and the Abu Dhabi Serious Collision Investigation Section (ASCIS). These data included the start and end of each time interval, the total accident duration, temporal, geographical, environmental and other accident characteristics. To analyse the total duration, the analysis was conducted using three time intervals. Accordingly, fully parametric Accelerated Failure Time (AFT) models were created for the purpose of reporting time, response time, and clearance time (all urban roads) and response time (rural freeways), depending on the data available. Analysis showed that the time intervals had different distributions. In addition, there was no similarity in the variable that affected each interval. The results also revealed that weaknesses exist in the current practices of TIM in Abu Dhabi. **ARGUE**: The results of the analysis were used to create decision trees to aid traffic controllers with decisions regarding traffic diversion and disseminating traffic information to travellers.

Al Kaabi, Abdulla Mohammed Saeed Khalaf, 2013, Newcastle University

the book offers a range of practical advice about how to organise reading materials and how to construct a text. Eco does not offer a default thesis structure, although he does suggest that the Humanities and Social Sciences theses may differ in important ways from each other – the first being about texts and ideas, the second about reporting and interpreting empirical work. He argues persuasively for form following function and thinking about the relationships between the two early on.

Eco's approach is to first write the introduction to the thesis and then an extended outline. This could be achieved through storyboarding. While Eco's outline begins as a table of contents, it becomes a larger working text with a short abstract for each chapter. Each chapter abstract could follow our Locate, Focus, Report and Argue format.

Eco proposes that writing an early thesis introduction sets the direction for the thesis, and convinces the supervisor that the DR knows what they are doing. Eco's early introduction is really the same as a research proposal, which is now routinely required for entry to most doctorates and which is often rewritten as an extended text, sometime towards the end of the first year, and assessed through some kind of symposium or viva.

It is striking that Eco proposes writing the thesis introduction as an organising strategy once the fieldwork has been completed. He argues, as do we, that the overall thinking about the thesis structure – we would suggest as an abstract as well as an introduction and chapter abstracts – is a working document. As Eco puts it

> it should be clear that you will continuously rewrite the introduction and the table of contents as you proceed in your work. This is the way it is done. The final table of contents and introduction (those that will appear in the final manuscript) will be different from these first drafts. This is normal. If this were not the case, it would mean that all of your research did not inspire a single new idea. Even if you are determined enough to follow your precise plan from beginning to end, you will have missed the point of writing a thesis if you do not revise as you progress with your work.
>
> (Eco, 1997/2015, p. 112)

Eco also suggests, as do we, that writing the actual text, putting the chunks together, doesn't have to start at the beginning. You start with the chunk about which you feel most familiar and comfortable, and then go on to the chapter that will help clarify and crystallise the overall argument. However, you don't do that in a vacuum. You have memos, storyboards, chunks, introduction and chapter abstracts as working texts to support the development of the final structure. The form will, through these strategies, grow with the content. Each chapter will perform its own function to carefully stage the argument and present the evidence for your contribution, your entry into the scholarly conversation.

Structure revisited

We have been critical of IMRAD and other templates that encourage DRs to engage in premature chapter formation. But let's be very clear. We are not against structure. On the contrary. The best theses are elegantly structured. The various components

1 **Establishing** the problem/puzzle/problematisation

2 **Situating** the study in the relevant literatures and prior research

3 **Explaining** the basis on which the research was conducted

4 **Presenting and analysing** data, **reporting results**

5 **Teasing out key patterns in the data,** connecting these with literatures

6 **Drawing out** the implications of the results for scholarship and/or policy and/or practice

7 **Making a case** and arguing that this research constitutes a contribution to knowledge

FIGURE 7.2 Research actions that comprise a thesis

connect well and build upon one another to make the thesis argument in a carefully staged and convincing manner.

The weakness of IMRAD and other templates is that they encourage you to think of chapters as a set of content holders – methods, literature, findings – for containing stuff. They treat writing as an object – a vehicle for displaying knowledge rather than an action that has purpose and effect.

In Chapter 2 we argued that language is social action. We say that again here – writing is social action. Figure 7.2 specifies seven key research actions in a thesis. We never just write – we write something – an argument, a description, an abstract. Writing is a form of doing. It achieves particular purposes in specific contexts. Something happens as a result of it being read. You therefore need to make sure to capture the key actions that comprise your doctoral thesis, regardless of whether you follow the IMRAD structure or not.

What might these actions looks like in an IMRAD structure (see Table 7.1)?

And what might they look like in an alternative structure? In Table 7.2, for example, we suggest a structure based on theses we've read in the field of politics.

The key point is this: there is NO single correct structure for the PhD thesis. There are structural options. DRs have agency and choice. You don't have to treat structure

TABLE 7.1 IMRAD Thesis structure by actions

Introduction	Establishing the problem
Literature review	Situating in prior research literatures
Methods	Explaining how the research was conducted
Results x 3	Reporting and analysing data
Discussion	Drawing out implications of results
Conclusion	Making a case for the contribution

TABLE 7.2 Alternative thesis structure by action

Introduction and methodology	Establishing the problem
Explaining how the research was conducted	
History and literatures	Situating in prior research and literatures
Case one	Reporting and analysing data
Case two	Reporting and analysing data
Case three	Reporting and analysing data
Case four	Reporting and analysing data
Discussion and conclusion	Drawing out implications of results
	Making a case for the contribution

as an arbitrary set of conventions or rely on pre-fabricated forms because you are nervous. Having worked through the strategies in this chapter, you will have a fairly good idea about what you want to say in your thesis; as you write, your ideas will evolve and change. The aim is to create a set of chapters that carry the argument you want to make. If you are using a version of IMRAD, you must decide how to foreground argument across chapters so it doesn't get lost. You can develop structure around the argument you want to make. Form works with content.

Carter, Kelly and Brailsford (2012) argue that even if IMRAD isn't the final structure that you choose to use, it can still be helpful in thinking about structure. They say

> Even the most risk-comfortable researcher, however, should also use the basic model (IMRAD) as a checklist for the work which needs to be demonstrated in their written thesis. One very obvious consideration is where the literature will be reviewed. . . . Even if you use the basic outline as one to resist and work against, knowing what it declares to be appropriate will help you to produce a more elaborate artifice. (p. 19)

We agree. Our point is about you not rushing early to a structure, but rather focusing on understanding how to structure your particular content. It's a question, we suggest, of thinking form and content together, not separately or sequentially.

In sum

We've considered the temptation to reach for a ready-made thesis structure. Instead, we've argued, it's helpful to think about form and function working together. We've proposed some ways to achieve this by writing chunks, storyboarding and writing thesis and chapter abstracts.

8 Writing the researcher into the text

The problem: getting beyond the dispassionate objective researcher

Most doctoral researchers understand that it is now acceptable to write as an 'I'. Writing 'I' was once seen as poor academic writing and poor research. It was said to indicate a researcher suffering from a lack of objectivity. An 'I' writer could not detach themselves from their research and therefore their work was bound to be biased. Third-person writing gave the 'right' impression of detachment and objectivity. This view is no longer as widely held, but it still lurks around many doctoral training programmes and conversations.

Much of the credit for tackling attitudes to the use of 'I' goes to feminist scholars who argued that the use of the third person in academic writing is a masculinist strategy intended to create the impression of an objective view that does not exist. Instead of resorting to what Donna Haraway (1988) described as a 'god trick', in which the researcher appears nowhere and everywhere via the use of the third person, researchers ought to explicitly situate the researcher in the text. If the reader can find out about the writer, then they can make judgements about the situated and particular nature of what is being offered to them. One way for the researcher to make herself visible is through the use of the first person. The use of 'I' allows the reader to understand that the research is a social construction, just like any other form of knowledge.

The understanding that research is never neutral is now so taken for granted in many disciplines and locations that it may well seem out of step to be arguing and writing otherwise. But the argument for 'I' is now accepted if not agreed – writing in the first person is seen as a legitimate form of academic writing, just perhaps not in 'my' discipline.

However, understanding research as situated does not equate to simply writing as an 'I'. Confining the personal to a matter of pronouns is a mistake. If, as Haraway and countless others have argued, the research enterprise cannot be separated from the researcher, then the tangle of researcher and research is not resolved by simply advocating or abhorring the use of 'I'.

Some commentators suggest that writing as 'I' is easier than writing in the third person. Here is a fairly typical view, taken from an advice website.

> Writing in third-person perspective is hard – much harder than first-person. Why? Because we see and experience the world through our own perspective – our patterns of beliefs, experiences, hopes, fears. We have opinions, thoughts, ideas, and desires. When we write, it is natural to tell our story from our own viewpoint.
>
> (www.elusiva.com/research/thirdperson.php)

We beg to differ with this view. We think that writing as an 'I' is often much easier said than done. DRs wanting to write in the first person are often on the receiving end of feedback from supervisors that suggests they have somehow got the 'I' wrong. It's used inappropriately, the 'I' is nowhere to be found, or there is too much 'I'.

Alex Seal is a first-year PhD student and graduate tutor at the University of Surrey in the Sociology department. His PhD explores why UK students choose to study abroad. Alex is also deeply interested in research methodology, particularly the objective/subjective divide. He has frequently found himself talking to other doctoral peers about writing in the first person (see Commentary: Alex Seal).

You may feel uncomfortable about putting yourself into the text and finding the right degree of reflexivity. You may feel uneasy about claiming what you've done in your thesis. But it is essential to highlight your contribution to knowledge, claiming it as 'my', not 'the', contribution.

So why is it so difficult to write as an 'I'?

The reframing idea: writing the right I

Not all 'I's are the same. Some are acceptable in academic writing and some are not. It might seem that once you have made the decision to write as 'I' it's just straightforward. Unfortunately, this is not so. There are conventions about the use of 'I' in academic writing that must be followed – or which you might consciously choose to disobey.

The 'I' who writes an academic article is not the same 'I' who makes dinner, picks the kids up after school, goes shopping, and chats with their friends on Facebook. This is a personal 'I'. Academic writing requires an academic 'I' (Giltrow, 1995). The academic 'I', not surprisingly, does a range of academic activities – academic 'I's argue, infer, suggest, propose, conclude, offer, deduce, analyse, assess,

COMMENTARY

Alex Seal

Writing as 'I' is about how you understand research

I have always been fascinated with the views of others when it comes to writing in the first person. In my (albeit limited) experience of the academy I have already come across those in my own discipline (Sociology) who label it 'bad practice', those who 'don't mind it', and those who 'actively promote it'. As a PhD student writing, researching, and teaching, I have always, and will continue to, remain within the 'actively promote it' camp.

I agree that writing in the first person with 'I' is linked to issues in objectivity. But the hostility of some towards it also serves to remind us that the objective/subjective divide within the social sciences is alive and well, with objectivity maintaining a subtle supremacy in research and writing.

This is because labeling the use of 'I' as 'bad practice' reinforces a view of the social sciences that distancing yourself within the research is both possible and desirable. But this objective conception of research is simply not achievable. For ethnographers, it is the researcher who recreates 'images' of the people, settings, and interactions for the reader to interpret. For qualitative interviewers, it is the researcher who takes snippets of the interview data and effectively becomes the biographer of their participants. However, and this is so important, the objective/subjective distinction is not something that is restricted to qualitative research.

Quantitative researchers choose the variables for analysis and how their data sets are used. Similarly the statistical tests used on quantitative data are often named after their creators, thus demonstrating that these tests are human creations set in values and particular ways of thinking – SPSS can therefore never be an autonomous instrument that 'uncovers' the reality of social life.

The key point here then is that data does not speak for itself. It is we as researchers who interpret and organise our findings, proceeding to speak through it. So the critique that the 'researcher can affect the research' is an argument that cannot exist because we are 'involved' in our research from the moment we choose a topic through to coding, analysis, and the write-up process.

Some would argue these views are not new or revolutionary for the social sciences.

However, if the view I have presented was widely accepted, I cannot see how anyone could object to writing with the 'I'. Perhaps the only logical argument against it is that any mention of the researcher as 'I' is seen as subjectivity triumphing over objectivity. And this inevitably goes back to objectivity as THE way to do 'real' science, whilst subjectivity is seen as something that hinders that goal.

Ultimately, if writing with the 'I' is actually just a signifier of the subjective elements within our research, is it not more appropriate to work with it, therefore giving greater authorship in our voice behind the writing? And by doing this, we may just begin to bridge the objective and subjective together, enabling ourselves to become more accountable for the claims we make.

http://patthomson.net/2013/08/22/writing-with-i-is-subjective-and-thats-ok/

evaluate, concur, trace, design, address, signal, signpost, flag up, situate, locate, affirm. These verbs capture the actions that are associated with scholarship.

Now there isn't a simple division between the academic and the personal, so you do need to think about where and when you might be more 'personal' in your academic writing. Blogging is a place where the personal 'I' and academic 'I 'blur. The academic blogging 'I' is not the same as the conventional academic 'I'. It's quite possible in blogs to write about yourself in a more journalistic way. In a blog it's perfectly plausible for an academic 'I' to laugh, cry and scream – acts that are well-nigh impossible in most conventional journal articles. Blogging is just a more personal kind of writing altogether, more relaxed, less distanced (see Chapter 6).

Academic writing, as in the thesis or a journal article, requires a more formal 'I' – the academic 'I'. And there are some common ways in which you can get this wrong.

Take the verbs 'believe' and 'feel' as an example. We often see first draft theses where 'I believe' and 'I feel' are liberally strewn about. Most often these phrases can be crossed out and eliminated altogether, without losing anything from the text. For example:

Sentence One: I feel that current explanations of bullying are not adequate
Sentence Two: Current explanations of bullying are not adequate

Nothing is lost by the deletion of 'I feel'; the meaning is maintained. In fact, the second sentence is more assertive and assured without the cover of 'I feel' – but it requires evidence to substantiate the claim. Scholarship is not just a matter of what you feel – your opinion – it has to be backed up.

Sentence Three: Current explanations of bullying are not adequate (reference 1, reference 2).

The addition of supporting citations results in stronger academic prose.

And saying 'I believe' and 'I feel' are often not appropriate in academic writing. This is because readers are not looking for what you think, but rather what you've done – they are looking for the 'evidence' you have generated to support your argument. This is either analysed data, or what you've taken from the literature. In these instances, saying 'I believe' invites the response 'Well if this is simply your belief and there is no evidence for it, why should I trust you?'

There *is* a place to discuss beliefs in most academic research – when you address the question of researcher position and reflexivity. Beliefs are often made explicit in the Introduction or Methods chapters, so readers know where the writer is coming from. But readers also want to know what processes DRs have put in place to be critical about their beliefs and their practice.

At this point, two caveats. There are disciplinary traditions that use 'I believe' quite regularly. Philosophers frequently write in this way. Some scientists do too. So, as always, it's important to check out your discipline-specific conventions for academic 'I' writing. And feelings can also have a place in research. A researcher might want to say 'I feel' and explain their own feelings/emotions in relation to a person, a situation, or an aspect of their research, in order to develop a particular analysis. If this is the case, you need to explain in the methods chapter why you are making explicit your feelings and what intellectual tradition(s) you are drawing on in doing so.

It can take time to develop the right academic 'I'. Writing Sample 8.1 is a draft text written by a DR in the social sciences. It contains a mix of the academic and personal 'I'. We put in bold the verb phrases that follow the 'I'.

WRITING SAMPLE 8.1

DR draft

I **believe** that this thesis demonstrates my capacity for independent inquiry, originality in my methods and makes new contribution to thinking. I **support** this claim throughout with examples and evidence drawn from my practice. This is particularly evident in the middle chapters of the thesis where I **outline** the content of the inquiry. I **believe** that my work reflects my own epistemology of practice that is situated in dialogical and holistic ways of knowing (McNiff & Whitehead, 2006).

In presenting this study I **intend** for others to engage with my ideas, to respond to them, and to support me on my continuing learning and professional journey. The structure of the thesis reflects the phases of both my own development as a novice researcher as well as the research itself. As a result of this I **feel that I can share with the reader the processes that lead to the claims that I make.** This also enables me to offer a real life explanation for my practice.

DR 8.1 has apparently used the academic I in three places – 'I support', 'I outline' and 'I intend'. The personal 'I' also appears three times – 'I believe' twice, and 'I feel'. However, even the apparently academic 'I' is doing rather un-academic things.

The DR is attempting to explain that her research meets the doctoral requirements for independent inquiry. She explains that in her research she draws on her own professional practice in order to produce the evidence for this claim. She provides a reference to the intellectual tradition in which this work is based. This section of the paragraph could be easily rewritten so that only the academic 'I' is used in the text.

> This thesis demonstrates my capacity for independent inquiry, and originality in my methods, and makes a new contribution to thinking. **I support** this claim throughout with examples and evidence drawn from my practice. The epistemology of practice **I adopt** is situated in dialogical and holistic ways of knowing (McNiff & Whitehead, 2006). This approach is particularly evident in the middle chapters of the thesis where **I outline** the content of the inquiry.

This is not the most elegant writing, but its rewritten form no longer signals that the DR doesn't know what she is doing. However, the second half of the paragraph is more problematic.

The DR imagines a reader with whom she will share the processes of researching and writing. The reader is being addressed as a trusted friend who will help the DR to continue to learn about themselves and their practice. This is a mistake. The thesis reader is first and foremost the examiner who is not there to support continued learning, but to judge whether the thesis is of the required quality. This is not the 'dear reader' of Jane Austen novels. The DR does not 'share' with their examiner. A more substantive rethinking and rewriting is required for this latter half of the paragraph to remove traces of this inappropriate reader.

> The structure of the thesis reflects the phases of both my own development as a novice researcher as well as the research itself. I show **the processes that lead to the claims that I make which** allows a real life explanation for my practice.

Our rewritten version has removed all references to the reader and retained the information about the DR showing their process and learning through their text. As in the first rewrite, this is far from polished writing, but removing the personal 'I' and the inappropriate reader provides the basis for further revision.

Writing Sample 8.2 shows a piece of 'I' writing from a Methods chapter that uses the academic 'I' appropriately. The DR is an ethnographer investigating children's food experiences in schools. Here she explains her choice of study sites.

WRITING SAMPLE 8.2

DR draft

I spent a significant amount of initial time, during the design stages of this project, thinking about the 'ideal' school site. This site was informed by my reading of the literature on whole school approaches and in particular, the design of The Edible Schoolyard in Berkeley. At the time, I was not aware of Jamie Oliver's Kitchen Garden Project which had recently started in the UK and so I looked to the nearest available model – that of the Food for Life Partnership (FFLP) – to inform my shortlisting of possible schools to work in. I was specifically looking for schools that were already teaching cooking and gardening – schools that were implementing the recommendations of *Turning the tables* (2005) and adopting the growing public attitudes towards food education. The schools I chose needed to provide particular cases that were 'vital to understand because of their particular significance in policy formulation and implementation' (Walford, 2008a, p. 20).

I drew up a shortlist of 12 potential schools, using the FFLP website and the (city name) Eco Schools. I cross-referenced schools on the list with their school websites and Ofsted reports (which often highlight extra activities like food growing or cooking). I was initially not concerned with the food being served at lunchtime – I did not specifically look for schools that ran the kitchens in-house or rather belonged to the Council or had private companies providing their lunches and so this was not a factor in the original choice of schools. I approached the initial 12 schools first via email (to either the general admin email address or where possible, directly to the head teacher). I suspect the initial letters were slightly too long, making an amateur mistake, as Walford notes:

'Instead of a short letter that raised interest in the proposal without giving too many details, I wrote fairly long letters that included far too much information. Every additional piece of information gives a chance for an objection or problem to be raised in the mind of the reader. Detailed letters make it far too easy to find a "good reason" to object. Thus, if a letter is to be used, it should be brief' (Walford, 2008a, p. 23).

This was exactly what I did. It is perhaps unsurprising then that I heard back in the negative, or not at all.

All DRs who do fieldwork of any description have to justify their sample and most of them do it using the third person. Many also opt for somewhat abstracted and distanced writing. Writing Sample 8.2 shows how the academic personal pronoun can be used to good effect to explain research decisions. It also demonstrates a degree of reflexivity and demonstrates precisely the kind of learning that the DR in Writing Sample 8.1 aspires to make clear to their examiner.

Writing the academic 'I' takes practice and thought. The DR needs to strike a balance between the focus on the self and the focus on the people or things that are being researched. Too much 'I' and the writing is all about the researcher. That's fine if the research is an autobiography or auto-ethnography. But lots of 'I' is not OK if the research is about something or someone else. Too much 'I' is narcissistic. Me, me, it's all about me. And the most startling/ironic/inappropriate use of the solipsistic 'I' is when a researcher writes about participatory research, going on and on about being collaborative while writing exclusively about themselves in the first person.

Then of course, there is the trap of writing in first person plural.

Some people think that they should write about themselves as a 'we'. Barbara, for example, was advised to write her PhD in this manner. We have seen a few DRs write about themselves as 'the researcher' – the researcher does this and that. When asked to revise this way of writing they often opt for 'we'. It is an illusion, however, to think that 'the researcher' or 'we' is more objective, less personal. It is strange to write about yourself as a plural when there's only one of you.

However, there are three academic uses of 'we' that do make sense. The first and most glaringly obvious is when research has been done by a team, a 'we'. A second use of 'we' is when there is an appeal to or an assumption of commonality or agreement – as in 'we in the academy', or 'we the people'. While this is pretty common in blogs (where 'we' can probably get away with it) it is also relatively common – and acceptable – in academic writing. However, the writer always runs the risk of someone asking 'Who is this we? What is the evidence that there is a we?' William Germano (2013), a veteran publisher and now academic has strong views about the use of an inappropriate first person plural (see Commentary: William Germano).

A third and more defensible use of the academic 'we' signals membership of a community. It is often used when a writer wants to discuss what a particular scholarly group does on the basis of shared conventions or convictions. 'We' examiners always look for theses that are well argued and structured. 'We' scientists never write as 'I'. But in this 'we' usage, there is the danger of universalising too much about the 'we' group. And what does it mean to speak for 'we'? What about all of those who are 'not we'?

Writing Sample 8.3 is from an eminent feminist psychoanalytic geographer, Liz Bondi (2003), writing as a member of an epistemic group. 'We' is not a bid to include the reader, but signifies a claim to membership of a particular scholarly community (see Writing Sample 8.3). We have put in bold her pronoun use.

Throughout the paper Bondi switches between 'we' and 'I' depending on whether she is writing as a member of the feminist geography community or as herself, the individual scholar. She alerts the reader at the outset that this is her

COMMENTARY

William Germano

'As we have seen', begins the dissertation, and so I find myself looking around quickly to see who is peering over my shoulder. The imaginary collective reader is a commonplace of collective writing. Thousands of dissertations, as well as scholarly articles and monographs, appeal to the slippery 'we'. Is the writer using an intimate 'we' – just herself-as-writer and me-as-her-reader? Perhaps her 'we' is more crowded, a pack of like-minded scholars of which she is, however modestly, at the vanguard? Or is the 'we' meant to write me, too, into this larger scholarly community? I might be flattered that the writer thinks I'm smart enough to join in, but as a reader I don't much like being told what I think.

Germano, 2013, p. 105

WRITING SAMPLE 8.3

Liz Bondi

Before proceeding to the main body of the paper, I have two preliminary points to make. First, feminist researchers in geography and other disciplines frequently address multiple audiences from multiple positions. For example, feminist geographers endeavour to communicate with geographers who take up a variety of positions in relation to different feminisms, with those outside as well as inside the discipline geography, and with activists as well as academics. In so doing, **we** draw on our own multiple positions and identities as geographers, feminists, academics, and much else besides. Negotiating such plurality presents **us** with numerous problems and dilemmas, including decisions about the 'voice' **we** adopt in particular contexts, whether orally or in writing. **My** use of the first person plural here signals **my** sense of belonging within the category of 'feminist geography'. However, the first person plural necessarily excludes as well as includes: it differentiates 'us' from 'not us', whether 'not us' is construed as 'them' or 'other' or something else. **I** imagine that readers will position themselves variously: included, excluded, elsewhere, affronted and so on. This positioning invokes processes of identification (identifying with) and dis-identification (identifying as "other than" or "against"), which are central to **my** concerns in this paper.

(Bondi, 2003, p. 65)

intention, and that she is cognisant of the effects of delineating boundaries of community in this way.

Bondi's use of 'we' and 'I' is self-conscious and reflexive. It's not done merely for stylistic purposes and it is done explicitly. This is what makes it academically acceptable. This is what 'we' academics do, 'we' make and justify 'our' syntactic choices. Furthermore, the Bondi example illustrates nicely our point that writing 'I' is often not just a matter of choice of verb. It is that, but usually much more. Her use of personal pronouns not only signals an epistemic decision about the researcher and their research, but quite also their relationship to disciplinary communities and/or research traditions and/or their position in the academy (Layer 3, see Chapter 2).

Getting the academic 'I' right is thus highly complex work. There are places in the thesis where it matters a great deal. Using the wrong 'I' can cause the DR, their research and their positionality to come unstuck. Two of the most important sites for potential 'I' trouble are at the beginning and end of the thesis.

We therefore offer a strategy to help you write as an authoritative 'I'. We do this in two parts, looking at the two places in the thesis where getting the 'I' right is critical. Examiners read both your thesis introduction and conclusion to see if you have avoided all of the hidden 'I' traps and made the most of its benefits. They look in these two key parts of your text to see whether you have the syntactic 'I' niceties right.

Strategy: writing as an authoritative 'I' – the introduction

The old adage 'first impressions count' holds true when it comes to writing the thesis introduction. After the title and the abstract, the introduction is the first thing the examiner sees. They form an opinion – sometimes quite a strong one – on what the rest of the text will be like, based on what comes at the start. They also make judgements about you, the writer.

The Introduction is a significant place where your writing must engage the examiner-reader and bring them into your research. It is here that you offer things that have been in your head for so long and make them explicit. The reason for your topic and project are not self-evident. Your text must make the reader understand why the research is important, and why they should keep reading. This is a key moment of social interaction and exchange.

The Introduction sets the *warrant* for the thesis – the mandate, the rationale for doing the research. That is, you must establish that not enough is known about a particular topic, and that it is worthwhile and important to know it. But it is not sufficient to simply say that there is a 'gap'. There are always gaps in knowledge;

the question is, why you are addressing this specific knowledge niche here and now? You could do this using the CARS approach we discussed in Chapter 4.

The research warrant can be of different kinds, depending on the discipline and the topic. Here we outline six possible types, to illustrate, rather than provide an exhaustive list (note our use of the academic 'we'):

1   We need to understand a particular social phenomenon, process or practice better (because . . .)

2   We don't know enough about a natural phenomenon or manufactured process or practice (and if we do . . .)

3   We could benefit from knowing more about a particular policy or professional practice (because . . .)

4   We could do with knowing more about the history of a particular topic (maybe for its own sake)

5   There is a scholarly debate about a particular topic which might benefit from being looked at in a different way (because . . .)

6   It would be helpful to develop a new method to examine this particular site, topic, population (because . . . but we don't know yet whether it will do what we hope)

A warrant for research is actually a claim backed up by 'evidence'. The 'evidence' you use to justify the claim can come from any number of sources. In the social sciences and humanities, it may come from current events, media or professional experience, with the scholarly literatures largely left until later in the thesis. However, if appropriate to the topic, there might be some literatures at the outset. There's no rule here. The kind of 'evidence' you use to justify your claim that the research is needed depends on the topic and argument you are making. Importantly, this 'evidence' is more than just a background to the study, its purpose is to persuade the examiner of the intrinsic or extrinsic necessity and/or benefits of your project.

The Introduction sets out the *specific focus* for the research in the form of a thesis statement, aims and objectives, hypothesis or a question. Examiners generally get frustrated if they have to wait too long for this information. They want to know early on what your research project is about and the kind of research that was undertaken. So a short statement that names *the approach* taken to the research is also generally included alongside the focus, e.g. this is ethnography, case study, action research, mixed methods.

The introduction always includes an *outline* of the thesis itself. The examiner expects to see some kind of road map about how the thesis will unfold. The outline shows how you have developed the argument. This has implications for chapter headings and the way you demonstrate the flow of your reasoning, as we show in Chapter 9.

As we discussed earlier, the Introduction also locates *the researcher*. Some disciplines in some countries have a convention of always beginning the thesis with a personal narrative that shows the examiner how they are implicated in the research. This is particularly the case in doctorates that arise from practice in a professional context.

The Introduction should clarify any key *definitions* that are important for the reader to know before they read any further. Some definitional work may be so extensive that it needs to be left to a discussion of the literature, but there are often terms that can be clarified quickly. Providing key definitions means that the examiner knows your particular take on the terminology that is being used in your question and warrant. Some theses provide a glossary separate from the Introduction.

The Introduction not only states what you will do, but also what you won't do and why. Establishing *boundaries* around the research makes it clear at the start what the examiner can expect. You don't want to give them any reason to later say, 'Well why isn't this here?' because you've already told them it's not going to be.

We now look at one researcher's thesis Introduction to see how she handles some of these elements. Dr Erin Mackay's research examined a specific area of legal practice – therapeutic jurisprudence. Writing Sample 8.4 shows how she introduces the reader to the topic and leads into her research question.

This text is written as the scholarly 'I'. Because the thesis is grounded in a professional problem and in the personal professional history of the researcher, it makes little sense to broach the topic as if it was divorced from her life experience. We think that the succinct statement of the personal-professional problem creates a compelling warrant for the research question. This is research that arises from everyday legal work and therefore seeks to have some influence through the research undertaken.

The Dr notes a polarised debate between academics and some senior members of the law – she refers to their disdain for therapeutic jurisprudence – and legal practitioners on the frontline. She informs the reader of her approach – she chooses potentially one of the most difficult sites through which to test out a new theoretical framework. The combination of the personal-professional problem and the deficiency in scholarship creates a niche for her to occupy as an emerging scholar.

After introducing the research question, the Introduction goes on to the methods used in the study. Writing Sample 8.5 shows how Erin Mackay establishes boundaries around her project.

In answering the anticipated question 'Why didn't you do empirical work?' Mackay also refines her critique of existing scholarship, saying that it lacks a sound

WRITING SAMPLE 8.4

Completed thesis introduction

Introducing and justifying the topic

I first encountered the term 'therapeutic jurisprudence' four years ago, when I was working on a national inquiry into violence against women at the Australian Law Reform Commission. I observed how therapeutic jurisprudence tended to polarize; a relatively new term in Australia, it was regarded with disdain by many academics and those in the upper echelons of the legal profession. The Commission noted these debates, and decided not to adopt it in that inquiry. Yet magistrates, and those non-lawyers who had heard of it, were exceptionally positive. My initial impression was that therapeutic jurisprudence had the potential to make a humane contribution to the law. While working as a nighttime solicitor at community legal centres in Sydney's Redfern and Kings Cross, I had realized that my simple acknowledgement of a client's challenging situation would visibly affect their wellbeing, resulting in what a client would tell me was a positive legal interaction for them, and sometimes even rendering a cathartic experience. In foregrounding how legal interactions could affect the wellbeing of those who interacted with the law, therapeutic jurisprudence seemed to reveal a reality about the operation of the law which was lacking from my legal education. In emphasizing how the law should do no harm – and where possible, try to do good – it also justified a compassionate approach to legal analysis, practice, and reform.

Given all of this, I wondered: why was therapeutic jurisprudence so divisive? Intrigued, I decided to embark upon a PhD to dig deeper, and this thesis is the result of that consideration. I chose a 'tough' case study – the legal response to Indigenous women who have experienced sexual violence - in order to really test the boundaries of what therapeutic jurisprudence has the capacity to achieve in justice terms. As a non-Indigenous person living in contemporary Australia, I have been committed to understanding the historical relationship between Indigenous peoples and the state, and through my work, contribute to improving the current situation of Indigenous peoples. I also share a sense of injustice about the way the law does not adequately respond to victims/survivors of sexual violence, a matter which became clear to me while working in family and sexual law reform, and which I discuss at length in Chapter 5 of this thesis. I had noticed that, in focusing on offenders, therapeutic jurisprudence seems to make assumptions about what it could deliver to victims/survivors, and I wondered what it actually offered to this category of legal participant.

With this as background, my research question for the thesis is as follows:

Can a therapeutic jurisprudence framework for the development, implementation and reform of the law, provide a more 'just' legal response to sexual violence experienced by Indigenous women?

WRITING SAMPLE 8.5

Completed thesis introduction

Offering a rationale for the approach

I note that a reader may wonder why I am not embarking on an empirical analysis in this thesis. I have not omitted empirical work because I do not see it as important: quite the opposite. As I argue at length in the thesis, theoretical analysis is what is lacking in the discourse of therapeutic jurisprudence. In my view, it is essential to ensure that the conceptual analysis of therapeutic jurisprudence is correct in justice terms before conducting empirical work. In other words, conceptual analysis is a necessary prerequisite to empirical research. Researchers need to get the conceptual and justice questions right before launching into further empirical work and perpetuating the same problems that I have identified in the therapeutic jurisprudence literature. Thus, in situating my thesis on a conceptual level, I certainly do not dismiss the importance of empirical research.

theoretical analysis. She is thus concerned to fill this gap, rather than undertake more of the same.

We note too the authoritative way in which this Introduction is written. 'In my view . . . it is essential, I have identified problems . . . '. The researcher is taking a contrary position to academics and senior colleagues who are disdainful. She is also critical of advocacy research that has not taken adequate account of theory. This places the researcher in a position where she needs to be assertive if she is to be taken seriously. She not only has to persuade the naysayers, but also convince those who already believe in the approach that they need to do something different. This research will provide the 'evidence' for this work. This is a good example of a researcher wanting to 'speak truth to power'. Even in these two extracts the Dr's skill in answering back is apparent. We discuss writing authoritatively further in Chapter 9.

You need to think about crafting the Introduction because having a lively thesis beginning will set the reader-examiner up well. If what you write at the start is dull and plodding then they will, rightly or wrongly, assume that the rest of the thesis will be the same. No matter how solid the warrant, focus, approach and outline are, the writing itself also does important work in predisposing the examiner to read on past the introduction, either with anticipation or dread.

This all suggests, of course, that the time you devote to the Introduction is time well spent!

Strategy: writing as an authoritative 'I' – the conclusion

The Conclusion is one of the most important sections of the thesis, yet it is often done quite badly. The Conclusion is a key part of the text and DRs need to spend time getting it right. It is the place where you argue that you have made a contribution to knowledge, where you show what it is, and where you discuss its implications. While it doesn't have to be as long as other chapters, the Conclusion has significant work to do.

It is useful to think, first of all, about what NOT to do in a thesis conclusion. There are six common mistakes that DRs make.

1   The DR attributes all of the strengths of the research to 'the research' or the thesis. They do not write as an 'I'. They do not claim the work.

2   The DR laboriously plods through all of the findings from previous chapters. Examiners really hate this. They've just read 90,000 words and now you want them to read exactly the same thing again! It is a déjà vu they can better do without. The conclusion does need to recap the results, but succinctly and elegantly. This summary is made only in order to go on to do the real work of naming the contribution(s).

3   The DR introduces new data. This is really confusing for examiners who wonder why they haven't encountered this material before. If the new material is needed to make the case for the contribution, it must come earlier. At the outset you establish the case for the research and in the conclusion you show that you've gone some way to addressing this deficit. When new material is introduced at the end, it also gives the examiners the impression that the writer has either run out of time or is too lazy to go back and do the necessary rewriting to insert the material in the right place.

4   The DR does not discuss the limitations of the research. This does not need to be an extended discussion of deficiencies – let the examiners do this – but it is very important to state what the research does and doesn't do. This establishes the basis for the claims that are made. Some DRs make a quick nod at the notion of acknowledging the limitations of the research and then fail to include themselves in this account. Limitations to research are not simply a result of sample, location or method, but are also about the DR – their capacities and blank and blind spots. Many examiners expect to see some reflexivity at the end of a long period spent thinking and writing research.

5   The DR overclaims or underclaims. It is critical in the conclusion to move from summarising the results to saying what they mean. This is the 'so what' and the 'now what'. Why was it important to do this research? The conclusion *must* provide the answer to this question. Sometimes DRs who have undertaken a relatively small study – because this is possible in a doctoral timeframe – go on to suggest that their findings demolish government policy, or offer the right way to do something. Grandiose, universalising claims need to be avoided, unless the research really is groundbreaking. Most doctoral research doesn't change the world but can raise questions about policy.

6   The DR does not return to the niche in the scholarly literatures or the problematisation that they initially established. Too often DRs rush through the implications of their study. They may offer some suggestions about policy or practice and a brief speculation on a future research agenda but don't refer back to the literature. As a result the actual contribution to scholarly knowledge is left hanging. Making sure that the conclusion connects back to the space in the literature is a crucial component of the thesis conclusion. The DR who fails to specify how their research reduces our ignorance about a topic, as it appears in the literature, is likely to be told to remedy this omission.

In order not to make these mistakes, it's important for DRs to get themselves well prepared for the tasks of writing a strong conclusion, for writing what 'I' have achieved and now have to offer the world. It's imperative to be clear about what the examiner is expecting. Cally Guerin, who works in Researcher Development at The University of Adelaide, makes this clear in her summary of what the conclusion has to accomplish (see Advice: What goes in a thesis conclusion).

Given what's at stake in the conclusion, it's important not to approach it as something to be rushed. It is a high-stakes piece of writing, and adequate preparation is in order.

Preparing for the conclusion

Any of you who watch cooking programmes will know the 'cheffy' expression *mise en place*. It's a term used to describe all the various kinds of preparation that need to be done in order to whip up something that can be described as 'freshly cooked to order'. In reality many restaurant meals have components that are pre-cooked and cut into the right portion sizes – they need only to be added, heated, stirred and assembled, with a minimum of actual cooking time between order and service.

The notion of *mise en place* is a helpful strategy for thinking about the thesis conclusion (see Advice: Preparation for writing the conclusion). There is a lot of

ADVICE

What goes in a thesis conclusion

It is important to remember that the conclusion plays a crucial role for the reader in reflecting back on the entire project. Of course, in the case of a thesis, the 'readers' are the examiners, so this is a high-stakes moment for the doctoral writer. Mullins and Kiley (2002) make it very clear that it is dangerous for an examiner to reach the end of the thesis and feel unsure what it was all about. The concluding chapter needs to make it impossible to miss the main findings about what this thesis is contributing to knowledge in the discipline, explicitly stating and drawing attention to the central message of the whole project.

The conclusion needs to match the introduction of the thesis, like a pair of bookends. It can be very helpful to go back to the original aims/objectives/hypotheses as outlined at the beginning of the thesis to show how each of the research questions set up at the beginning has now been answered. Repeating those initial questions in the conclusion can structure the discussion in ways that make it easy for the reader/examiner to see that the research has indeed achieved what it set out to do. Depending on the disciplinary conventions, presenting the aims or questions as numbered statements or dot points – as a kind of checklist – can highlight that each of these points has been addressed and completed.

In situations where the thesis is presented as a collection of articles, the conclusion is even more important in its power to bring together the findings of the project into a coherent, unified whole. Even though each article/chapter has its own conclusion (sometimes this might be just the last paragraph of the Discussion section, depending on the requirements of the intended journal), the conclusion of the thesis needs to do meta-level work on top of summarising the findings.

This is the moment in every thesis to address the implications of those findings – the 'so what?' part of the process. What does it all mean? Why does it matter? Finally, after all that work, it becomes clear where the whole argument is going to end up.

In the process of reflecting on the overarching meaning of the research, it may be necessary to return to the previous chapters and scrutinise what has been presented there. Sometimes it is necessary to adjust the content or interpretation of earlier work in light of what is known at the end. The emphasis may have shifted for the overall project along the way, rendering some passages of writing redundant or others requiring more prominence.

https://doctoralwriting.wordpress.com//?s=conclusion&search=Go

ADVICE

Preparation for writing the conclusion

Here is a set of questions to guide your conclusion *mise en place*.

1   How did you create the warrant for the research in your Introduction? Was there a policy or practice problem you were addressing? Is there a current debate that you want to address? Is there something about the ways in which the topic is currently understood or researched that you want to change?

2   What niche did you identify in the literature? How do your results speak to this niche?

3   Check the methods. Was there anything about the way that this research was conducted that was new, different or significant?

4   What were your key results? Do they challenge, disrupt, add to what is already known?

5   What are the implications of this new knowledge? Who needs to know what you have to say? Why? How could this knowledge be of interest/use to them?

6   What further research might now be done as a result of your work? What research agenda might your research open up? How might your work be a building block for further work that you, or someone else, might do?

7   Are there any implications for your own research practice? What did you learn about researching from this study?

Now write a page using this sentence skeleton. It is not a formula for the thesis conclusion. It is preparatory work to help you identify the material you have to include. It is getting all the vegetables washed and chopped. Once done, you still have to put them together to make a tasty dish.

Write only two or three sentences per statement. The goal is to produce a rough guide to the conclusion:

My research addressed the following issue/problem/debate/problematisation . . .

My research question was . . .

To answer this question I conducted (type of study) and the most important things I found were . . . (no more than three)

My work contributes to the literature on . . . (name any key types of literature or key authors) by . . .

These findings will be of interest to . . . benefit to . . . concern to . . .

As a result of my study, further research into . . . might be conducted in order to . . .

If I was going to do this research again I would . . .

preparation that can be done before a draft text is begun. And just as in cooking, the more preparation you do, the quicker and less painful the actual writing time involved. The conclusion to the thesis may appear to need less *mise en place* than other chapters, because there is *no new data, no new literature*.

Writing the conclusion

We go back to Erin Mackay's thesis to show how she began the work of concluding her thesis. The Conclusion (Writing Sample 8.6) is relatively short, about half the size of the other chapters, but about the same length as the Introduction.

WRITING SAMPLE 8.6

Concluding the thesis

Making the claim for contribution

In this thesis, I have been concerned with ascertaining the nature and scope of therapeutic jurisprudence, which highlights the relevance of the wellbeing of those who interact with the law. The therapeutic jurisprudence literature reveals a lack of clarity about its character. It is also preoccupied with offenders; in its nascent engagement with the victimological literature, the relevance of therapeutic jurisprudence to victim/survivors has not been clearly elucidated. I have addressed these matters in this thesis, in order to contribute to the ongoing development of therapeutic jurisprudence. In particular, I have contributed the following to the literature:

1 A more critical examination of the application of therapeutic jurisprudence to victim/survivors than evidenced in the literature to date, through an in-depth analysis of the claims of therapeutic jurisprudence in relation to victim/survivors, and especially those 'structured' in accordance with a particular gender and race (that is, Indigenous women who experience sexual violence).

2 Clarification of the status of therapeutic jurisprudence as a descriptive and normative theory, and the revelation of the normative limitations of therapeutic jurisprudence, when measured against the criterion of justice and applied to a case study where the interests of parties may conflict rather than converge.

3 A strong foundation for the argument that there should be a new normative basis for therapeutic jurisprudence to deal with 'tough' cases before the law.

In this concluding chapter, I bring together the key findings from preceding chapters that relate to the above concerns, and expound my core thesis argument – that a therapeutic jurisprudence approach to sexual assault and practice could contribute to a partial realisation of justice, but that without a more developed justice perspective, it fails to deliver justice for Indigenous victim/survivors of sexual violence. I conclude the thesis with a section that explores the implications of my findings for therapeutic jurisprudence more generally, and suggest a direction for the ongoing theorizing that I argue is necessary for the most useful development of therapeutic jurisprudence.

Mackay makes a clear link back to the problem she identified at the very beginning of the thesis. She not only returns to the literature but explicitly states her three contributions. She then indicates the 'evidence' – results – that she will summarise in order to justify these claims for her contribution. She is crystal clear about her argument and reminds the examiner what it is – *my core thesis argument*. She outlines at the very beginning what is to come in the conclusion, highlighting the key implications for practice and for future theorising.

We are not suggesting that this thesis is a template to be followed, or a model of exemplary writing. Indeed, the conclusion beginning is somewhat repetitive and also demonstrates the formality of expression associated with the core discipline. But Writing Sample 8.6 shows that it is possible to cover all of the elements needed in a conclusion in a relatively short piece of writing.

It also shows an authoritative and appropriate use of the scholarly 'I'. 'I have been concerned with, I address, I have contributed, I bring together, I conclude, I argue'. Even just listing these uses of the 'I' hints at the moves that Erin makes in establishing the shape of her research, its place in the field, its importance and implications.

In sum

We have suggested that tackling the question of writing as 'I' is tricky. In a thesis it is important to use the academic 'I' not the personal 'I', but this is not just about choosing appropriate verbs to accompany the 'I'. The use of the 'I' also establishes your relationship with your research, epistemic and disciplinary traditions and your reader. This is Layer 3 work and requires careful thought and practice. Nowhere in the thesis is it more crucial for you to get this right than in the Introduction and the Conclusion.

CHAPTER 9 Revising the first draft

The problem: all I have to do is tidy up

DRs are often elated when they complete their first draft. At the start it didn't seem possible to write an entire text that hung together. Eighty to one hundred thousand words on your research topic seemed an unreachable goal only a few months earlier. But you've done it! You've written the full draft of your thesis. Now all you have to do is tidy up the text. Get rid of awkward phrasing and syntax, check for consistency, eradicate spelling and citation errors, be sure your tables and diagrams are correct. Then you're done. It should only take you a few weeks. Right?

No. Not right. We'd all like our first drafts to be close to the finish line, but sadly, this is not the case. When DRs and their supervisors read the first completed draft, it generally turns out to be less coherent and polished than either of them imagined. It is clear there is a great deal more work to do. And a few weeks will never be enough. Unfortunately, there is no quick thesis fix.

At the point where they realise that there is still a long way to go, many DRs want to give up. They feel inadequate. It took so much effort to get the first draft done, and this is still not enough. They are hopeless – the PhD will never be done. How can they rally the required will power and knowhow to start the text all over again?

It's really important for the DR on the point of giving up to understand that the first draft is never enough. Never. It is just the beginning. And this is not a personal deficiency. A poor first draft is not the result of an inadequate mind and a hopeless DR. It is the way writing works.

A few people do produce brilliant prose early, and consistently. They are good with words and seem to gallop off a chapter or paper with relatively little effort. But these writers are the exception, rather than the rule. The vast majority of DRs will produce a draft that needs a great deal of attention. So don't be distressed or surprised by the time it takes and the amount of work involved in turning a first draft into the kind of text an examiner will find acceptable. This is the work of revising.

DRs can learn much about the importance of revision from creative writers such as Anne Lamott, author of the much admired creative writing book *Bird by bird* (Lamott, 2008) (see Advice: Anne Lamott).

You will note that Lamott talks about multiple drafts. The editing or dental draft comes last. In Chapter 10 we will discuss editing strategies to finalise and make your thesis text shine for examiners. Here, our concern is drafting and redrafting for meaning – Lamott calls this the updraft – and for flow of narrative or argument.

ADVICE

Anne Lamott

Almost all good writing begins with terrible first efforts. You need to start somewhere, start by getting something – anything – down on paper. A friend of mine says that the first draft is the down draft – you just get it down. The second draft is the up draft – you fix it up. You try to say what you have to say more accurately. And the third draft is the dental draft where you check every tooth, to see if it's loose or cramped or decayed, or even, God help us, healthy.

Lamott, 2008, pp. 25–6

Reframing idea: revising the text

There are still not enough conversations about the complexity of revising or the inevitability of the poor first draft. If you only read finished articles and never see work in progress – and how many of us actually do get to see the work of experienced writers along the way – then you have no idea how much revising good academic writers actually do.

It's always reassuring and instructive to look at manuscript collections in public and university libraries to see how much revision creative writers actually do. Some revise their work until the last possible moment. Pat works at the university attended by the once notorious British writer D.H. Lawrence, and there are extensive archives of his work available. Even at the proof stage, Lawrence made fairly major decisions about inclusions and exclusions in his manuscripts, something that must have driven his publisher to distraction, as each proof change cost money to achieve. The page proofs from his short story *The odour of chrysanthemums* are online (see http://odour.nottingham.ac.uk/index.asp) and they show the extent of his proof corrections – more like complete rewriting! In fact, Lawrence went on to change this story further between published versions. He saw that his writing could always be revised to become better.

Interviews with experienced academic writers provide another window into the extensive work required to produce good academic writing. Stephen Ball, a leader in the field of sociology of education, is a prolific writer who produces sharp, elegant prose. In interviews, he describes the process of writing multiple drafts as reworking and refining the text – an integral and enjoyable part of the work (see Experience: Stephen Ball).

Many a thesis completion timetable has come unstuck because DRs do not grasp the fact that real revising takes time. Most academic writers have to do more than one draft. In reality, very few of us write the scintillating introduction, the elegant conclusion, the persuasive argument right from the start. It takes several iterations. Revising is not minor rewriting, fiddling with grammar and moving a few paragraphs around. Sometimes it requires radical textual surgery – cut and cut again.

EXPERIENCE

Stephen Ball

I'm usually working with bodies of data, and then bodies of theory, so I read theory and I read the data, and move between the two in an iterative and cumulative process. One informing the other. To improve and amend and adapt theory in relation to data, and to explore data using the tools of theory. So there comes a point from that, when I think I have a sense of what I'm going to write in a chapter or a paper or some headline ideas or themes, then I start to write . . . And I like to write drafts, so for each piece of writing I do have a notebook, which I use for thoughts, reflections on data, comments, ideas and key quotations from literature, fragments of analysis and other writing, possibilities to explore. I go through the notes and I put together a very rough draft. So some bits would be written out, some bits would be notes, some bits would just be headings. But once I've got the whole thing mapped out then I print it out and rework it, and then produce another draft, which is a much fuller draft, and that may involve moving things about, dropping things, bringing new things in, elaborating and refining. And then when I've got that, I usually go through it again and, given the time that's available, I will do that again and again until I'm at least temporarily satisfied with the outcome. So I see writing as a continual reiteration process, drafting and redrafting, until a draft stands as finished, at least for the time being.

Carnell, Macdonald, McCallum, & Scott, 2008, pp. 71–2

But DRs are often afraid of cutting text. You may be attached to what you've written. You may have struggled to produce the first draft and are worried about 'losing' words in case you can't get them back again. It's as if words are somehow irreplaceable – as if the writing can't be done again.

More experienced writers, by contrast, are prepared to write over and over because they don't see words as a finite resource – as something precious, which, once produced, need to be kept and just 'edited'. We think of words and writing more like *The magic pudding*. Let us explain for those of you who haven't encountered this most distinctive of Australian children's books.

The magic pudding, written by Norman Lindsay (1918/2006), known as a somewhat risqué Australian artist, is the story of Bunyip Bluegum, a young koala who leaves home to have an adventure. Setting out somewhat unprepared in the morning, Bunyip finds himself hungry by lunchtime and fortuitously encounters Bill Barnacle (a sailor) and Sam Sawnoff (a penguin) eating from a delicious pudding. The pudding has one magic quality. No matter how much it is eaten, it remains a complete pudding. Unlike oil, or coal, or many other natural resources, the magic pudding replenishes itself continually.

> A peculiar thing about the Puddin' was that, though they had all had a great many slices off him, there was no sign of the place whence the slices had been cut. 'That's where the Magic comes in,' explained Bill. 'The more you eats the more you gets. Cut-an'-come-again is his name, an' cut, an' come again, is his nature. Me an' Sam has been eatin' away at this Puddin' for years, and there's not a mark on him. (p. 17)

The pudding is an excellent metaphor for revising. Words are malleable. You can cut them and come again. It's not a question of losing, but rather of working to produce the right words, getting the writing right. You can mould words, sentences, paragraphs, sections, slice them up, bash them around and rework them until they form a shape that is pleasing.

There is actually *nothing* to be lost from trying radical textual surgery, because you can keep your original file as you attempt a new version. There is everything to gain from finding the courage to refuse to accept first draft writing that you know isn't right. If it feels terrifying to even contemplate radical change, think of the writing and the words as the magic pudding – able to withstand whatever treatment you hand out. Cut and come again is a motto to hold onto.

But what do you look for when cutting and reshaping the text? If you're not just tidying and fixing, what are you doing?

According to Mike Rose (2009), a Professor at UCLA and an academic writing specialist, if a writer starts to edit a text without having a useful set of syntactic strategies – such as using headings and subheadings or manoeuvring topic sentences for paragraphs – they cannot bring a logical order to what is written. Over-editing and attending to fine detail too soon can compound problems for DRs. You get glued to the first draft and are reluctant to make substantial changes to meaning. What you need is a way of tackling the overall text and its argument.

It is useful to think about revising work at three different levels: aerial, ground and close-up. The *aerial* view is an analysis of the whole text and the way chapters build to make the whole argument. Such diagnostic work always relates to the particularities of your discipline, research topic and argument. This needs to be done with your supervisor and/or committee and cannot be further specified by us. We have suggested some strategies, such as storyboarding (see Chapter 7), which can be used to look again at your chapter organisation and flow. You may, as we have done in writing and revising this book, re-chunk your chapters, break them up in different ways to help the argument and coherence of the overall text.

While the aerial view work entails looking within chapters for coherence, flow, argument, readability and credibility, the *ground* work looks at the level of the paragraph to ensure these make sense and proceed logically one after another. The *close-up* work involves fine-tuning the text for stance, quotations, grammar, spelling, typos, references and citations in order to project the confident and capable scholar you have become.

In this chapter we offer four strategies to accomplish the ground work and close-up work. These are:

1   Rethinking headings
2   Working with paragraphs
3   Nominalising text
4   Balancing active and passive voice

Strategy 1: rethinking headings

Headings and subheadings play a significant role in academic writing. They act as a kind of road map to the sections of a chapter. It is easy for a reader to see what is important within a section just by reading the subheadings. There are sometimes even subheads within subsections – three levels of headings! When this happens, each subsection and sub-subsection becomes more detailed and focused.

In workshops, we often ask DRs to read the title of a paper, its abstract, the headings and subheadings and the conclusion, and then say what they think the article is about. Many DRs are surprised by how much they can tell about the point of the paper simply by doing this very quick activity. This activity doesn't work well if the headings are all generic (Findings, Results, Discussion), or if they are so clever, erudite and elusive that it's impossible to know what they might refer to. But when the headings are specific, they are surprisingly informative.

DR first drafts often suffer from two kinds of headings trouble. Either they are not informative enough or there is a quantity problem. That is, they either have too many headings or too few.

How many headings are enough?

If you think of the thesis as a landscape, as a topography, then a text without enough headings is like a landscape without any prominent features. Readers are frustrated by long stretches of text that cover a number of topics and ideas. They may ask themselves: How long is this going on? Where is the text going? What is the writer saying that is most important?

The text with too many headings, by contrast, is like travelling on a road with too many speed humps. You can't see what's in front of you for all the jostling and interruption. If your text has many short sections that are disconnected, readers will also be frustrated. They may ask: What do each of these pieces add up to? Which is more important than others? What is the point?

Either way, DRs need to do something about their use of headings. You can't leave your evolving draft in this condition. You need to find a more coherent way to divide your thesis text. The first thing to do is to actually count how many chunks or sections you have and do wordcounts for each. This is an initial check for balance. If the sections are wildly out of balance with each other, this signals that you might have a division problem, you might need to create more or fewer headings.

Once you see the overall shape of your chapter, you can then ask more specific questions about each of the component pieces and about the subheadings that capture their meaning. You can diagnose which sections are needed, which might be amalgamated or rebalanced, which might be added and which might be renamed or omitted. You can assess the degree of your problem by asking:

- What is each major piece of writing about?
- How much space is devoted to each?
- Are these pieces in the right order?
- What can be removed or combined?
- What needs to be added?
- How can each piece be labelled more effectively?

You want to ensure that the headings are designed around coherent chunks of meaning; that they capture the overall argument as intended, and have the required sequence in order to make sense.

Do the headings carry the meaning?

Headings that are informative tell the reader what's coming up. They not only allow readers to follow the argument more easily, but signal its various building blocks and overall organisation. Generic headings do not do this. They tell the reader nothing other than the general nature of what is to come. You do sometimes read articles where writers do both things – they use a generic label, but then add a semi-colon and a runner to say what is in the section. Methods: something specific. Discussion: something specific. The writer not only signals what is coming up, but also shows that the paper conforms – or not – to an expected structure. However, this is not helpful in a thesis. Thesis headings should be specific.

So what might this look like? Writing Sample 9.1 is a chapter from Tracy Skelton's Geography thesis reporting on a study conducted in Montserrat in the Caribbean. This chapter is an analysis of the gendered nature of employment in Monserrat.

Skelton's thesis was written in 1989. This numbered format was dominant at this time. Many supervisors and examiners now prefer not to see theses numbered in this way, as it distracts from the meaning and flow of ideas. At its worst, the numbered thesis produces disjointed segments that are named but not linked. However, some universities do expect DRs to use numbered templates they provide. But even if you do have to use such templates, the headings can still work to advance your argument, as Skelton's outline shows.

Within this strict numerical framing, Skelton's headings and subheadings clearly name the big ideas that she addresses. The subheadings specify the content and are focused. The reader can guess from each heading the kinds of content that will be presented and also see that the material has been well sorted. The use of questions for some of the subheadings in Section 6.6 sets up points of debate and engagement for the reader. The structure also shows that Skelton provides a brief conclusion to each section. While not all DRs will do this, it is immediately apparent that Skelton is building up her argument piece by piece.

In revising your first draft you will need to pay particular attention to whether your headings are working effectively for your argument. One way to do this is to reproduce the contents outline, as we have done in Writing Sample 9.1. Put all of the headings, subheadings and even those pesky sub-subheadings from the thesis together. Now read them as if they are a road map to a document that you don't know well. Do they carry your argument as effectively as Skelton's headings? Do there seem to be headings that don't say much? Headings that seem out of order? Big gaps in the sequence of material? This will help you see if there are any problems with your actual headings, and provide some useful pointers to look at sequencing and flow.

WRITING SAMPLE 9.1

List of chapter contents, completed thesis

(Tracy Skelton, 1989, University of Newcastle (Australia))

Strategy 2: working with paragraphs

The paragraph is the basic building block of academic writing. Most DRs know that a paragraph consists of:

1   an opening topic sentence, which sums up what the paragraph is about;

2   sentences that offer further explanation, evidence, contested ideas and so on; and

3   a concluding sentence, which completes the idea and anticipates where the next paragraph is going.

However, many DRs are often more worried about the length of their paragraph – it has to be less than half a page, or it can only be five sentences, no more, no less – than actually focusing on the internal structure. When revising, it's important to check both the sequencing of paragraphs and the moves within them. Poor paragraph structure and sequencing are frequently the root of many a poorly written chapter or chunk (for support on writing paragraphs see http://second language.blogspot.dk/2012/11/what-to-do.html; and https://medium.com/advice-and-help-in-authoring-a-phd-or-non-fiction/how-to-write-paragraphs-80781e2 f3054).

Rachael Cayley offers the Reverse Outline strategy for assessing the position and utility of headings, while simultaneously checking the flow of paragraphs (see Advice: Rachael Cayley).

Numbering paragraphs and working with topic sentences, ensuring there is only one topic per paragraph, can assist the flow of the argument, as well as the ordering. Cayley's strategy, and other similar approaches to outlining, treat the first draft as a piece of text to be examined and analysed, rather than simply read and rewritten.

One of the most common places where paragraphs go awry is when DRs discuss literatures. Literature chapter troubles, in particular, are often down to poor paragraphing. If you want to avoid producing unreadable text it's helpful to understand how and why the problems arise.

So here's another strategy to try, this time on a single paragraph. We introduced sentence skeletons as a way to step in the shoes of good writers (see Chapter 5). Here we show you how to use skeletons to diagnose your own paragraph pickles.

We've manufactured a set of dense sentence skeletons; that is, we've stripped out the content from a paragraph in a draft paper that we could barely follow.

Here is the problematic paragraph set out as a sentence skeleton.

According to A & B (date), Professors in . . . at . . . C & D's argument derives from E's view that . . . In a move similar to A & B, F (date) matches C & D's (date) concept of . . . with that of G's (date) concepts of . . . Writing in (title of book) G, (date) a professor in . . . , states: 'two line quotation' (p.). Like C and D's . . . , G's notion of . . . is . . . G's concepts of . . . are very similar to C and D's (date) concept of . . . and . . . , 'three line quotation' (p.).

Below we've numbered the sentences and set them apart so that they now read like a list.

ADVICE

Rachael Cayley

Reverse outline

My favorite strategy is the **reverse outline**. Reverse outlines are outlines that we create from an existing text. Regardless of whether you create an outline *before* you write, creating one *after* you have written a first draft can be invaluable. A reverse outline will reveal the structure—and thus the structural problems—of a text. The steps to creating a reverse outline are simple:

1. Number your paragraphs. (Paragraphs are the essential unit of analysis here.) 2. Identify the topic of each paragraph. At this point, you can also make note of the following: a. Is there a recognizable topic sentence? b. How long is the paragraph? i. Does the topic seem sufficiently developed? ii. Is there more than one topic in the paragraph? 3. Arrange these topics in an outline. 4. Analyze this outline, assessing the *logic* (where elements have been placed in relation to one another) and the *proportion* (how much space is being devoted to each element). 5. Use this analysis to create a revised outline. 6. Use this revised outline to reorganize your text. 7. Go back to your answers in **2a** and **2b** to help you create topic sentences and cohesion in your paragraphs.

This strategy is effective because it creates an objective distance between you and your text. A reverse outline acts as a way into a text that might otherwise resist our editorial efforts. We often find our drafts disconcerting: we know they are flawed but making changes can seem risky. A reverse outline can give us purpose and direction as we undertake the valuable process of restructuring our work.

http://explorationsofstyle.com/2011/02/09/reverse-outlines/

---

1   According to A & B (date), Professors in . . . at . . . C & D's argument derives from E's view that . . .
2   In a move similar to A & B, F (date) matches C & D's (date) concept of . . . with that of G's (date) concepts of . . .
3   Like C and D's . . . , G's notion of . . . is. . . .
4   Writing in (title of book) G (date) states: 'two line quotation' (p.). G's concepts of . . . are very similar to C and D's (date) concept of . . . and . . . , 'three line quotation' (p.).

So what's wrong with this paragraph? Well for a start, once you make the paragraph into a laundry list, you can see that's probably how it started. However, the list is only one part of the paragraph's troubles. One major problem is that it's not immediately clear what the paragraph is about. This is because *there's no topic sentence*.

The paragraph is actually about a concept that C and D use, and its origins. The paragraph claims that C and D developed their idea from E (according to A and B). However F says that this isn't what happened at all – C and D got their idea from G. F produces a quotation from G as evidence to show the similarity with C and D's.

It wouldn't be too hard to start the paragraph with a topic sentence that read something like this:

The source of C and D's concept of . . . is contested.

This makes it clear what the writer is going to discuss. Once the topic sentence is sorted, it could be followed by something like . . .

On the one hand A and B say that it is derived from E. E wrote about . . . and . . . . However, an alternative view (F date) is that it is actually a reworking of G's work. F for instance shows the similarity between . . . and . . .

We now have a clearer meaning – and in doing so, we've got rid of every sentence starting with an author's name (the 'he said, she said' list). We've also eliminated the quote dumping. But doing this rewriting means that we can now see two other problems.

There is unexplained information in the original paragraph. There's some miscellaneous information about the people concerned – Professor of – and it's not immediately clear why that needs to be included in the text. It may perhaps signal disciplinary differences or countries of origin or periods of time, but the writer doesn't say why they've put this detail in. The reader thus has no idea why this information is important. If it's pertinent then the writer needs to provide some commentary.

But hang on, the revised version reads as if it's only half a paragraph. That's because we don't know where it's going. Why does the contestation about the idea matter at all? *The point of the paragraph is unclear.* Why does the reader need to know where C and D's ideas come from? Does one source offer something that the other doesn't?

The writer probably can't answer those questions in this one paragraph. But they can do something towards building an answer, otherwise the paragraph has no purpose. Even if *this* paragraph isn't going to give the reader all of the answers to the 'so what', 'who cares' questions, the reader needs to know that there is some point to including the differences of opinion. The writer has provided the evidence for their opening claim about contestation – but why?

At the very least, we'd expect a last sentence in the paragraph that summarises the evidence presented and provides some clue about where the argument is going. So, *there needs to be a concluding sentence.*

So, to sum up, there's no topic sentence, and no crunch at the end. The writer has jammed a lot of information – names, dates, quotes, locations – into very little text. It's this combination of *too much naming and not enough framing* that makes this paragraph difficult to understand.

But the ultimate problem with the paragraph is that the writer hasn't constructed a thread through the text. They haven't used a meta-narrative that explains to the reader what is going on. Writ large over several pages or an entire chapter, the problem of no framing and all naming means a discussion of literature that goes nowhere, fast. When the thread of argument created by those topic and concluding sentences is missing, the overall text won't make any sense. And that's why it is crucial to get naming and framing in balance.

This problematic paragraph is symptomatic of a writer submerged by their content. They know what they want to do, but they haven't moved far enough away from the material to take charge of the conversation. They've produced some bits of text out of which an argument might be crafted, but they haven't yet taken the leap to sort out what they want to make of their assembled bits. The writer is not yet evaluating, arguing, telling the reader why this matters. The writer is simply reporting some differences between texts and doing so in a way that is barely readable.

And that means that the reader is left to fight their way through the names, dates and quotes, and draw their own conclusions.

Strategy 3: nominalising text

But problems also occur at the level of the sentence, in the way nouns are used. Many critiques of academic writing focus on nouns. The critique goes something like this. Academic prose is densely packed with nouns and nominalisations that make it hard to understand. Nominalisations are nouns that have been made from verbs – pacify to pacification, to be responsible to responsibilisation. Linguists call this *thingifying*, the act of creating an abstract concept and then proceeding as if it were a material entity subject to physical laws and having the properties of a physical thing (Halliday & Martin, 1993).

Thingifying can obscure context, agency and actions. When you make lively words into abstract things, you not only hide who does what, but you create what Helen Sword (2012b) calls 'zombie nouns'. Sword, an academic at the Centre for Academic Development at the University of Auckland, says that

> zombie nouns cannibalise active verbs, suck the lifeblood from adjectives and substitute abstract entities for human beings . . . At their best, nominalisations

help us express complex ideas: *perception, intelligence, epistemology.* At their worst they impede clear communication.

(Sword, 2012b)

A similar critique is made by Michael Billig, an academic psychologist from Loughborough University (Billig, 2013). His target is what he calls 'nouny prose'. Billig argues that when social scientists use abstract nouns in order to generalise, they gloss over important ambiguities and difficulties. The nouns and nominalisations don't always communicate the idea that academics think they've encapsulated. Perversely, nouny prose can make it harder for readers to understand what has happened, how and why.

We agree with much of this critique. Passages padded with nominalisations are hard to grasp and they can obscure meaning. When you string lots of heftily nominalised sentences together readers can't work out which are key to your argument. However, some nominalisation *is* necessary to capture the key concepts that you are working with.

We stress that nominalisation is a linguistic process – a process by which verbs and adjectives in a text are changed into nouns and more information is packed into noun groups. This is neither a good thing nor a bad thing in itself. It is part of how writing differs from speaking. And we don't speak as we write.

Typically, we use speech interactively to achieve some social action. Our language is fairly spontaneous and unrehearsed. It is most often organised as a dialogue, where the participants take turns speaking and build up meaning together. When we write, by contrast, we typically use language to reflect or analyse, so it is more formal. We don't have the visual or aural dimension of face-to-face contact. We draft, revise and edit our writing for an absent audience who will engage with our words when we are no longer present.

For the most part we are unaware of the differences between speech and writing (see also Chapter 6). But it is useful for DRs who are revising first drafts to become more aware, because if you write as you speak, your text will sound immature and unscholarly. Writing is more nominalised than speaking, and much of the content occurs as 'things' or nouns, whereas in speaking, much of the content occurs as 'action' or verbs.

It's more accurate, however, to think of these differences as a continuum. When you give a conference keynote, you speak to an audience, but it is like writing, in terms of being an uninterrupted monologue of ideas and information. When you blog you are writing, but the writing is often more speech-like, informal, personal and relaxed. We can illustrate by considering a post on the Patter blog that described one of Pat and Barbara's many struggles in producing the first draft of this book.

Today has been wading through mud. Gloopy, sticky, thick, hard to get clear of mud. We struggled to get going again after our break. We couldn't find out how to start off the next, new chapter. We had several goes at ordering the contents. We made many false starts. There was a lot of cutting and pasting, moving about, rewriting and patching up as we went along. It wasn't until the very end of the day, in fact just before Barbara went off for Nana duties with the grandchildren, that we felt that we actually had something that was OK.

This is chatty writing with some of the characteristics of speech. It is verb-centred: *struggled, wading, find out, made, went off, went along, felt*, but is not the kind of academic writing you'd find in a thesis. If we wanted to make it sound more thesis-like, we'd have to create more complex sentences, get rid of colloquial expressions and do some nominalising.

Our struggle with writing was evident today. Beginning the next chapter was difficult and our progress improved marginally with content re-ordering. After many false starts, cutting and pasting, rewriting and repairing, the text began to take shape. It was not until the end of the day, however, just before Barbara's departure, that we achieved some degree of satisfaction.

The text is now recognisable as something that could appear in an academic book about writing. We use noun phrases such as: *struggle with writing, beginning the next chapter, content reordering, departure, satisfaction* to capture our activity. That is, we turned actions into things. We've made the passage more formal by deleting phrases such as *mud, gloop, went off, ok, nana duties*. And we've reduced 100 words to 56. It's more succinct, we've condensed the meaning.

You can see from this example that when you pack more information into noun groups you can expand the content of a text. Nominalisations tighten meanings, make information more concise and foreground abstract ideas and concepts, rather than people and actions (Hammond, 1990). Abstract concepts are central to the research endeavour. It would be hard to write about research without these conceptual tools.

Janet Giltrow argues that nominalisations provide high levels of abstraction. Once introduced, these abstractions can be reinstated and used across a text to compress information and make it portable.

Scholarly writers need a concentrated expression they can reinstate to bind together parts of their discussion and to control extensive stretches of lower-level information. These expressions are like elevated platforms from which the extent of the argument can be captured at a glance. There is not much standing-room on these platforms, so, when the arguments are complex, the expression can be complex.

(Giltrow, 1995, p. 238)

These viewing platforms or nominalisations, Giltrow suggests, are crucial in academic writing because 'they compact a vast array of events and conditions, and hold them steady for scrutiny' (p. 242). They have rhetorical force and conceptual force. As Giltrow puts it, 'They engage readers' interests as Big Issues, matters of concern, and persuade them to pay attention' (p. 242).

It's therefore not useful for DRs to be told to avoid nominalisation. But too much *will* make writing stodgy and impenetrable, just as the critics of academic writing suggest. It is also true that too little will not only make doctoral writing sound childish and immature, it will reduce the DR's capacity to build up hierarchies of assumed knowledge in a text.

Finding the right balance with nominalising can be tricky. DRs need to learn the right textual balance of not too heavy–not too light nominalisation. When diagnosing your first draft, you can assess whether you have achieved balance in your use of nominalisation. You can nominalise up (making the text more dense and less speech-like) or nominalise down (thinning the text for accessibility and clarity). We illustrate the process by looking at some doctoral writing.

Nominalise up

Writing Sample 9.2 is an extract from a methods chapter in a DR draft thesis that is verb-centred. We highlight the verbs in bold to show how many there are and why it sounds more like speech than writing.

WRITING SAMPLE 9.2

Methods writing

There **was** a need to be sure that what I **heard was** what **was** actually **said,** and that my response **was** appropriate and true as there **was** the possibility that **could introduce** bias into the discussion. During the transcription of the taped discussions it **had not been** my original intention **to transcribe** verbatim, but I **decided** this **was** necessary as one way of checking how much influence I **had** during the discussion and if it **was** appropriate. This then **enabled** me **to take** more care during the next focus groups **to ensure** the data **remained** true. During this process, I also **reflected** on my emotional and also unconscious responses where I **let go** the facilitator role and **became** a participant in the discussion, **drawing** on my own experiences of the discussion subject. (130 words, 20 verbs)

In order to nominalise up this 'speech-like' prose so it becomes more like what the examiner will expect to read, we will rewrite it. Our aim is (1) to reduce the number of verbs and particularly forms of the verb to be (was, is) and (2) repackage the verbs as noun phrases and nominalisations.

> I **needed to ensure** the transcription **contained** no inaccuracy or bias. I **had not initially intended to transcribe** the taped discussions verbatim, but I **adopted** this procedure in order **to ascertain** my influence on the discussion. Careful listening to my comments in the focus groups **enabled** me to be more self-conscious of my role. I **gained** a new awareness of my emotional and unconscious responses and the way I **steered** the discussion. Consequently, I **stepped back** from facilitation and **participated** more equally with the group. (86 words, 11 verbs)

We have not introduced a large number of complex nominalisations in this revision. Instead we have reduced the number of verbs by half, and created noun phrases (*no inaccuracy*, *this procedure*, *my influence*, *careful listening*, *new awareness*, *facilitation*) to capture more precisely what the DR has done. So for example, we replaced the phrase 'to be sure that what I **heard was** what **was** actually **said**, and that my response **was** appropriate and true' with the noun phrase 'no inaccuracy'. In making these relatively small changes, the text has changed from sounding clumsy and naïve to sounding more concise and authoritative. A more controlled and precise persona is projected through this more balanced text.

Nominalise down

But what happens when the text is over-nominalised and too dense? Writing Sample 9.3 is an extract from the literature chapter of a DR thesis on higher education submitted for examination. We put the verbs in bold.

WRITING SAMPLE 9.3

Literature writing

The expansion and diversification of the doctoral student body

Over the last decade or so, the massification of the UK higher education sector generally **has been** consistent with a greater demand for advanced degrees, **resulting** in an enlarged and more heterogeneous doctoral student body and with it, a diversification of student experiences and ethnographies and learning trajectory and expectations.

This text is written as one sentence of fifty words, but it only has two verbs because it relies heavily on the process of nominalisation. Verbs have been changed into nouns to produce a dense text whose meaning is not always self-evident. To unpack the text and let it breathe, we can do the reverse process. That is, we can rewrite the extract by inserting verbs and actors and create more sentences, so it is clearer who is doing what and with what consequences.

> Over the last decade or so, the UK higher education sector **has changed** from an elite to a mass system. As many more students **have enrolled** in higher degrees, the student population **has become** much more diverse. This **has resulted** in an enlarged and more heterogeneous student body whose different experiences, learning trajectories and expectation **have brought** new challenges to the sector.

Here we've only slightly increased the number of words to sixty-two and broken the text into three sentences. It is certainly easier to read because we've added another three verbs. But in unpacking the nominalisation *massification*, we've also made the meaning more explicit. We've identified the shift that happens when moving from an elite to a mass system – a system that once catered for a few now has to cater for the many. We've also added the idea that *massification* and *diversification* create new challenges to the system, something the writer left implicit. Our changes illustrate Billig's point – that nominalisations can obscure as much as they reveal.

We've already made the point that nominalising obscures agency. You can become more aware of the ideological effects of removing agency by excavating the action buried in the nominalisation. A simple sentence can illustrate this point.

> The detonation of bombs in the London tube system in 2005 resulted in widespread mortality.

There are two nominalisations ('detonation', 'mortality') in this sentence and they remove actions and actors. There are no identifiable people who either set off the bombs ('detonation') or who died ('widespread mortality'). These events just happen; who is doing what to whom remains implicit. If we want to make the agents explicit, we need to re-insert verbs.

> When terrorists *detonated* the bomb in the London tube system, thirty-seven people *died* and another 700 were injured.

In this less nominalised form, the ideological reasons for omitting agency and hence responsibility are made visible. We see who is responsible and we see the consequences. The text is not sanitised. Obscuring agency is a common characteristic of bureaucratic text – or if we de-nominalise our own language we can say: 'Bureaucrats create obscure texts in order to . . . '. We're sure you can fill in the blank.

Knowledge about nominalisation is a useful tool for your revising toolkit. It allows you to diagnose where your text is too dense and obscures meaning, or where it sounds too immature, chatty and speech-like. The aim is to revise for clarity; to create pithy, economical and authoritative prose that makes your argument persuasively.

Strategy 4: balancing active and passive voice

When you start revising your first draft you might decide to use a grammar check. One of the things that computerised grammar systems really dislike is the passive voice. However, before you rush to change every single passive voice to the active, it's worth stopping to think about how much passive voice is actually too much.

Much academic writing is characterised by the use of the passive voice. The passive voice converts the object of the action into the subject of the sentence. So, for example, 'The researcher found puzzling correlations in the survey' becomes 'Puzzling correlations were found in the survey'. The one who is performing the action (the researcher) disappears from view (see Commentary: Michael Billig). If the passive voice carries on regardless, page after page after page, it *can* be tedious to read. It can also create long, over-complicated and awkward sentences that trip the reader up.

It is too simplistic, however, for DRs to avoid the use of the passive voice. The passive voice *is* important in presenting research findings and in conducting discussions – as is the active voice. Both are required in doctoral writing. When revising your text for clarity and meaning, you are looking to achieve a balance.

Here is an example we have devised to illustrate an effective use of active and passive voice.

> Access to higher education is adversely affected by escalating fees. Fear of accumulating debt often reduces young people's enthusiasm for further qualifications. When prospective students calculate the sum they will be required to pay back for fees, housing and living expenses, a significant number refuse the university place they are offered.

We put the issue 'access to higher education' in the topic sentence using the passive voice. This draws the reader's attention at the outset to the topic discussed in the paragraph. Subsequent sentences use active voice to make the case in an uncluttered manner.

COMMENTARY

Michael Billig

Scientific writing and the passive voice

By using the passive voice, scientific writers can clear the stage of human actors, permitting the chosen fictional things to be the stars of the show. Formulaic phrases using 'it' followed by a verb in the passive voice, can be particularly useful: 'it can be seen that . . . ', 'it has been demonstrated that . . . ', 'it is argued that . . . ', 'it will be shown that . . . ', and so on (Hewings & Hewings, 2006). Whoever is doing the showing, demonstrating or arguing slips into the background. The object of the showing demonstrating and the arguing stands there in the rhetorical spotlight in full objective glory, ready to take the applause.

Modern scientists tend to use passive verbs in the results and methods sections of their research papers (Biber & Conrad, 2009). Scientific writers did not always write in this way. When Isaac Newton described what he did in his various experimental investigations, he had no hesitation in using the first person singular. In his *Opticks*, Newton described how *I* held the prism, how I looked through it, how *I* observed the image etc. (Halliday, 2006, pp. 145f). Nowadays, a scientific writer is unlikely to write quite like this, but will learn to use agentless passive verbs: an image *was* observed, the prism *was* positioned, chemicals *were* refined etc.

When it comes to describing results, modern researchers are also unlikely to be as personal as Newton was. If a research team is publishing their results – and many scientific papers these days are multi-authored – they are unlikely to indicate who precisely did what. Team leaders will not use their positions of command to write: 'My statistician/research assistant/postgraduate student found significant results.' The person who ran the statistical tests, will remain rhetorically absent: 'significant results were found . . . '

Billig, 2013, pp. 128–9

It is important to avoid passive constructions that obscure connections and lack specificity. However, deciding whether to use the active or passive voice is not just a matter of producing clarity. When passive voice combines with nominalisation, the potential for stodgy prose increases exponentially. Take for example the following extract, Writing Sample 9.4, from an article on men's health (Banks, 2004). We have numbered the sentences for ease of discussion.

WRITING SAMPLE 9.4

Journal article

[1] Understanding masculinity is crucial for analyzing men's health problems. [2] For instance it is important to appreciate that many men take risks with their health because risk taking is one way men are brought up to prove their maleness to each other and themselves. [3] The long-standing and largely unresolved debate about the extent to which traditional characteristics of masculinity are pre-determined by biology should however be set aside if progress is to be made. [4] The attitude that there is an inherent and thus inevitable relation between maleness and poor health could distract from the chances of changing male attitudes and behaviour to bring about improvements in health.

(Banks, 2004, p. 156)

The writer here takes an assertive stance by saying 'is crucial', 'is important' and 'should'. But the use of nominalisation and the passive voice in the third sentence, for example, creates an overly complex subject: 'The long-standing and largely unresolved debate about the extent to which traditional characteristics of masculinity . . .'. As Sword (2012a) would put it, there is too much distance between the heavily packed nominalisation around *debate* and the passive verb *are predetermined*. This makes it hard to get the crucial importance that the writer wants to convey.

The use of the passive voice also leaves many unanswered questions. In sentence 1, who should understand men's health problems? In 2, who should appreciate male risk-taking behaviour? In 3, who should set aside preconceived ideas about maleness and biology? And in sentence 4, whose attitude is likely to distract from changing male behaviour and thus bringing about improvements in men's health?

We could rewrite sentence 1 in the active voice:

[1] It is critical that the medical profession understands masculinity in order to analyze men's health problems.

The sentence now has a critical and vaguely accusatory tone: wagging a finger at the medical profession and telling them what to do. This may be a more provocative stance than the writer wishes. It may be more productive to attend to unpacking the nominalisation. Sentence 3 might become:

[3] There are long-standing and largely unresolved debates about masculinity. Disputes about the effects of biology hinder progress and should be set aside.

Unpacking the nominalisation creates the opportunity to insert new verbs (are, hinder) and produce the urgency the writer wants to communicate. Clarity and assertiveness are enhanced, without attributing blame.

Some academic writing suffers from an excess of the passive voice. While passives are necessary, too much creates a kind of stuffy distance. If you always write in the passive then you'll produce the kind of pseudo-scientific style that many contemporary readers find alienating.

We conclude our strategies for producing clearer and more authoritative writing with an example of passive overload – a final reminder of what to avoid! Writing Sample 9.5 comes from a conference abstract, a site where it is very tempting to cram as much as possible into a limited word allowance. The researcher is discussing how she generated the results that she is going to report. We've highlighted the passive verbs in bold.

The three sentences are complex, choked with phrases and clauses separated by commas. When the writer, presumably for economy's sake, over-relied on nominalisations – presentations, legitimations, systematic analysis, interrogation and so on – they then had to use the passive in order to string a complex set of interrelationships together. The researcher herself is obscured in this move. She is the one doing the capturing, using and enhancing in order to generate her data and analysis. But she is nowhere evident in the text.

We have used only three sentences here to illustrate the passive problem. It's worse when there are whole paragraphs of these complex sentences strung together one after the other. It makes the reader and eventual examiner feel as if they are swallowing cotton wool.

We hope you can see that both active and passive voice have their purposes and effects. Making them the focus of active attention in revising your text is a better tactic than following blanket rules and prohibitions.

WRITING SAMPLE 9.5

DR conference abstract

Successive government presentations and legitimations of the academies policy **were captured** through a systematic analysis of policy document, speeches and government collated evidence dating back to the birth of the policy. A critical policy analysis approach **was used** to draw out and problematise the two core aims of the policy and to highlight shortcomings in the academies evidence base. The interrogation of the academies policy **was enhanced** by including in the analytic framework concerns about equity, school improvement and inclusion.

In sum

It's a big mistake for the DR to think that once they have finished their first draft, the thesis is nearly done. Several weeks, if not months, of revision, may now be required. We've offered four strategies that can help the revision process. They work from the aerial view of the outline, through the middle level of the paragraph, to the syntactic work required on sentences, verbs and nouns.

Don't think that revision is something that only DRs have to do. It took us about three times as long to revise this book as it took to produce the first draft! The trick is to understand – and accept – that academic writing is always rewriting.

10 Writing as the expert scholar

The problem: am I really ready?

You've completed the first draft. You've been working hard on the revision. Now you're at draft three, four, maybe even five. But even with all the revising work, there's still more to be done.

But you not only feel that the process is never-ending. The more you go on, the more you feel like a perpetual student, stuck on some kind of thesis treadmill. Will it never end? Make it stop – now! Will you ever get it right? Will you ever be good enough?

The last leg of the PhD can be hard, as Sophie Coulombeau, a lecturer in literature at Cardiff University, remembers (see Experience: Sophie Coulombeau 1).

Coulombeau offers some good advice on the need to take extra physical care during the last stages of the PhD. It is easy to become so obsessed with getting done and moving on that the various strategies employed at the start of the PhD – eating properly, exercising, having a well-organised office, planning and taking time to think – all fall by the wayside. Taking physical care of yourself can make the difference between feeling completely overwhelmed or feeling in control.

However it is not enough. There is psychological work to do as well.

You've been a student for so many years. A candidate. Under the supervision of expert scholars. You have been evaluated and assessed in your coursework. Your dissertation research and writing have been discussed, scrutinised, criticised, put under the microscope. You're still working hard on a text that by now you are heartily sick of. You're still getting feedback and feeling your thesis will never be good enough. What to do? How to juggle the need to be responsive to feedback, keep working on the text, revising, refining, and develop whatever it is that still seems to be lacking. Strange as it seems, DRs need to make a textual shift from student to scholar.

Writing the thesis, we've argued, is always about textwork/identitywork. The completed thesis reports and represents your research. It argues your contribution

---

EXPERIENCE

Sophie Coulombeau 1

I was prepared for Writing Up to be a mental strain. I was prepared for feelings of inadequacy, frustration, and nerves. What I wasn't prepared for was how physically tough it was. It all stemmed from lack of sleep, I think. I found it very hard to get a good night's sleep where I wasn't dreaming about tracking changes, and eventually I found myself, near my three deadlines, sleeping and working in shifts – six hours' work, two hours' nap, repeat ad nauseam. What this means is that I stopped doing any exercise at all, because I was always too tired. And near my deadlines I ate whatever was in the fridge or takeaways, which made me feel even worse. Smoking didn't help either.

By the time of my third deadline, the sleep deprivation got to a point where I was actually hurting myself quite badly. I fell over in the street because my balance was constantly off – hilarious pratfall, but was in pain for days. My face was always aching because I was grinding my teeth when I did sleep. I had a constant agonising crick in my neck. My stomach was a mess. My immune system was buggered, and I picked up a hideous cold in the final weeks.

This is one thing I really think I could have managed better. If I'd controlled my diet better (maybe by getting a job lot of fruit and veg once a week) and tried to make sure I jogged just 20 minutes every few days, I think it would have paid dividends further along the line. The time spent at the supermarket or in the park feels like a big sacrifice at the time, but trust me, you don't want to end up as physically knackered as I was.

https://sophiecoulombeau.wordpress.com/2014/08/06/writing-up-the-phd-thesis/

---

to knowledge. But it also projects you the scholar. You may not feel like an expert in your subject, but there is no one else who has spent three or more years totally focused on answering your research question. You *are* the authority on your topic. Now at the end of the thesis you must step back from your text and ensure that you project this confident scholar – and erase the textual traces of the tentative and less-developed student you. This may not seem easy, but it's necessary. You must 'style' the expert you into the text.

Reframing idea: styling the confident scholar

Creative writers often talk about a stage of writing, before they get to the final editing and proofreading. This is sometimes called styling. Styling means attending to textual matters that give the writing 'voice', your particular stamp on the text. We want you to think about this work as not only crafting the text, but also projecting your identity as a confident scholar.

This is the stage of writing when you have to be utterly self-conscious about what your reader will make of the scholar who writes the thesis text. If you don't have a viva, the examiners may never meet you in person. And if you do, it's well after they've read your text. If your examiners are members of your advisory committee, they need to see the writer as someone different from the student they've been mentoring for years.

You might also at this point in time, although the examination is first and foremost in your mind, remember that there will be other readers to come. People who are researching in the same area and will find your thesis through a search engine, and those who will find your digital thesis on the web or in the library. Many of the examples we've used in this book have come from theses we've found in digital thesis collections. Like us, your thesis readers expect to encounter someone who knows what they are talking about, not someone who still seems to be a student writing for approval.

A helpful way for DRs to think about this task comes from a drama strategy used in schools. It's called 'The Mantle of the Expert': it was invented and taught to generations of English drama teachers by Dorothy Heathcote (see www. mantleoftheexpert.com). The Mantle of the Expert approach asks students to stop thinking about themselves as learners and start thinking of themselves as experts in a particular area – scientists, archaeologists or historians. With the expert role come particular ways of being, talking, thinking and acting. Through acting as experts, students take on some of the responsibilities, challenges and problems that real scientists, archaeologists and historians face in everyday life. Teachers often introduce this approach by asking students to put on an imaginary mantle – when they are wearing it, they must be in role. When they wear the mantle of the expert, their student self is invisible.

The idea of a mantle can be helpful for anxious DRs in the last throes of thesis writing. It suggests that the expert is not yet part of the DR, but is something to be assumed while the writing is going on. You sit down at the keyboard, and mentally put on your expert robes. These are, of course, an imaginary set of the real doctoral robes you will wear at graduation! Sophie Coulombeau, who earlier described her anxieties during the last stages of the PhD, also aptly captures the pleasure that comes from taking on the mantle of expertise (see Experience: Sophie Coulombeau 2).

There are two aspects to assuming the role of expert scholar that we think are important. We point them out here because they underpin the strategies we offer later in the chapter.

EXPERIENCE

Sophie Coulombeau 2

In one very bizarre way, the last six months was one of the best times of my life. I was almost exclusively focused on one thing, one project, one goal. To be working towards it, with few other distractions, was a buzz: I could lose track of time while writing and realise at the end that I had finally made that breakthrough; managed to express that tricky paradox or link up those two awkward thoughts. Finally, at the end of four years of study, I felt that I knew my field very well indeed, and knew where my argument fitted into it. I felt confident that I could defend my thoughts and inform those of my colleagues, and that I was making a genuinely original contribution to knowledge. That is a precious, exquisite feeling. That's why we do this.

So, if you're in the home strait (or approaching it) – bon courage. You can do it. Try to stay healthy, and try to enjoy it along the way. This is why we do this. Keep swimming.

https://sophiecoulombeau.wordpress.com/2014/08/06/writing-up-the-phd-thesis/

First, being an expert does not assume that you know everything, and that you know better than everyone else. Scholars are also learners. To stop being a student does not mean the DR is no longer a learner. The nature of scholarship is about learning, about creating knowledge, about pushing your – and other people's – thinking further. But it is also, as we noted in Chapters 4 and 5, being cognisant of what can be learnt from other people's intellectual endeavours.

Umberto Eco, in his advice on writing a thesis (Eco, 1977/2015), nicely sums up the mix of humility and pride that are required (see Advice: Umberto Eco).

Eco talks about a specific combination of expertise and learning and humility and pride, and we agree. Too much hubris in the scholar is just as alienating to the reader as too much obsequiousness to the work of others.

Second, being an expert involves making a strong commitment to your reader. The kind of expert scholar we are imagining is scholarly and accessible. They make complex arguments, but guide the reader through their moves. Their writing is engaging and informative. They have something new to offer and are not afraid to make the argument. We've already highlighted some critiques of academic writing (see Chapter 9). Academic writing is obscure, difficult, abstract, self-indulgent, lifeless, of little interest to the public. This is not what you want to produce.

ADVICE

Umberto Eco

Academic humility: the knowledge that anyone can teach us something

Perhaps this is because we are so clever that we succeed in having someone less skilled than us teach us something: or because even someone who does not seem very clever to us has some hidden skills; or also because someone who inspires us may not inspire others. The reasons are many. The point is that we must listen with respect to anyone, without this exempting us from pronouncing our value judgements: or from the knowledge that an author's opinion is very different from ours, and that he is ideologically very distant from us. But even the sternest opponent can suggest some ideas to us . . . (Eco, 1997/2015, pp. 143–4)

Academic pride – confidence in writing

What do you mean you are not qualified? You have devoted months and years to the topic you have chosen. You have presumably read everything there was to read on it, you have reflected on it, taken notes, and now you say that you are not qualified? But what have you been doing all this time? If you do not feel qualified, do not defend your thesis. If you defend it, it is because you feel ready, and in this case you have no right to make excuses. Once you have illuminated other scholars/opinions, once you have illuminated the particular difficulties of the issue, and once you have clarified that there can be alternative answers to a specific question, *jump in at the deep end . . .* When you speak *you* are the expert.

Eco, 1997/2015, p. 183

Steven Pinker, a well-known psychologist and popular science author, articulates the bad writing problem in an article titled 'Why academic writing stinks' in the *Chronicle of Higher Education*. Pinker combines an analysis of writing with findings from cognitive science and sociology (see Commentary: Steven Pinker 1).

We don't want to pretend that all academics write well. However, we don't think this kind of critique is particularly helpful for DRs. It is important for you to understand the popular view that by virtue of being a researcher this automatically means you are going to write obscure, difficult, potentially meaningless prose. However, what you do need are strategies for editing the final text. Not the glib, arrogant tone that characterises much popular writing on academic writing.

Some of the serious critiques, like Pinker's (see Pinker, 2014), do point to the kinds of text work you need to do and we're going to call on them. A key point generally made is that academic writers need to distinguish between the writing you do when you undertake research – this is writing that helps you to discover, analyse

COMMENTARY

Steven Pinker 1

Bad academic writing

The familiarity of bad academic writing raises a puzzle. Why should a profession that trades in words and dedicates itself to the transmission of knowledge so often turn out prose that is turgid, soggy, wooden, bloated, clumsy, obscure, unpleasant to read, and impossible to understand?

The most popular answer outside the academy is the cynical one: Bad writing is a deliberate choice. Scholars in the softer fields spout obscure verbiage to hide the fact that they have nothing to say. They dress up the trivial and obvious with the trappings of scientific sophistication, hoping to bamboozle their audiences with highfalutin gobbledygook.

Though no doubt the bamboozlement theory applies to some academics some of the time, in my experience it does not ring true. I know many scholars who have nothing to hide and no need to impress. They do groundbreaking work on important subjects, reason well about clear ideas, and are honest, down-to-earth people. Still, their writing stinks.

. . . People often tell me that academics have no choice but to write badly because the gatekeepers of journals and university presses insist on ponderous language as proof of one's seriousness. This has not been my experience, and it turns out to be a myth. In *Stylish academic writing* (2012), Helen Sword masochistically analyzed the literary style in a sample of 500 scholarly articles and found that a healthy minority in every field were written with grace and verve.

http://chronicle.com/article/Why-Academics-Writing-Stinks/148989/

and make meaning – and the writing you do to communicate your results to readers. Writing for readers involves translating, converting your earlier writing-to-understand into the kind of text that will make your ideas comprehensible for your examiner.

This is what styling and editing is all about. You go through the text again to do the necessary translation and conversion work. You've already done the revising work to make sure your argument is well ordered and presented appropriately. Now you need to take the perspective of the examiner/reader. You need to imagine the reader who will engage with your writing. Earlier drafts were for you. This final draft is first and foremost written for the examiner and for posterity. Does your thesis as a whole project the argument and the expert scholar that the examiner, and future readers, need to see?

To help you assume an expert scholarly stance expressed in clear, straight-forward prose, we offer four strategies. They address problems faced by many DRs and may be a useful guide in specifying the final styling work to be done:

1   hedging your bets
2   guiding the reader
3   careful quoting
4   proofreading tactics

Strategy 1: hedging your bets

Critics of academic writing often complain that academics are generally not prepared to say anything absolutely certain (see Commentary: Stephen Pinker 2). Why do we do this? Do we simply love complexity and being vague? Well of course not. We want to show that things are rarely straightforward and utterly conclusive.

Our apparent indecision is a recognition that our claims to knowledge are always our best interpretation at the time – always open to challenge and reinterpretation. Research is always limited by time, place, focus, scope, method, sample, analytic process and so on. Thus there are caveats to put around most research results.

COMMENTARY

Steven Pinker 2

Hedging

Academics mindlessly cushion their prose with wads of fluff that imply they are not willing to stand behind what they say. Those include almost, appar-ently, comparatively, fairly, in part, nearly, partially, predominantly, presumably, rather, relatively, seemingly, so to speak, somewhat, sort of, to a certain degree, to some extent, and the ubiquitous I would argue. (Does that mean you would argue for your position if things were different, but are not willing to argue for it now?)

Consider *virtually* in this sentence: 'She is a "quick study" and has been able to educate herself in virtually any area that interests her'. Did the writer really mean to say that there are some areas the student was interested in but didn't bother to educate herself, or perhaps that she tried to educate herself in those areas but lacked the competence to do so?

Writers use hedges in the vain hope that it will get them off the hook, or at least allow them to plead guilty to a lesser charge, should a critic ever try to prove them wrong. A classic writer, in contrast, counts on the common sense and ordinary charity of his readers, just as in everyday conversation we know when a speaker means in general or all else being equal. If someone tells you that Liz wants to move out of Seattle because it's a rainy city, you don't interpret him as claiming that it rains there 24 hours a day, seven days a week, just because he didn't qualify his statement with relatively rainy or somewhat rainy. Any adversary who is intellectually unscrupulous enough to give the least charitable reading to an unhedged statement will find an opening to attack the writer in a thicket of hedged ones anyway.

Sometimes a writer has no choice but to hedge a statement. Better still, the writer can qualify the statement – that is, spell out the circumstances in which it does not hold rather than leaving himself an escape hatch or being coy as to whether he really means it. If there is a reasonable chance that readers will misinterpret a statistical tendency as an absolute law, a responsible

writer will anticipate the oversight and qualify the generalization accordingly. Pronouncements like 'Democracies don't fight wars,' 'Men are better than women at geometry problems,' and 'Eating broccoli prevents cancer' do not do justice to the reality that those phenomena consist at most of small differences in the means of two overlapping bell curves.

Since there are serious consequences to misinterpreting those statements as absolute laws, a responsible writer should insert a qualifier like on average or all things being equal, together with slightly or somewhat. Best of all is to convey the magnitude of the effect and the degree of certainty explicitly, in unhedged statements such as 'During the 20th century, democracies were half as likely to go to war with one another as autocracies were'. It's not that good writers never hedge their claims. It's that their hedging is a choice, not a tic.

http://chronicle.com/article/Why-Academics-Writing-Stinks/148989/

The need to be cautious presents DRs with a dilemma. The requirement to 'hedge your bets' – not to overclaim on the basis of the research that's been done – creates one of the underlying difficulties in writing the thesis. The thesis is meant to be an authoritative argument. You must make the case that your work represents a contribution to knowledge. You must show the expertise and depth of knowledge gained after spending years on a single problem. But because you know the limitations of your work, and must address these in the thesis, your writing may sound unduly tentative.

Hedges are one of the ways to signal your level of authority *and* caution. A linguistic hedge is a way of taking precautions, of dealing with the risk of being wrong. Hedges guard against criticism. Using hedges creates trust between the reader and the text; readers know that the writer/researcher has carefully considered their work, and is not simply advocating, preaching or ranting.

There are many different kinds of hedges. You have choices about how powerfully you represent yourself and your propositions. Here are some hedges to think about: *verbs* such as: seem, tend, appear to be, indicate, propose, prove, show, will, must, would, could, might, believe, assume, suggest, demonstrate; *adverbs* such as: often, sometimes, always, clearly, definitely, probably, possibly, conceivably; *adjectives* such as: certain, definite, probably, possible; and *clauses* such as: it might be the case that . . . , it is possible that . . . , it is crucial to . . . , it is useful to . . .

DRs often underclaim. They create a tentative stance through phrases such as: it is likely that, it seems obvious here, one tentative conclusion that might be drawn . . . If you qualify every statement, this will lead to weak, unconvincing prose. It will create a text that does not convey the expertise you actually have. Tentative text doesn't produce a convincing argument for contribution – and it doesn't produce the right impression for the examiner-reader. So it's important to get the hedging balance right. Not too certain, not too cautious.

We call this the 'Goldilocks dilemma' (Kamler & Thomson, 2006/2014). How much assertiveness is appropriate? *Not too cold:* passive, tentative, overcautious or evasive. *Not too hot:* overly confident, too brash and assertive. *But just right:* confident, in charge, leading the reader through the dissertation.

You can take a playful approach to this dilemma by experimenting with the extremes of hedging. Writing Sample 10.1 is taken from a journal article on education policy in Scotland (Mackie & Tett, 2013). We've edited out some bits, but you'll get the general idea. We've put in bold the markers of certainty and/or caution.

WRITING SAMPLE 10.1

Hedging in a conclusion

In this paper **we have shown** how the policy discourse in Scotland has been framed through our analysis of key categories and labels for young people. . . . As such, it **would appear** that the government's strategy for young people falls short in two domains. The policy **appears strong** on 'enabling' but **is weak** on the relationship between economy and society, **ignoring** the structural factors that marginalise young people from the employment market in the first place.

(Mackie & Tett, 2013, p. 398)

The extract has a strong opening statement 'we have shown', and some confident assertions with no hedges – 'is weak', 'appears strong', and 'ignoring' – with a hedge modification, the use of 'would appear'.

If we rewrite the same text to be more tentative, it might look like this. We've bolded the key changes we've made.

> In this paper **we have offered a beginning analysis** of the policy discourse in Scotland by focusing on key categories and labels for young people ... **We believe** our analysis **might suggest** that the government's strategy for young people **could fall somewhat short** in two domains. The policy **can be seen as** strong on 'enabling' but **we propose** that **it could potentially be regarded as** weak on the relationship between economy and society; it **could perhaps be argued** that it ignores the structural factors that marginalise young people from the employment market in the first place.

How much notice would you take of this research? Too much *believe, propose, could be seen as ... maybe, if only, you wish ...* But if we rewrite it again to be much more (way too) definitive, it might look like this:

> In this paper we have **unequivocally demonstrated** that the policy discourse in Scotland has been framed through the development of key categories and labels for young people ... It **is absolutely obvious** that the government's strategy for young people **falls drastically short** in two domains. The policy is **clearly strong** on 'enabling' but is **risibly weak** on the relationship between economy and society, **blithely ignoring** the structural factors that marginalise young people from the employment market in the first place.

This reads more like a newspaper column than research; there's too much opinion, too much personal-position to be trusted.

As you analyse your dissertation to see how much hedging you do, it's worth experimenting with text in this way. You can rewrite a passage so you sound too bold, overstating what you've done – or too cringing, underplaying your claims. A good place to try this out is in your conclusion chapter.

Find a passage where you make a claim about your research contribution. First, rewrite the text with high assertiveness. Be extremely confident and sure of your propositions. Use all the language resources you can muster to assert the truthfulness of your claim. You are aiming for maximum impact. Then rewrite the same passage with low authority. Be as tentative, cautious and careful as you can. Emphasise your unequal power relationships in the academy.

Working on the extremes like this does help DRs find the middle ground, which reads authoritatively, and accurately reflects the research that has been undertaken.

It is one way to address the Goldilocks dilemma. It makes light of the difficulty of getting the hedging balance right, but raises the serious identity consequences of dissertation text work. If you are to be a successful scholar, you must come to the 'just right' combination of certainty, humility, personal claim, dis/agreement and authoritative stance. You need to edit your text to project a confident stance about your contribution.

Strategy 2: guiding the reader

The expert DR skilfully guides their reader through the thesis to make the argument and evidence accessible. You must do this too – put the expert scholar mantle on and examine your signposting. This requires you to shift from being the writer of an all-too-familiar text, to a reader encountering your work for the very first time. What's more, you are not just any reader, you are the examiner.

If examiners read a text that offers no assistance, they can forgive it for a bit, but after a while they get really irritated because they don't know where you're going. They are lost in the chapters, drowning in bits that you can't or won't fit together.

The usual way to help the examiner see how the thesis is organised is through the use of signposts and headings. Academic writers usually produce a road map to the thesis, but also to each chapter, section and subsection. This is an opening move that orients the reader to what they are about to read (see Advice: Claire Aitchison). There also needs to be a closer at the end of a chapter. Ask yourself: What do I want the reader to most remember from this chapter? Where does this logically lead next? The answer produces the closer. A closer comes at the end of the chapter/section/subsection: it summarises the key points made and anticipates where to next.

Signposting is not all that matters. Your examiner also needs to be guided through the moves of your argument, especially as it is to be maintained over 80,000–100, 000 words. Graff and Birkenstein (2010) point to the importance of a 'meta-commentary', which makes explicit what the writer is doing. The metaphor they use is that of a Greek chorus which stands to one side of the stage telling the audience what is going on under the spotlights. They talk about two texts joined at the hip, one of which makes the argument. The other distinguishes

> your views from others they may be confused with, anticipating and answering objections, connecting one point to another, explaining why your claim might be controversial and so forth (p. 130).

A meta-commentary does significant work. Because it's easy for readers to get lost in a complex argument, you want to avoid provoking reactions you don't intend. You have to ensure your argument isn't mistaken for one you don't want to make.

ADVICE

Claire Aitchison

Where's this going? Metadiscourse for readers and writers

We've all heard good teachers and orators lay out what they're going to cover in their talk. It usually happens early on, and when done well, it is unobtrusive and incredibly useful to help us 'get' what it is they are going to talk about. Depending on the situation, this bit of chatter may remind listeners of what was covered previously (where they're coming from), of the scope and nature of their current talk, and indicate how they're going to proceed (where they're going). This bit of talk ensures everyone is 'on the same page' and acts as a launching pad from which things can proceed . . .

Linguists call this chatter 'meta-discourse' – that is, talk about the talk, or 'discourse about discourse' (Feak & Swales, 2009, p. 38) . . . Metadiscourse features a lot in academic writing – and especially in thesis writing . . . Metadiscourse is most commonly found at the beginning and end of chapters and as a segue between different parts within chapters. At its most basic, it aims to foreshadow what is to come and how, and perhaps also connect backwardly to what has been covered/ argued. Metadiscourse is a feature of a *reader-friendly* text (Paltridge & Starfield, 2007).

Not surprisingly, we can expect to find a fair bit of metadiscourse in the average dissertation or thesis, although some disciplines favour it more than others . . . Evans and Gruba (2002) outline a useful structure for the beginnings of chapters: that is the three moves of: backward reflection to the previous chapter, to state what's in the current chapter and to foreshadow what follows. The rendition of these steps or 'rhetorical moves' will vary – for example they might appear as three distinct paragraphs, or be combined in one paragraph, or even as one sentence.

Here are some examples of sentence structures or 'skeletons', as Kamler and Thomson (2013) call them, that may be located at the beginnings or endings of chapters or between segments of a text.

Current orientation

The focus of this chapter is . . .

This chapter reviews the literature on . . . , beginning with an overview of the key disciplinary influences . . .

Backwards orientation

This chapter follows from a detailed report of the findings that . . .

The previous chapter provided an historical review of the evolution of these models. To recap, the main . . .

Future orientation

Having established the central argument, the next chapter . . .

. . . and thus, the next chapter explores the key themes . . .

Combination orientations

This chapter analyses the environmental drivers first identified in Chapter 4. It begins by . . . , and then . . . , thereby establishing the context for a more thorough discussion in Chapter 7.

Some readers object to this kind of directional voice, finding it intrusive and simplistic, even insulting. Certainly if it is formulaic and repetitive, reoccurring at regular intervals when it simply isn't necessary, it can become tedious.

As a writer myself, and as a writing teacher, I make frequent use of metadiscourse as a writing tool. My early drafts often have lots of metadiscourse signalling for me what it is (I think!) I'm doing. Later, I remove most of this writing.

When working with others, I often ask them to include explicit metadiscursive text between new sections of writing because this forces writers to clearly articulate their intentions for any particular section – and how these relate to what has come before, and what will follow. Sometimes, together, we read only the metadiscourse or sentence skeletons to gauge the logic and rhetorical integrity of the writing.

https://doctoralwriting.wordpress.com/ 2014/11/15/wheres-this-going-metadiscourse-for-readers-and-writers/

The use of meta-commentary prevents readers from just focusing in on details of the argument and missing its overall significance. As Graff and Birkenstein say

> no matter how straightforward a writer you are, readers still need you to help them grasp what you really mean. Because the written word is prone to so much mischief and can be interpreted in so many different ways, we need meta-commentary to keep misinterpretations and other communication misfires at bay (p. 131).

There are different kinds of meta-commentaries, and Graff and Birkenstein offer some templates as a guide to their formulation and use. In Figure 10.1 we adapt one of their exercises, which DRs can use to practice writing meta-commentary.

Strategy 3: careful quoting

We talked in Chapter 4 about including too many quotations in your literature chapter and the need to express things in your own words. DRs can also get into quotation trouble when they're reporting the results of their analysis. The problem

---

Complete each of the following meta-commentary templates in any way that makes sense.

- In making a case for_____, I am not saying that_____.
- But my argument will do more than prove_____. In this chapter, I will also_____.
- My point about the _____reinforces the belief held by many_____ that_____.
- I believe, therefore that_____. But let me back up and explain how I arrived at this conclusion:_____. In this way I came to believe that _____.

FIGURE 10.1 Meta-commentary template exercise

(Adapted from Graff & Birkenstein, 2010, p. 138)

involves either putting in large slabs of quotations from interviews or very frequent grabs of smaller quotations. The DR's intention in presenting these bites from participants may be soundly based. They may want to allow the perspective of participants to have prominence in their chapter. This is usually explained as giving voice to participants, particularly if the chosen participants have been silenced in research up to this point. DRs also want to provide evidence that they have talked to real people. It can be a sign of respect.

There are two mistakes here. The first is the view that the interview is 'authentic', ignoring that it has been produced in a particular context in response to a request from the researcher, transcribed and then selected. The researcher is all over the participants' words. There is nothing pure about these words at all. The second mistake is the assumption that if the researcher rewrites what the participant has said, this does not provide a truthful representation. This is not correct. You can selectively misquote and you can accurately retell and rephrase. The point is to be 'truthful'.

Creative writers often talk about the importance of 'showing not telling'. But in academic writing, both showing and telling are necessary. Showing is displaying the material, the quotations. Telling is offering an analysis. Academic writing always consists of both showing and telling. In the data chapters what's needed is a judicious combination of quotation, the researcher's retelling of participant's views and experiences and the researcher's analysis.

There is no one best way to show and tell using quotations. It is, however, worth looking at how expert writers handle participants' words and their own interpretations. Rarely do they use the hit and run quotation, but find ways to integrate quotations into a coherent discussion.

WRITING SAMPLE 10.2

Embedding a quotation

Once young people assumed increased financial responsibilities, many parents started giving them more decision-making authority. For example, when Anna Kahan was only sixteen, she had a job making hats for twenty-five dollars a week in a small shop with pleasant conditions and a friendly forelady. 'For the first time, I had no aggravation,' she recalled, 'for the first time I enjoyed my work, and it was a pleasure to go and pleasure to come.' But her father was sick and the family needed more money. A distance relative who had a 'dirty little shop' came and offered her a job as a hat designer for thirty-five dollars a week. 'I knew I'd have a harder time,' Anna recalled, 'but ten dollars a week more! I couldn't refuse.' Yet, her mother did not tell Anna to take the job. 'You have to decide,' she told her daughter. The girl knew that for financial reasons she had to accept the better-paid position, but again, the final choice was hers to make. The obligation was thus assumed by the daughter rather than imposed by the parent, as it may have been among parents in other immigrant groups for whom working did not elevate daughters to the status of adults.

(Weinberg, 1998, p. 191)

We illustrate two different approaches – one where the quotation is embedded (Writing Sample 10.2: Weinberg) and the other where it is separated out from the interpretation (Writing Sample 10.3: Walkerdine *et al.*).

Sydney Stahl Weinberg is an historian whose work is based on oral history interviews. Writing Sample 10.2 shows a skilful combination of Weinberg's analysis and retelling of the words of her informant, Anna Kahan. The text reads seamlessly. It is engaging and yet also conveys the point about how young Jewish immigrant women assumed financial responsibility as a rite of passage.

Valerie Walkerdine and her colleagues are known for their explorations of social class and gender in Britain. In this extract, the authors are countering a common myth about working-class parents. They follow a more conventional indented presentation of interview material than Weinberg. Theirs, however, is not a quotation sandwich, where the researcher explains the point, theoretical or otherwise, then shows the data and then explains what the data means. Walkerdine *et al.* use a non-formulaic approach to illustrate and expand the point that they are making about the difficulties of working-class parents expressing anger in a school context. After the quote they then elaborate the argument, referring back to Zoe's mother's words. This is not descriptive reporting, but uses highly analytic and evaluative terms – grave danger, profound sense, desperate attempt – to make an argument.

WRITING SAMPLE 10.3

Separating out the quotation

While one set of defensive strategies often employed by the working-class parent in home-school interactions included silence, withdrawal or compliance, others mobilised feelings that allowed for the possibility of a different section of actions. However those working-class parents who did insist on voicing their concerns about their children's education were in grave danger of being viewed as demanding and unreasonable. Feelings of inadequacy and unfairness were coupled with a profound sense of not being heard, so it was not surprising that some parents' attempts to defend against and overcome those feelings manifested themselves in an angry way:

> She'd hate parents evenings, she'd say 'don't come', because we always ended up having an argument . . . or I'd start shouting at somebody [laughs]. I'd start having a row. It doesn't do any good, does it? [Laughs] (Zoe's mother)

The routes by which anger can be expressed depend on where the individual is located in the discursive positioning of the subject, and therefore the power and effectiveness of their response. Zoe's mother's anger drove her voice outwards in a desperate attempt to be heard, and yet, as she said, 'it doesn't do any good does it?' She was seen as stroppy and aggressive

(Walkerdine, Lucey, & Melody, 2001, p. 129)

When styling your final draft you should analyse the way in which you have used quotations from participants. Are you doing hit and run? Have you over-relied on the sandwich? Or are you in danger of 'quotitis'? Nick Hopwood, a researcher of learning and pedagogy at the University of Technology Sydney, talks about the perils of quotitis in qualitative research (see Advice: Nick Hopwood).

Naïve use of quotations gives the examiner the impression that even at the end stage of their research, the DR is still hesitant and unsure of themselves. This is a judgement to be avoided – so checking for hitherto undiagnosed quotitis is an important part of styling the thesis.

Strategy 4: proofreading tactics

There is nothing worse for examiners than to be confronted with 80–100,000 words full of typos, spelling mistakes, poorly laid out prose, incomplete citations, missing

ADVICE

Nick Hopwood

Underlying causes (assumptions) of quotitis

Any of the following assumptions might well give the writing doctor cause for concern:

- No one will trust or accept your claims unless you 'prove' each one with evidence in the form of quotes from raw data
- Participants express themselves perfectly, and your own words are never as good, and lack authenticity
- Not to quote participants directly is to deny them appropriate 'voice'
- Raw data is so amazingly powerful it can 'speak for itself'.

All of these assumptions are false. Perhaps at times, in certain kinds of research that place high emphasis on sharing knowledge production with participants, you may take issue with point 3. But still, I would suggest that an academic text will be more valuable by virtue of you developing ideas around data rather than just reproducing it.

Of course, the really uncomfortable truths around some cases of quotitis are as follows:

- You may have a fear of your own voice and words (whether self-doubt, uncertainty, insecurity), and prefer to rest in the safety of the words of others.
- Simple laziness, for example using quotes to pad out a text and increase the number of words.
- Lack of analytic insight. Lots of cases of quotitis seem to reflect the fact that the researcher hasn't gone much further than coding her or his data, coming up with a bunch of themes, and wishing to illustrate them with quotes from data in the text. Coding is sometimes useful as a starting point. It is rarely an outcome of analysis.

So the way you introduce quotes is important – is this 'typical', 'illustrative', or chosen for some other reason? How does it relate to other quotes you could have chosen? And you need to provide a commentary on each quote. What work is it doing in the development of your argument? What do you want readers to take from it? Why is it important?

Raw data speaks most powerfully when you speak on its behalf . . .

http://nickhop.wordpress.com/2014/02/02/do-you-have-quotitis-how-to-diagnose-treat-and-prevent/

and inconsistent references. Poorly edited text says the DR is sloppy, haphazard and unscholarly. Examiners are often required to list all of the corrections that they want the DR to make. If the text is in poor shape, then they not only spend a lot of time on this secretarial task, but it also takes their attention away from the substantive content. They are likely to get cranky and irritable. They are not being paid to be a proofreader.

Proofreading always comes at the very end of writing the thesis. It's your last work on the text. Some researchers pay for a professional proofreader to do this job, because it is time-consuming and not an easy thing to do. Most writers are inclined to see what they think they've written, rather than what they actually have. They miss the odd spelling mistake, missing comma, overlong sentence, the too often repeated word. It's hardly surprising they miss these slip-ups as most pieces of writing that are ready for proofreading have been through multiple drafts and revisions. The proofreading trick is to try to make the text appear unfamiliar and strange, almost as if someone else had written it.

Most universities do allow DRs to use professional proofreaders as long as their involvement is limited to correction of surface features and they do not address the content of the research. DRs who do pay for such services are also required to state this at the start of the thesis text. While professional proofreaders have the advantage of not being familiar with your work, problems can arise. If they are not used to working with academic texts in your discipline they may well not do the kind of repair work that is needed (see Advice: Proofreading checklist).

The most difficult aspect of proofreading is getting sufficient distance on your text. There are a number of tactics to help you find and identify the errors you have made:

- *Leave the text* for a week or so before reading it. It is then less close and immediate and the time may allow you to get some distance on it.
- *Print it out.* If you're used to reading the text on the screen, then printing it out can give you a new view.
- *Print it out in a new font.* You've looked at the text in your usual font for a long time – changing it might provide you with a new look.
- *Read the text aloud.* This can help you to hear klutzy syntax, missing and misplaced words, and you might also spot commas and full stops in the wrong places.
- *Get the computer to read the text to you.* The strange voice is stilted, monotonous and unforgiving about overcomplex sentences or clunky phrases. It is especially good at exposing missing or repeated words.
- *Read the text backwards.* Because you can't read for content, reading backwards focuses attention on the marks on the page, not the meaning.

ADVICE

Proofreading checklist

- Is the manuscript in a coherent style? This includes the references – check the style guide for rules about brackets, stops, commas, capital letters and italics.
- Do all citations have dates and page numbers, if appropriate?
- Do you suffer from shifting verb tense, overuse of particular words, incorrect subject-verb agreements – even poor spelling?

- Have you got some shockingly long sentences? Break them up.
- Have you got some shockingly long paragraphs? Break them up too around the key ideas/moves, and make sure your topic sentences are well focused.
- Have you got pages and pages of prose where all the sentences are the same length? (Zzzzz) Get some variety in there.
- Typos typos typos.

- *Ask someone else to read* the text for errors. Get them to mark the things you need to check.

- *Use a ruler* to guide your reading, either silent or out loud. The ruler forces you to read line by line rather than skip through.

- *Check your known common mistakes.* Keep a list of the things you do incorrectly and use this as a checklist. Also pay particular attention to the end of the text as you're getting tired.

- *Change location.* Some people find the shift from the familiar writing environment to somewhere different very helpful in making the whole experience of reading the text seem new.

- *Use the computer to check* for obvious grammar and spellos. Even if it picks up things that you don't agree to, it still allows you to look at selected bits of text more closely.

- *Circle all of the full stops* and check each one. This forces you to look at whether the stops are in the right place, but it also shows you sentences, short and long. Holding the paper at arm's length allows you to see how many sentences you've crammed into one paragraph – are there too many or too few do you think?

The most important thing of course is *not to rush*. Rushing almost always means that there are things you won't see. Do make the time it takes. Proofreading matters.

In sum

In this, our last chapter, we've addressed the transition that all DRs need to make – from student to expert. We've offered textual strategies that can assist in making that shift from tentative tone to authoritative voice. We've addressed key aspects of the thesis that can give away a nervous DR waiting for their grade, to a confident researcher who oozes just the right amount of humility and pride. This thesis end work is crucial, and mustn't be rushed, even though the temptation to get the text out of the door can be almost overwhelming. It's crucial, we've suggested, to take the necessary time to ensure that the text – and you – are styled and ready to be judged and evaluated as a fully-fledged scholar.

Coda

This book has been arranged around the notion of the detox, a time to stop and try a few new strategies in order to address bad habits and sticky problems.

It's important, we think, to understand the challenges that writing the doctoral thesis brings. With understanding comes the realisation that you are not alone, that others have been here too. Taking a break to try out some reframing thinking, combined with some alternative strategies, puts you back in control. The writing and its associated problems are not in charge, you are.

We have designed the book to combine understanding with reframing ideas and with strategies. Our aim has been to lessen the panic, and to restore a strong sense of you, the DR, as a scholar able to analyse issues and take the necessary steps to address them.

At the end of a book centred on problems, we want to end with one last challenging idea. That is, at least some of the writing that you do should be pleasurable. We take our lead here from the late Ray Bradbury (see Advice: Ray Bradbury), the acclaimed science fiction writer.

Now Bradbury was talking about and to creative writers. His references to commercial publishers and the avant-garde clearly don't apply to academic writing per se. But there is a relationship between advice for creative writers and the concerns of academic writers. Bradbury is arguing against writing purely for extrinsic reasons – for approval, for career success, for acceptance. Of course, these things are important. However, there must also, Bradbury argues and we agree, be intrinsic reasons for writing.

As a researcher you want to communicate your research. You want to convey your passion for your topic, the excitement you have about the insights you have to offer, the take you have on an old topic, the new text/concept, frame you've developed. You want that enthusiasm to be on the page. In order to do this, you do have to come to love the writing too, not just the fieldwork. The writing is part of your research, as we've suggested. The writing is research.

Writing the thesis is not all going to be smooth and problem-free – far from it. But it's important we think, and we know from our own experience, for the writing not to become a continuous and ongoing burden. You need to get to love the moments when you write white-hot and when you have the zest and gusto that Bradbury urges. The joy of language and the pleasure of text are what makes the scholarly community a fine place to work, and live with and within.

ADVICE

Ray Bradbury

Enjoy writing

If you are writing without zest, without gusto, without love, without fun, you are only half a writer. It means you are so busy keeping an eye on the commercial market, or one eye peeled for the avant-garde coterie, that you are not being yourself. You don't even know yourself. For the first thing a writer should be is – excited. He (sic) should be a thing of fevers and enthusiasms. Without such vigor, he might as well be out picking peaches or digging ditches; God knows, it'd be better for his health.

(Bradbury, 1994/2013, p. 4)

References

Aitchison, C. (2009). Writing groups for doctoral education. *Studies in Higher Education*, 34(8), 905–16.

Aitchison, C. (2010). Learning together to publish: Writing group pedagogies for doctoral publishing. In C. Aitchison, B. Kamler & A. Lee (eds), *Publishing pedagogies for the doctorate and beyond* (pp. 83–100). London: Routledge.

Aitchison, C., & Guerin, C. (eds) (2014). *Writing groups for doctoral education and beyond*. London: Routledge.

Aitchison, C., & Lee, A. (2006). Research writing: Problems and pedagogies. *Teaching in Higher Education*, 11(3), 265–78.

Alvesson, M., & Sandberg, J. (2013). *Constructing research questions: Doing interesting research*. Thousand Oaks, CA: Sage.

Andrews, R., & England, J. (2012). New forms of dissertation. In R. Andrews, E. Borg, S.B. David, M. Domingo & J. England (eds), *The Sage Handbook of digital dissertations and theses* (pp. 31–46). Thousand Oaks, CA: Sage.

Bakhtin, M. (1981). *The dialogic imagination: Four essays* (C. Emerson & M. Holquist, Trans.). Austin, TX: University of Texas Press.

Banks, I. (2004). New models for providing men with health care. *The Journal of Men's Health and Gender*, 1(2–3), 155–8.

Barthes, R. (1975). *The pleasure of the text* (R. Miller, Trans.). New York: Hill and Wang.

Bayard, P. (2007). *How to talk about books you haven't read*. London: Granta.

Becker, H. (1986). *Writing for social scientists: How to start and finish your thesis*. Chicago: University of Chicago Press.

Belcher, W.L. (2009). *Writing your journal article in 12 weeks. A guide to academic publishing success*. Thousand Oaks, CA: Sage.

Berger, A.A. (2008). *The academic writer's toolkit. A user's manual*. Walnut Creek, CA: Left Coast Press.

Billig, M. (2013). *Learn to write badly. How to succeed in the Social Sciences*. Cambridge: Cambridge University Press.

Boblett, N. (2012). Scaffolding: Defining the metaphor. *Teachers College and Columbia University Working papers in TESOL and Applied Linguistics*, 12(2), 1–16.

Bondi, L. (2003). Empathy and identification. Conceptual resources for feminist fieldwork. *Acme: An International E-Journal for Critical Geographies*, 2(1), 64–76.

Booth, W., Colomb, G., & Williams, J. (2008). *The craft of research*. Chicago: The University of Chicago Press.

Bradbury, R. (1994/2013). *Zen in the art of writing*. Santa Barbara, CA: Joshua Odell Editions.

Bulman, R.C. (2005). *Hollywood goes to high school. Cinema, schools and American culture.* New York: Worth.

Burke, K. (1941). *The philosophy of literary form.* Los Angeles: University of California Press.

Bushnell, C. (1997). *Sex and the city.* New York: Warner Books.

Carnell, E., Macdonald, J., McCallum, B., & Scott, M. (2008). *Passion and politics: Academics reflect on writing for publication.* London: Institute of Education.

Carter, S., Kelly, F., & Brailsford, I. (2012). *Structuring your thesis.* London: Palgrave Macmillan.

Clarke, I. (2006). *Writing the successful thesis and dissertation: Entering the conversation.* New York: Prentice Hall.

Cooley, L., & Lewkowicz, J. (2003). *Dissertaton writing in practice.* Hong Kong: Hong Kong University Press.

Currey, M. (2013). *Daily rituals. How artists work.* New York: Alfred A Knopf.

Dinkins, C.S., & Sorrell, J.M. (eds) (2014). *Our dissertations, ourselves. Shared stories of women's dissertation journeys.* New York: Palgrave Macmillan.

Du Gay, P., Evans, J., & Redman, P. (eds) (2000). *Identity: A reader.* London: Sage.

Eco, U. (1977/2015). *How to write a thesis* (C.M. Farina & G. Farina, Trans.). Cambridge, MA: The MIT Press.

Elbow, P. (2012). *Vernacular eloquence. What speech can bring to writing.* Oxford: Oxford University Press.

Ely, M., Vinz, R., Downing, M., & Anzul, M. (eds) (1997). *On writing qualitative research. Living by words.* London: Falmer.

Fairclough, N. (1992). *Discourse and social change.* London: Polity.

Fielding, H. (1997). *Bridget Jones's diary: A novel.* London: Picador.

Fielding, M., & Moss, P. (2010). *Radical education and the common school: A democratic alternative.* London: Routledge.

Foucault, M. (1977). *Discipline and punish. The birth of the prison* (A. Sheridan, Trans. 1991 ed.). London: Penguin.

Fuller, A., & Unwin, L. (2003). Learning as apprentices in the contemporary UK work-place: creating and managing expansive and restrictive participation. *Journal of Education and Work,* 16(4), 407–26.

Germano, W. (2013). *From dissertation to book* (2nd edn). Chicago: University of Chicago Press.

Giltrow, J. (1995). *Academic writing: Writing and reading across the disciplines.* Ontario, Canada: Broadview Press.

Giltrow, J. (1997). *Academic writing: Writing and reading across the disciplines* (2nd edn). Ontario, Canada: Broadview Press.

Graff, G., & Birkenstein, C. (2010). *They say, I say. The moves that matter in academic writing* (2nd edn). New York: W.W. Norton & Co.

Gunter, H. (2010). Dusting off my doctorate. In B. Cole & H. Gunter (eds), *Changing lives: Women, inclusion and the PhD.* Stoke on Trent: Trentham.

Halliday, M., & Martin, J.R. (1993). *Writing science. Literacy and discursive power.* London: Falmer Press.

Hammond, J. (1990). Is learning to read the same as learning to speak? In F. Christie (ed.), *Literacy for a changing world* (pp. 79–117). Melbourne, Australia: Australian Council for Educational Research.

Haraway, D. (1988). Situated knowledges: The science question in feminism and the privilege of partial perspective. *Feminist Studies,* 14(3), 575–99.

Hart, C. (2001). *Doing a literature search.* Thousand Oaks, CA: Sage.

Heath, C., & von Lehn, D. (2008). Configuring 'interactivity': Enhancing engagement in science centres and museums. *Social Studies of Science,* 38(1), 63–91.

Holt, J. (2005, 28 February). Time bandits. What were Einstein and Godel talking about, *New Yorker*.

Hughes, C., & Tight, M. (2013). The metaphors we study by: The doctorate as a journey and/or as work. *Higher Education Research and Development*, 32(5), 765–75.

Ingold, T. (2000). *The perception of the environment. Essays in livelihood, dwelling and skill.* London: Routledge.

Johnson, C.J. (2013). *Odd typewriters. From Joyce and Dickens to Warton and Welty, the obsessive habits and quirky techniques of great authors.* New York: Perigee.

Kamler, B., & Thomson, P. (2006/2014). *Helping doctoral students write: Pedagogies for supervision.* London: Routledge.

Kamler, B., & Thomson, P. (2008). The failure of dissertation advice books: Towards alternative pedagogies for doctoral writing. *Educational Researcher*, 37(8), 507–18.

Kamler, B., & Thomson, P. (2011). Working with literatures. In B. Somekh & C. Lewin (eds), *Theory and methods in social research* (pp. 16–24). Thousand Oaks, CA: Sage.

Keroes, J. (1999). *Tales out of school. Gender, longing and the teacher in fiction and film.* Carbondale, IL: Southern Illinois University Press.

Lakoff, G., & Johnson, M. (1983). *Metaphors we live by.* Chicago: University of Chicago Press.

Lamott, A. (2008). *Bird by bird. Some instructions on writing and life.* Melbourne: Scribe.

Lawler, S. (2008). *Identity. Sociological perspectives.* Cambridge: Polity.

Lee, A. (1998). Doctoral research as writing. In J. Higgs (ed.), *Writing qualitative research.* Five Dock, New South Wales: Hampden Press.

Li, X. (2008). Learning to write a thesis with an argumentative edge. In C.P. Casanave & X. Li (eds), *Learning the literacy practices of graduate school. Insiders' reflections on academic enculturation.* (pp. 14–31). Ann Arbor, MI: The University of Michigan Press.

Lillis, T. (2001). *Student writing. Access, regulation, desire.* London & New York: Routledge.

Lindsay, N. (1918/2006). *The magic pudding.* Mineola, NY; www.gutenberg.org/files/23625/23625-h/23625-h.htm: Dover.

Luker, K. (2008). *Salsa dancing into the social sciences. Research in an age of info-glut.* Cambridge, Mass: Harvard University Press.

Mackie, A., & Tett, L. (2013). 'Participatory parity', young people and policy in Scotland. *Journal of Education Policy*, 28(3), 386–403.

Mewburn, I., & Thomson, P. (2013). Why do academics blog? An analysis of audiences, purposes and challenges. *Studies in Higher Education*, 38(8), 1105–19.

Mullins, G., & Kiley, M. (2002). 'It's a PhD, not a Nobel prize': How experienced examiners assess research theses. *Studies in Higher Education*, 27(4), 369–86.

Noddings, N. (1986). *Caring. A feminine approach to ethics and moral education.* Berkely, CA: University of California Press.

Paltridge, B., & Starfield, S. (2007). *Thesis and dissertation writing in a second language. A handbook for supervisors.* London: Routledge.

Parè, A. (2010). Slow the presses: Concerns about premature publication. In C. Aitchison, B. Kamler & A. Lee (eds), *Publishing pedagogies for the doctorate and beyond* (pp. 30–46). London: Routledge.

Parè, A. (2011). Speaking of writing: Supervisor feedback and the dissertation. In L. McAlpine & C. Amundsen (eds), *Doctoral education: Research based strategies for doctoral students, supervisors and administrators* (pp. 59–74). Dordrecht: Springer.

Petrie, M., & Rugg, G. (2011). *The unwritten rules of PhD research* (2nd edn). New York: McGraw Hill, Open University Press.

Pinker, S (2014). *The sense of style: The thinking person's guide to writing in the 21st century.* New York: Penguin.

Rankin, E. (2001). *The work of writing. Insights and strategies for academics and professionals.* San Francisco, CA: John Wiley & Sons.

Richardson, L. (1994). Writing: A method of inquiry. In N. Denzin & Y. Lincoln (eds), *Handbook of qualitative research* (pp. 516–29). Thousand Oaks, CA: Sage.

Richardson, L. (1997). *Fields of play. Constructing an academic life.* New Brunswick, NJ: Rutgers University Press.

Richardson, L., & St Pierre, E.A. (2005). Writing: A method of inquiry. In N.K. Denzin & Y.S. Lincoln (eds), *The Sage handbook of qualitative research* (3rd edn), pp. 959–78. Thousand Oaks, CA: Sage.

Rose, M. (2009). *Writer's block: The cognitive dimension.* Carbondale, Ill: Southern Illinois University Press.

Schechner, R. (2013). *Performance studies: An introduction* (3rd edn). New York: Routledge.

Swales, J. (1990). *Genre analysis: English in academic and research settings.* Cambridge: Cambridge University Press.

Swales, J., & Feak, C. (1994). *Academic writing for graduate students: Essential tasks and skills.* Ann Arbor, MI: University of Michigan Press.

Sword, H. (2012a). *Stylish academic writing.* Boston, MA: Harvard University Press.

Sword, H. (2012b, 23 July). Zombie nouns, *New York Times,* http://opinionator.blogs. nytimes.com/2012/2007/2023/zombie-nouns/?_r=2010.

Thomson, P. (2014). The uses and abuses of power: Teaching school leadership through children's literature. *Journal of Educational Administration and History,* 46(4), 367–86. doi: 10.1080/00220620.2014.940858

Thomson, P., & Kamler, B. (2013). *Writing for peer reviewed journals: Strategies for getting published.* London: Routledge.

Thomson, P., & Walker, M. (2010). *The Routledge doctoral student's companion: Getting to grips with research in education and the social sciences.* London: Routledge.

Trier, J. (2002). Exploring the concept of 'habitus' with preservice teachers through the use of popular school films. *Interchange,* 33(3), 237–60.

Vygotsky, L. (1978). *Mind in society: The development of higher psychological processes.* Cambridge, MA: Harvard University Press.

Walkerdine, V., Lucey, H., & Melody, J. (2001). *Growing up girl: Psychosocial explorations of gender and class.* London: Palgrave.

Wegener, C., Meier, N., & Ingerslev, K. (2015). Borrowing brainpower – sharing insecurities. Lessons learned from a doctoral peer writing group. *Studies in Higher Education, ifirst.*

Weinberg, S.S. (1998). *The work of our mothers: the lives of Jewish immigrant women.* New York: Schocken Books.

Weston, A. (2001). *A rulebook for arguments.* Indianopolis, IN: Hackett Publishing Company.

Williams, J., & Colomb, G. (2006). *The craft of argument* (3rd edn). New York: Pearson Longman.

Index

Note: illustrations are denoted by italics.